The Video Poker Answer Book

The Video Poker Answer Book

How to Attack Variations on a Casino Favorite

John Grochowski

Bonus Books, Inc.
Chicago, Illinois

Except for appropriate use in critical reviews or works of scholarship, the reproduction or use of this work in any form or by any electronic, mechanical or other means now known or hereafter invented, including photocopying and recording, and in any information storage and retrieval system is forbidden without the written permission of the publisher.

04   03   02   5   4   3   2

Library of Congress Control Number 00-131754

ISBN 1-56625-141-9

Bonus Books, Inc.
160 E. Illinois St.
Chicago, IL 60611

Printed in the United States of America

Dedicated to the memory of Lenny Frome, a pioneer in video poker analysis who provided immeasurable support when I started to write about casino games. Lenny, you truly were the players' pal.

Contents

Acknowledgments

The approach of any book deadline is a harried, intense time—especially for those closest to the author. To my family, I can only say it's time to see the outside world again—the force field around the home office is down!

In addition to my usual playing time and searching through the casinos for video poker variations, I logged a good deal of computer time in researching this book, and many—most—of the answers would not have been available without some truly exceptional software. I used four different programs: VP Strategy Master by TomSki; Panamint's VP Tutor; Bob Dancer Presents WinPoker by Zamzone; and Masque's Video Poker Strategy Pro, using the strategies of the late Lenny Frome. For one game that most software won't handle, Multi-Pay Poker, I relied on a Chicago analyst named Howard Stern. Howard was one of the first readers to contact me when I began writing my newspaper column on gaming at the beginning of 1994, and has supplied his help and advice ever since.

Special thanks go to many in the community of gaming writers. I draw not only on the works, but also the friendship of Frank Scoblete, Walter Thomason, Henry Tamburin, Jean Scott, Anthony Curtis, Deke Castleman, John Robison, Alene Paone and many others.

That also goes for the magazine editors who put up with me on a regular basis—John Busam and Catherine Jaeger of *Midwest Gaming and Travel*, Buster Phillips of *Chance: The Best of Gam-*

ing, Rex Buntain at *Casino Executive,* Marian Green at *Slot Manager,* Paul Doocey at *International Gaming and Wagering Business* and, of course, Frank Scoblete at *The New Chance and Circumstance.* Their assignments, as well as research for my twice-weekly Gaming column in the *Chicago Sun-Times,* have brought a wealth of information that I hope shows up in this book.

Introduction

Video poker is one of my first loves among casino games.

I can date my infatuation to a couple of key events. One day in the 1980s, my wife Marcy and I were staying at Bally's Las Vegas, and decided to go casino hopping. From door to door to door we went, stopping at Bourbon Street, Barbary Coast, the Flamingo Hilton, Imperial Palace, the Holiday Casino, the Sands, the Riviera. And back we came down the other side of the Strip— Circus Circus, the Stardust, the Frontier, Caesars Palace, the Dunes.

All along the way, the game of choice was video poker. Quarter machines. Jacks or Better. I'd like to think we were playing the best games available, although I can't honestly say we knew the difference between 9-6 and 8-5 pay tables back then.

We had a good day. Marcy drew four of a kind at Bourbon Street. I hit a straight flush at the Sands. We lunched along the way, and by the time we got back to Bally's for dinner we found we had $65 more than we had when we started.

That was a revelation. That a couple of low rollers like us could have our day's entertainment and come out ahead a few bucks in the bargain... well, video poker moved high on the hit parade for both of us. Among the gifts under the tree that Christmas was a hand-held video poker game I bought for Marcy, and a video poker bank she bought for me.

Two years later on what had become our annual Las Vegas jaunt, we found ourselves playing in a video poker tournament at the Tropicana, which in those days was practically alone at the south end of the Strip. No Excalibur. No Luxor. No MGM Grand. No New York–New York. On the current site of the MGM Grand stood a tiny joint called the Marina. About a quarter mile south was the Hacienda. And that was the south end of the Strip.

By then we had learned the difference between 9-6 and 8-5 machines, read strategies—not all of which were correct—and practiced at home. There were no computer programs to warn you when you made mistakes, as there are now. I dealt hands from a deck of cards, made my decisions, then consulted a strategy sheet to see if I was right.

When we were invited to the tournament at the Trop, we both entered, plunking down our $99 entry fees. We drew different session times, so while Marcy was playing her round, I whiled away the time at—what else?—a video poker machine. Jacks or Better, with a 9-6 pay table.

Then it happened. Dealt a King and Jack of diamonds, a Queen of clubs and two low cards, I held the King and Jack and dumped everything else. Up popped the Ace, Queen and 10 of diamonds. A royal flush! My very first.

A fellow in cowboy gear passed behind me. Not so unusual—it was rodeo week. He stopped, looked at my screen and grinned, "Now ain't them purty!"

It was even purtier when the slot supervisor and a change person arrived and counted out 10 $100 bills. A thousand dollars! By the time I found my wife after her round, my hands were shaking.

"What happened?" she gasped, for I was just coming off a little health problem and apparently looked as if I was having a relapse.

"This!" I replied, and counted out those hundreds.

There have been more royals since, and toward the end of this book I'll tell you about the time I hit two in one day with my dad and brother on hand for a little Las Vegas getaway. But that first one is forever etched on my gray matter.

Those were simpler times for video poker players. Casino gambling still was confined to Nevada and New Jersey. Play in

Nevada, and you found 9-6 Jacks or Better and full-pay Deuces Wild games galore. In New Jersey, Joker Poker was the game of choice.

As video poker became the popular favorite it is today, dozens of other games appeared. Jacks or Better begat Bonus Poker, which begat Double Bonus Poker, which begat Double Double Bonus Poker. There's Money Fever, Multi-Pay Poker, Loose Deuces, Triple Bonus Poker—with pay table variations on every type of game.

Not only that. We can play them three, four, five, 10, even 50 hands at a time on new multihand machines.

The days are long gone when all players needed to know was to look for Jacks or Better games that pay 9-for-1 on full houses and 6-for-1 on straights, or Deuces Wild games that pay 5-for-1 on four of a kind. Today, we need a road map to get through the maze of video poker variations, and we need a guide to know how to adjust our strategy when playing games with different pay tables.

Different games demand different strategies. A lone Jack that is a reasonable starting point in Bonus Poker is just another discard in Deuces Wild, with no return on high pairs.

Different pay tables on the same game demand different strategies, too. In Double Bonus Poker, for instance, dealt two Aces, two Kings and a low card, what do you keep? Both pairs? One pair? It depends. Do full houses pay 10-for-1, 9-for-1 or less? It makes a difference, as you'll find out.

In *The Casino Answer Book*, which compiled answers on blackjack, video poker and roulette, I concentrated on four video poker games: 9-6 Jacks or Better, 10-7 Double Bonus Poker, full-pay Deuces Wild and full-pay Kings or Better Joker Poker.

This time, with a whole book dedicated to video poker, we'll explore more games, along with strategies to attack multiple versions of the most widespread games. There's so much variety out there that we can't possibly look at every game in one volume. But we'll hit a broad range of games, point you toward the best and explain what to expect from the worst.

xiv   THE VIDEO POKER ANSWER BOOK

Along the way, we'll try to have some fun checking out variations on a casino favorite.

CRUNCHING NUMBERS

Most of the video poker games we'll look at have hyphenated numbers associated with them, like "9-6 Jacks or Better" or "8-5 Jacks or Better." These numbers refer to paybacks on full houses and flushes when one coin is wagered. A 9-6 machine pays 9-for-1 on a full house and 6-for-1 on a flush. A "full-pay" machine is one whose paybacks are the highest you're likely to find for that particular game. You'll learn more about pay tables as you read on.

In chapters on video poker strategy, answers will include an "expected value" or "EV" on each sample hand. A little later, you'll find out just how these EVs are calculated. Don't get bogged down in the numbers. They are mere signposts, pointing toward which plays are close calls and which are no-brainers.

More important are the whys that go with each strategy. We save two pair in Illinois Deuces and not in full-pay Deuces because full houses pay more and four of a kind less in Illinois Deuces than in the full-pay game. Remember that, and you're on your way to applying the information given with the sample hands to similar situations when you play.

If you get stuck, don't panic. In the Appendix, you'll find basic strategies for the major types of games covered here. I hope you'll have fun exploring some the some of the changes we make in those strategies as the casinos throw different pay tables at us.

Shuffle No. 1: The Basics

1. **Video poker is similar to slot machines in that:**

    A. There's no way to tell a high-paying from a low-paying machine from the outside.
    B. Results are determined by a random number generator.
    C. The games give only the illusion of player skill making a difference.
    D. All of the above.
    E. None of the above.

2. **Video poker is different from slot machines in that:**

    A. The information we need to determine a payback percentage is clearly posted on the machine.
    B. Player skill makes a difference in outcome.
    C. Payback percentages usually are much higher.
    D. All of the above.
    E. None of the above.

3. **Casinos that want to change the payback percentage on video poker games:**

    A. Tighten or loosen a screw inside the machine.
    B. Run a program in a central computer out of sight of players.
    C. Change the pay table on the game.

4. **Getting the most from a video poker game requires:**

    A. Knowledge.
    B. Patience.
    C. Sufficient bankroll.
    D. All of the above.
    E. None of the above—it's all random chance.

5. **It is possible for a skilled player to gain an edge over the house on:**
    A. Any video poker machine.
    B. Some video poker machines.
    C. No video poker machines.

6. **A player who has an edge on a video poker game differs from a blackjack card counter in that:**
    A. The video poker player can never be barred from playing.
    B. The video poker player usually bets less money per hour.
    C. The video poker player endures more losing sessions than winners.

7. **Someone who wants to play video poker well:**
    A. Should first master table poker.
    B. Should learn Jacks or Better strategy first.
    C. Should understand that it's all chance and trust to luck.

8. **A video poker machine that pays 9-for-1 on full houses and 6-for-1 on flushes:**
    A. Is among the best games around.
    B. Should be avoided.
    C. Can be either high- or low-paying, depending on the rest of the pay table.

9. **On a Jacks or Better–type game with no wild cards, a decrease in the full house payoff from 9-for-1 to 8-for-1:**

    A. Hurts the player more than a three-of-a-kind decrease from 3-for-1 to 2-for-1.

    B. Hurts the player less than a three-of-a-kind decrease from 3-for-1 to 2-for-1.

    C. Hurts the player about as much as a three-of-a-kind decrease from 3-for-1 to 2-for-1.

10. A large bonus high on the pay table:

    A. Usually means a high-paying game.

    B. Usually is accompanied by decreases lower on the pay table.

    C. Usually is accompanied by an even larger decrease higher on the pay table.

11. On machines that pay bonuses for four of a kind:

    A. The games are programmed to pay four of a kind less frequently.

    B. Four of a kind turns up about as frequently as on non-bonus Jacks or Better.

    C. Four of a kind turns up more frequently than on non-bonus Jacks or Better.

12. Video poker pay tables:

    A. Are meant to reward winning hands according to the probability of hitting them.

    B. Are meant to make a game playable and enjoyable without precisely corresponding to the probability of hitting winning hands.

    C. Were originally determined by the number of times an engineer's pet hamster spun his wheel in intervals of nine and six minutes.

13. Casinos offer video poker games with payback percentages of more than 100 percent because:

    A. They are very popular.

    B. The casino is hoping they will draw customers who will then play other games, too.

    C. Most players don't play well enough to get 100 percent payback, and the casino still makes a profit on the games.

    D. All of the above.

    E. None of the above.

14. Players will find the biggest concentration of 100 percent payback machines:

    A. On the Strip and downtown in Las Vegas.

    B. In locals-oriented casinos in Las Vegas.

    C. In Atlantic City.

15. Multiple-game machines:

    A. Should be checked for "hidden" full-pay games.

    B. Usually have lower pay tables than single-game machines.

    C. Have a ceiling of 98 percent payback under Nevada law.

16. A casino that offers full-pay video poker games:

    A. Usually will have full-pay games on all its machines.

    B. Usually will hide the full-pay games in corners of the casino that draw less traffic.

    C. Usually will have a mix of full-pay and lower-paying games.

17. On multiple-hand machines, in which the customer plays three or more hands at once:

    A. The chances of hitting a royal flush in a given amount of time increase.

    B. The chances of hitting a royal flush after wagering a given amount of money increase.

    C. The chances of hitting a royal flush are lowered because of an inhibiting program.

18. On multiple-hand machines, players should:

A. Accept slightly lower pay tables because the chances of hitting a bonus are so much greater.
B. Seek out the same pay tables they'd want on a single-hand machine.
C. Ignore the pay tables, because multiple-hand machines are programmed to behave like slots, not video poker games.

19. On multiple-hand machines, the player should:

A. Play a more conservative strategy and never discard a winning hand.
B. Play a more aggressive strategy to further enhance chances of hitting a royal flush.
C. Play the same strategy appropriate to pay table as on a single-hand game.

20. Given a multiple-hand quarter game, a single-hand quarter game and a single-hand dollar game with the same pay tables, a player with a limited bankroll is better off:

A. Playing one coin per hand on the multiple-hand game, because of the increased likelihood of hitting a royal flush.
B. Playing maximum coins on the single-hand quarter game.
C. Playing one coin in the single-hand dollar game.

Shuffle No. 1:
The Basics
Answers

1. B. Video poker is similar to slot machines in that results are determined by a random number generator (RNG). Programmed into a computer chip inside the machine, the RNG runs continuously, even when the machine is not in use.

However, in video poker the random numbers correspond to cards in a 52-card electronic deck. In Nevada and many other gaming jurisdictions, each electronic card must have an equal chance of being dealt. That leaves a game that is the equivalent of taking a table poker game and putting it on a video screen. The odds are the same as if you were playing with a physical deck of cards. That allows us to calculate odds and devise strategies.

Laws in some states, including New Jersey, allow video poker programming to be more like that for a slot machine. One way such a program could depress payback percentages would be to have a high card or high cards appear less frequently than once in every 52 cards. For example, if the Ace of spades is programmed to appear randomly only once in 104 cards, that not only would lead to fewer royal flushes; it also would have a ripple effect on the rest of the pay table. There would be fewer high pairs because one of our high cards doesn't appear as often as it would in a regular deck of cards, and fewer three of a kinds because when we save two other Aces, we have a depressed chance of adding the Ace of spades.

As a practical matter, you're probably getting games that live up to Nevada randomness standards wherever you play. Most video poker machines are manufactured in Nevada and, when asked point-blank, operators in other states have told me the computer chips in their machines are the same as the ones used in Nevada. And that means a randomly shuffled, 52-card electronic deck in which each card has an equal probability of being dealt.

2. D. All of the above—video poker is different from slot machines in that the information we need to determine a payback percentage is clearly posted on the machine, player skill makes a difference in outcome *and* payback percentages usually are much higher.

All the information we need to calculate a payback percentage is contained in the pay table that is either painted on the machine glass or displayed on the video screen. Since we know video poker is dealt from a randomly shuffled 52-card electronic deck, we can calculate the frequency with which winning hands will occur, given a specific drawing strategy. We can then apply the pay table to those winners and calculate a payback percentage.

Player skill does make a difference. If I tell you a 9-6 Jacks or Better machine returns 99.5 percent with expert play, but you insist on discarding low pairs while holding single high cards from the same hand, your payback percentage will be lower.

If you play video poker well—and if you can answer all the strategy questions that follow in this book, rest assured that you will play well—you get a much better run for your money than the average slot player. Slot paybacks vary wildly across the country. Someone playing in downtown Las Vegas gets in excess of 95 percent on quarter slots and nearly 96 percent on dollar machines. Play in Joliet, Illinois, and it's more like 92 percent on quarters and 95 percent on dollars, while in Atlantic City you're looking at 91 percent on quarters and 93 percent on dollars.

A video poker player who knows what games to look for and plays well does much, much better. Some games approach, or even slightly exceed, 100 percent payback with expert play. Even weaker video poker games pay better than the slots. A game of Jacks or Better with an 8-5 pay table, meaning full houses pay 8-

for-1 and flushes 5-for-1, pays 97.3 percent in the long run with expert play.

The trick is learning to play well. Play poorly on a low-paying machine, and your money will go just as fast as on the slots.

3. C. Casinos that want to change the payback percentage on video poker games change the pay table on the game. If you see two Double Bonus Poker machines sitting side by side, with equal pay tables except that one pays 10-for-1 on full houses and the other pays 9-for-1, you know that the first machine returns a higher percentage in the long run.

In this way, the casino tips its hand and lets video poker players do a little comparison-shopping. In the late '80s, my wife Marcy and I were staying at the Tropicana. That truly seems like the dawn of time today: What is now the busiest corner of the Strip was all but deserted then. No need for today's overhead walkways—there wasn't any traffic. You could cross the Strip on foot against the light at virtually any hour.

Back then, the Trop had a large bank of Jacks or Better machines, alternating 9-6 and 8-5 pay tables. The 9-6 version returns 99.5 percent to players in the long run, while the 8-5 version pays only 97.3 percent. Marcy and I were surprised to see that players were taking machines at random, not even checking the pay tables. Those who landed at 8-5 machines were giving away 2.2 percent off the top.

If you want the best deal, it's part of your job as a player to check the pay tables before you play.

4. D. Getting the most from a video poker game requires knowledge, patience *and* sufficient bankroll.

We need the knowledge to make decisions on which cards to hold and which to discard. We need patience, because that royal flush that'll give us a big win turns up only once every 40,000 hands or so. There's no guarantee that even if we play all week we'll hit the royal, or even a nice secondary jackpot such as four deuces on a Deuces Wild machine.

To get the most out of video poker, we also need sufficient bankroll to withstand losing streaks. It sounds nice to say 9-6

Jacks or Better is a 99.5 percent game, and that if we bet five quarters at a time for 500 hands an hour, our expected average loss is just $3.12 per hour. (A 500-hand-per-hour pace is fairly easy, by the way; some video poker regulars play at 800 h.p.h. or more.) But anytime our session does not include a royal flush, the average payback drops to about 97.5, and in a bad streak we can drop $20 bill after $20 bill.

Just to give yourself a 50 percent chance of hitting a royal before you run out of money requires a bankroll of about $900. And that's on a good quarter machine. Imagine playing for dollars, or playing a bad pay table, or (horrors!) both.

That doesn't mean you can't walk into a casino with twenty bucks to wager and have a good time playing quarter video poker. You can, and there's nothing wrong with playing strictly for entertainment. You might even hit a royal, or at least a quick four of a kind to give yourself a little breathing room. Just understand that your good time also might be over in 10 minutes if you hit a cold streak right off the bat.

5. B. It is possible for a skilled player to gain an edge over the house on some video poker machines. Some pay tables are so high that a player who knows expert strategy can expect a long-term payback of more than 100 percent. One of the more common is 10-7 Double Bonus Poker, which yields 100.2 percent. Full-pay Deuces Wild is even better at 100.8 percent, but you'll find it only in Nevada.

I know video poker experts who will not play unless a machine returns at least 100 percent, whether by itself or combined with slot club benefits. They play for profit, and if there is no profit opportunity, they see no reason to play.

Most players, however, play for recreation and entertainment. I once wrote a diatribe about avoiding low-paying video poker machines, and received a letter from a riverboat customer who wrote, "I agree with what you say about low-paying machines, but when that's all there are on the boat, what are you going to do? I'm still going to play."

As long as they go into it with their eyes open, I can't really argue with those who play low-paying machines for entertainment. Whether you play the coin-gobblers is entirely up to you. Just do yourself a favor and walk through the casino first, check pay tables and get yourself the best deal available.

6. C. A player who has an edge on a video poker game differs from a blackjack card counter in that the video poker player endures more losing sessions than winners.

There are winning and losing sessions at any skill level at any game of chance. However, a blackjack card counter with the necessary knowledge, skill, discipline and bankroll can expect to win at more sessions than he loses.

In video poker, much of the long-term payback is tied up in a few rare hands. When you don't hit a royal flush, 10-7 Double Bonus Poker turns into a 98.5 percent game. The long-term average, including royal flushes, is 100.2 percent, but to get there, the player must endure a pack of losing sessions.

A few years ago, my own video poker ledger looked pretty grim. Why? Because it had been nearly two years since my last royal flush. Then one morning in Las Vegas, I hit a royal on quarter machine, and that night hit one on a $2 machine for $8,000. Suddenly my ledger looked much brighter.

That's the way video poker works. You can have winning sessions without a royal if you hit four deuces in Deuces Wild or one of the bonus quads in Double Bonus Poker or even a few full houses above the average in Jacks or Better. But you'll lose more often than you win, then make it back when the big ones hit.

7. B. Someone who wants to play video poker well should learn Jacks or Better strategy first. That's the foundation on which most video poker games are based. Whether the game is Bonus Poker, Double Bonus Poker, Double Double Bonus Poker or countless bonus variations, the game is essentially Jacks or Better with some pay table adjustments.

Take Double Bonus Poker. Expert strategy includes a lot of special cases, making Double Bonus a fairly difficult game to learn to play well. One adjustment that confounds players is that in Double Bonus, when we have a full house that includes three Aces, we break up the full house, just keep the Aces and hope to draw the fourth Ace for a 160-for-1 payoff. Another situation that causes some difficulty is that straights pay 5-for-1 in most versions of Double Bonus, leading us to draw to inside straights. In Jacks or Better, with straights paying only 4-for-1, we draw to inside straights only if they include at least three high cards. Then, if we don't draw our straight, we at least have the chance to pair up one of the high cards and get our money back.

There are many more adjustments to be made in Double Bonus. You know how much they add to our bottom line? Just 0.4 percent. If we apply the same strategy that brings us 99.5 percent in 9-6 Jacks or Better to 10-7 Double Bonus, we get 99.8 percent. Jacks or Better strategy works even better in Double Bonus than in Jacks or Better.

To get the maximum payback available from any game, you'll need to make some adjustments. But learn to play the basic game first, and you won't be far off on any Jacks or Better–based game.

8. C. A video poker machine that pays 9-for-1 on full houses and 6-for-1 on flushes can be either high- or low-paying, depending on the rest of the pay table.

Over the years, countless video poker players have heard that they should look for 9-6 machines. They've read it, heard it from friends, maybe even a friendly casino employee nudged them away from 8-5 Jacks or Better and toward a 9-6 machine.

That was fine and dandy in the days that Jacks or Better games made up the majority of games in the casino. Once Double Bonus Poker appeared, things changed. The full-pay version of Double Bonus, with a 100.2 percent payback with expert play, has a 10-7 pay table. Most 9-6 Double Bonus machines pay only 97.8 percent. (There is a version of 9-6 Double Bonus that pays 200-for-1 on four Aces instead of the standard 160-for-1. That raises the overall payback to 99.0 percent.)

Be careful. Each game has its own pay table variations. Be alert for both game and pay table.

9. B. On a Jacks or Better–type game with no wild cards, a decrease in the full house payoff from 9-for-1 to 8-for-1 hurts the player less than a three-of-a-kind decrease from 3-for-1 to 2-for-1.

The more frequently a hand occurs, the greater the effect of a change in the payoff. In Jacks or Better-based games, we draw three of a kind roughly once every 14 hands, while full houses occur only about once per 90 hands—a little more or less depending on game and strategy. We hit three of a kind more than six times as often as full houses, so the effect of a one-unit drop on the pay table is magnified.

I once walked through a newly remodeled casino. Not only had it been expanded and redecorated, but it had bought all new slot and video poker machines. I was about to make a note to praise it for raising the Bonus Poker pay table from 6-5 on the old machines to 8-5 on the new ones, when I noticed a quirk. Three of a kind paid only 2-for-1 instead of the common 3-for-1. They were giving me a couple of percent more on full houses, but taking away nearly 8 percent on three of a kind. Ouch. And double ouch.

10. B. A large bonus high on the pay table usually is accompanied by decreases lower on the pay table.

Let's look at Double Bonus Poker. Instead of the 25-for-1 payoff on four of a kind offered by Jacks or Better, it pays 160-for-1 on four Aces, 80-for-1 on four 2s, 3s and 4s and 50-for-1 on any other four of a kind. That's a huge jump. I've had many former slot players tell me that Double Bonus Poker sparked them to switch to video poker because they felt it gave them a shot at a worthwhile jackpot without having to hit a royal flush.

How did Double Bonus Poker balance off those big secondary jackpots? By reducing the payoff on two pair to 1-for-1, down from the 2-for-1 standard in Jacks or Better. That little one-unit drop depresses overall payback by more than 12 percent. Even the big four-of-a-kind bonuses weren't enough to make that up, so in the best-paying versions of Double Bonus, full houses also were raised to 10-for-1, flushes to 7-for-1 and straights to 5-for-1.

Any time a game gives you more at the top of the pay table, it's balanced out by giving you less nearer the bottom. That makes for a choppier, streakier game, since more of the overall payback is tied up in fewer, rarer hands.

11. B or C. If you use the same drawing strategy on a bonus game as on garden variety Jacks or Better, you will hit four of a kind with about the same frequency on both machines. However, if you adjust strategy to account for the bonuses, you actually will hit some fours of a kind more frequently than in the regular game.

For an example of why, check back to Answer No. 7. Notice that in Double Bonus Poker, we break up a full house that includes three Aces to go for the four-Ace jackpot. That increases the frequency with which we hit four Aces in Double Bonus. We get four Aces more often because we give ourselves more chances to draw them.

It is our strategy that makes the difference. There is no programming in the game to depress the number of fours of a kind. Cards still must be dealt from a randomly shuffled 52-card electronic deck.

12. B. Video poker pay tables are meant to make a game playable and enjoyable without precisely corresponding to the probability of hitting winning hands.

In 9-6 Jacks or Better, given expert strategy, full houses, flushes and straights occur with about the same frequency. Full houses actually occur the most frequently of the three, at once per 87 hands, while flushes occur once per 91 and straights once per 89. If video poker pay tables were meant to precisely reflect the odds, would full houses pay 9-for-1, flushes 6-for-1 and straights 4-for-1? No.

But players used to table poker are comfortable with full houses beating flushes and flushes beating straights. The pay table is designed to give the player the comfort of familiar hand ranks while at the same time giving enough back on those hands to sustain interest.

It's the same with Bonus Poker and its variations. Why should four Aces, worth 125 coins for five played on regular Jacks or Better, be worth 400 coins on Bonus Poker, 800 on Double Bonus or 2,000 if accompanied by a 2, 3 or 4 on Double Double Bonus? It's not because the odds of drawing those hands are radically different in different games. It's because offering those jackpots makes the games attractive to players.

13. D. All of the above—casinos offer video poker games with payback percentages of more than 100 percent because they are very popular, casinos hope they will draw customers who will then play other games, too, and most players don't play well enough to get 100 percent payback, so the casino still makes a profit on the games.

A classic example is full-pay Deuces Wild, which returns 100.8 percent with expert play. Despite attempts by casinos and manufacturers to wean players onto other versions of Deuces Wild, the full-pay version survives in Las Vegas because it is so popular. Most players don't know all the ins and outs of the game, so they don't really get 100.8 percent out of it. The casino makes a smaller profit than on other games, but the machines earn enough and draw enough business to justify their existence.

A small cadre of players know exactly what they're doing on full-pay Deuces, however, and the casinos don't want to just give money away. So dollar machines offering full-pay Deuces are becoming as rare as a Strip resort without a theme. Dollar machines attract the pros, who dominate the machines day and night so the amateurs can't get near them. With no amateurs, there's no profit, so the machines are quickly removed.

Full-pay Deuces survives mostly at the quarter level, where the potential profit per hour isn't high enough for the pros to take over.

14. B. Players will find the biggest concentration of 100 percent payback machines in locals-oriented casinos in Las Vegas. Those who look still can find 100 percent machines on the Strip and downtown, and 10-7 Double Bonus Poker turns up in New Jersey, the Midwest and South. There's even a special treat for quarter players at the north end of the Strip—Stratosphere Tower, where 9-7 and 10-6 pay tables turn Jacks or Better into a 100-percent-plus game and an 8-6 pay table does the same for Bonus Poker.

But if you really want a selection of high-paying games, rent a car on your next trip to Las Vegas and check out locals hangouts such as the Fiesta, Texas Station, Santa Fe or Arizona Charlie's in northwest Las Vegas or The Reserve southeast of Las Vegas

15. A. Multiple-game machines should be checked for "hidden" full-pay games.

Several years ago, I was staying at the Stardust on the Las Vegas Strip, and was checking out Double Bonus Poker machines. Most of the quarter games had a 9-6 pay table, and dollar machines were 9-7. But I came across a bank of quarter Bally's Game Maker multiple-game machines, and started pushing "buttons" on the touch screen to see what games were offered. Voila! Full-pay 10-7 Double Bonus Poker.

Fast forward to 1999, when I was checking out the Par-A-Dice Casino in East Peoria, Illinois. There, hidden on $1 Williams Multi-Pay Plus multigame machines, was the casino's only 100-percent game, good old 10-7 Double Bonus. Not only that, but there was also 9-6 Jacks or Better and a 99.7 percent version of Deuces Wild on quarter Triple Play Poker multigame, multihand machines.

Don't just stop at multigame machines that offer only video poker games. Check out the ones that hide a few poker offerings among slot and keno games. On a trip to Trump Casino in Gary, Indiana, I found 7-5 Jacks or Better on quarter IGT Multi-Poker machines, with only video poker games, but was able to improve to 8-5 by looking on Williams Multi-Pay Plus machines that also included slots and keno. A few months later, the same casino added quarter Triple Play Poker machines with 9-6 Jacks or Better.

If you find what you're looking for on a single-game video poker machine, great! If not, check out the multigames before you settle for a lesser pay table.

16. C. A casino that offers full-pay video poker games usually will have a mix of full-pay and lower-paying games.

Even if you're knowledgeable enough and picky enough to stay with the full-pay games, the casino still wants your business. But if you're willing to play the lower-paying games, hey, any business wants to add a little extra to the bottom line. It's up to you to search out the best deal before you play.

17. A. On multiple-hand machines, in which the customer plays three or more hands at once, the chances of hitting a royal flush in a given amount of time increase.

If I bet 800 hands per hour on a single-game machine, and hit a royal an average of once per 40,000 hands, on the average I'll hit one per 50 hours of play. If I stay at 800 plays per hour on Triple Play Poker, I'm getting three hands per play, so in effect I'm playing 2,400 hands per hour. Now it takes me only 16.67 hours to get in 40,000 hands, so I hit a royal an average of once per 16.67 hours. (Actually, it will take slightly longer because of added time required to get three separate draws for tallying larger numbers per winning hand on the meter. But it won't take *much* longer.)

In that 16.67 hours, though, I've still seen 40,000 hands— and, more importantly, bet just as much money as if I'd bet the 40,000 hands one at a time.

18. B. On multiple-hand machines, players should seek out the same pay tables they'd want on a single-hand machine.

I can't possibly emphasize this enough. For some players, multiple-hand games make a quantum leap in the entertainment factor of video poker. They're fun to play, with lots of instant gratification. Some casinos count on the allure of that instant gratification to offer substandard pay tables.

Don't fall for it. If you're playing maximum coins at Triple Play, you're betting 15 coins at a time instead of the five coins at a time on a single-hand game. The last thing you want to do is complicate the effect of larger bets with a low pay table.

One casino on my regular rounds has 9-6 Jacks or Better on $1 single-hand machines. On $1 Triple Play machines, it has 6-5—that's right, 6-5!—Jacks or Better. Play 800 hands per hour, five coins at a time, on a single-hand 9-6 Jacks game, and you bet

$4,000 per hour, with an expected average loss of $20. Play single-hand 6-5 Jacks, with an average payback of 95.1 percent with expert play, and those average losses jump to $176 per hour. Make it 6-5 Triple Play, and the losses leap to $528 per hour. Ouch! And triple ouch!

Casinos asking players to bet 15 coins or more per play have no business shorting their customers on the pay table. And customers who should know better have no business settling for that one-way trip to the poorhouse.

19. C. On multiple-hand machines, the player should play the same strategy appropriate to pay table as on a single-hand game.

Seeing three or more hands at once doesn't change the odds of the game. Look at it this way: If you have Ace-King-Queen-Jack of diamonds and a 10 of clubs on a single-hand game, you break up the straight, discard the 10 of clubs and hope for a royal flush, right? Of course you do. It's not even a close call. If you saw that hand three times, you'd discard the 10 three times. Same thing if you saw it four times, or five, or 10, or 50. The best play is always to discard the 10.

Well, on multihand machines, we see that hand three times, or four, or five, or 10, or 50, only they're all at once. (Yes, Virginia, there is a Fifty Play Poker.) Break up a straight that pays 4-for-1 in Fifty Play Poker, and you toss away 200 coins at once. Isn't it worth it for the chance that at least one of your 50 draws will give you a royal flush for 4,000 coins, not to mention other possible winners? Of course it is.

The best percentage play is always the best percentage play, no matter how many hands are involved.

20. B. Given a multiple-hand quarter game, a single-hand quarter game and a single-hand dollar game with the same pay tables, a player with a limited bankroll is better off playing maximum coins on the single-hand quarter game.

The payback percentage on video poker games is highest with maximum coins wagered because of the jump in the payoff on royal flushes. Typically, if you hit a royal with one coin wagered, you get 250 coins back, but if you hit a royal with five coins wagered the payback doesn't rise proportionately and give you 1,250 coins, but skyrockets to 4,000 coins.

As a consequence, the payback percentage with fewer coins wagered is always lower than the percentage paid with maximum coins bet. Not only that, but the portion of the wager covered by the fifth coin almost always returns more than 100 percent. A 99.5 percent return on 9-6 Jacks or Better breaks down to 98.4 percent on each of the first four coins, and about 104 percent on the fifth coin.

In plain English, if you play 1,000 hands, betting one coin on each, on a $1 9-6 Jacks or Better machine, your average expected loss is about $16. Play on a quarter Triple Play machine instead, betting one quarter on each of three hands for a 75-cent bet per play, and your average losses are $12. But bet five quarters at a time on a single-hand 9-6 Jacks machine, and your expected losses drop to $6.50.

You risk $1,250 per 1,000 hands betting maximum coins on the single-hand quarter machine, which is higher than the $1,000 you'd risk betting one coin at a time on the single-hand dollar machine or the $750 you'd risk betting three quarters per play on Triple Play. But the difference in payback percentages means you're getting a much better run for your money betting the max.

If your bankroll is limited enough that you can afford only to play one coin at a time at the lowest denomination in which a game is offered, that's fine. It's never a good idea to overbet your bankroll. And sometimes, if the disparity in pay tables is wide enough, you'll get a better return betting one coin at a time in a higher denomination game than betting maximum coins at a lower denomination. That 98.4 percent return for one-coin play on 9-6 Jacks or Better beats the 97.3 percent return with max coins bet on the 8-5 version. So if your casino offers 9-6 Jacks on dollars and 8-5 or worse on quarters, you may want to bet one coin at a time in the 9-6ers rather than settle for the weaker quarter game.

But given equal pay tables, you're better off stepping down a denomination and playing maximum coins than playing one coin at a higher denomination.

Shuffle No. 2:
The Match Game, Part I

Match the following video poker games with their descriptions:

1. **Jacks or Better**

2. **Bonus Poker**

3. **Double Bonus Poker**

4. **Double Double Bonus Poker**

5. **Double Double Jackpot Poker**

6. **Aces and Faces**

7. **Multi-Pay Poker**

8. **Big E Poker**

9. **Money Fever**

10. **Triple Play Poker**

11. **Triple Bonus Poker**

12. **Lucky Draw Poker**

13. **All-American Poker**

14. **Reel Deal**

15. **Super Bonus Poker**

16. **Spin Poker**

17. **Double Down Stud**

18. Pick 'Em Poker

19. Five Deck Frenzy

20. Pick Five

A. This four-hand game involves four different pay tables and four separate draws. A single base hand is dealt, but the player is given the opportunity to hold different cards for each pay table. It attempts to draw players into making maximum-coin bets by offering the best pay table on the fourth hand.

B. The customer plays three hands at once. The base hand is at the bottom of the screen. Cards that are held in that hand then appear in all three. When the player hits the "draw" button, the hand is played out with the same cards held, but with three different draws.

C. Pays a 1,600-coin jackpot for five coins wagered if the fifth card to go with four Aces is a face card. Enhances other four-of-a-kind payoffs and full houses, but not flushes or straights. Pays only 1-for-1 on two pair. A volatile game, with much of the overall payback tied up in certain rare hands.

D. Mimics multiline video slots by putting cards on video slot reels. The five cards that stop on a center payline serve as a base hand. The player chooses which cards to hold, then spins the reels to draw the remaining cards on nine paylines.

E. Two stacks of five cards each are dealt. The player sees the top three cards in each stack. The player then picks one of the two hands, and the remaining two cards in that stack are turned face up. Winning hands start at a pair of 9s or better.

F. The first game to offer enhanced payouts of four of a kind, it reduces paybacks on full houses and flushes. Offers increased payoffs on four Aces or four 2s, 3s or 4s. It still pays 2-for-1 on two pair, leaving a fairly steady game.

G. All four-of-a-kind payoffs are enhanced, with four Aces paying 1,200 coins for a five-coin bet, four 2s through 4s paying 600 and other quads paying 375. Full house and flush payoffs are enhanced, but straights pay the same 4-for-1 as Jacks or Better, and two pair pays only 1-for-1.

H. Pays a 2,000-coin jackpot for five coins wagered if the fifth card to go with four Aces is a 2, 3 or 4. Enhances other four-of-a-kind payoffs, but does not enhance full houses, flushes or straights. Pays only 1-for-1 on two pair. A real roller-coaster ride—the player either wins big or loses fast.

I. An early four-of-a-kind bonus game, it offers enhanced paybacks on four Aces or four Jacks, Queens and Kings. Reduces payoffs on full houses and flushes, but still pays 2-for-1 on two pair. For a bonus game, a fairly steady play.

J. The player receives only five cards. There is no draw. However, after the first four cards are dealt, the player has the option of doubling his bet.

K. The video screen includes slot reels as well as cards. The pay table on the basic game is low by video poker standards, but some winning hands give the player the opportunity to spin the slot reels to multiply the payoff.

L. Starts the pay table with a pair of Kings or better, and does not pay on two Jacks or two Queens. Pays on all types of winning combinations contained in the player's final hand. A royal flush, for example, gives the player payoffs for a royal flush, straight flush, flush and straight.

M. Full houses, flushes and straights all pay 8-for-1, a big leap on flushes and straights and a slight decrease on full houses compared with most Jacks or Better–based games. Four-of-a-kind payoffs are also enhanced, but two pair pays only 1-for-1.

N. This is video poker with a Western theme, from old-fashioned-looking cards and Old West graphics to the gunshots and twangy guitar themes that accompany winning hands. The customer plays four hands at once. The base hand is at the bottom of the screen. Cards that are held in that hand then appear in the other three. When the player hits the "draw" button, the hand is played out with the same cards held, but four different draws.

O. The first video poker game to offer a progressive jackpot in the hundreds of thousands of dollars, the big payoff is on five Aces of spades.

P. Enhances the bonus payoff on four Aces to 160-for-1, leaving a frequent-hit 800-coin jackpot for five coins wagered. Also enhances payoffs on other fours of a kind, full houses, flushes and straights, but reduces the two-pair payoff to 1-for-1, creating a much more volatile game.

Q. The player sees a total of 10 cards, two at a time. As each two cards are shown, the player picks one on the way to building a five-card hand.

R. A low-paying game most of the time, it kicks into overdrive whenever the player hits a flush. For the next seven hands, the game not only pays off winning combinations according to the pay table, but also awards a bonus for each card in the flush suit.

S. The classic video poker game on which most others are based. Often called simply "Draw Poker" on the machine glass, it offers no fancy bonuses on rare hands, just a solid pay table starting at a pair of Jacks that keeps the player and bankroll on more of an even keel than most games.

T. The player arranges 17 cards into four five-card hands along one vertical column and three horizontal lines. Cards at the left ends of the horizontal lines also are used in the vertical column. At any given time, the player sees a card to be placed and a preview of the next one in the stack of 17.

Shuffle No. 2:
The Match Game, Part I
Answers

1. S. Jacks or Better is the game that started the video poker boom. Earlier 10s or Better games, with lower overall pay tables, showed small promise, but once 9-6 Jacks or Better hit the floor, customers crowded around for a chance to play. Jacks or Better still has a place in nearly every casino, although it seems almost sedate in comparison with games that offer big bonuses on rare hands.

I still enjoy Jacks or Better, as long as I can find a machine with a 9-6 pay table on full houses and flushes. Just ask my wife, who to this day insists on leaving for the airport an hour or more early because a few years ago we wound up running for our plane after I was caught up in a good run on a 9-6er at Treasure Island.

You'll not have as many big wins as on a flashier game with big bonuses, but you'll walk away with more small wins and usually have a good run for your money even when you lose.

2. F. Bonus Poker, in its full-pay version, takes basic Jacks or Better and reduces its full house-flush payoffs to 8-5. That would reduce the overall payback percentage to 97.3 percent, except that Bonus Poker enhances payoffs on certain four-of-a-kind hands. Bet five coins on Jacks or Better, and any four of a kind brings you 125 coins. That's still true with Bonus Poker if the four of a kind consists of 5s through Kings. Hit four 2s, 3s or 4s, and the payoff goes up to 200 coins, and on four Aces, it's 400.

25

That brings the payback on 8-5 Bonus Poker up to 99.2 percent with expert play, far better than 8-5 Jacks or Better. Some casinos reduce the pay table still further, to 7-for-1 or even 6-for-1 on full houses. You lose a little more than 1 percent of your payback for each unit the full house or flush payback is reduced.

3. P. Double Bonus Poker is a touchstone in the history of video poker. It made converts of a segment of slot players who wanted a little better run for their money, and still wanted to have a shot at a jackpot they deemed worth taking home.

One former slot player told me, "I used to think video poker was boring. You never won much of anything unless you hit a royal flush, and how often does that happen? But with Double Bonus Poker, you get $200 (for a five-quarter bet) when you hit four Aces. Then you feel like you've won something."

It's not just the payoff on four Aces that's enhanced. Bet five coins, and you get 400 back on four 2s, 3s or 4s, and 250 on any other four of a kind—a giant leap from the 125 on all quads on Jacks or Better. Full house–flush–straight payoffs also are enhanced to 10-7-5 in the 100.2 percent–return full-pay version, up from 9-6-4 in full-pay Jacks or Better. Double Bonus also is available in 9-7-5, 9-6-5 and 8-5-4 versions. (Tip: Don't play Double Bonus if straights pay only 4-for-1.)

To make up for the bonuses and other pay table enhancements, the two-pair payoff was dropped from 2-for-1 to 1-for-1. In Jacks or Better, two-pair hands account for about a quarter of our paybacks, so the effect of cutting the payoff in half is enormous. Concentrating more of the payback in fewer, rarer hands makes Double Bonus a very volatile game.

4. H. If you're going to play Double Double Bonus Poker for long, the quads better be coming. As on most video poker games, the big jackpot is on a royal flush, where you take away 4,000 coins for a five-coin wager. But four Aces with either a 2, 3 or 4 as the fifth card are worth 2,000 coins—fully half the royal flush value. Not only that, but if you hit four 2s, 3s or 4s with an Ace, 2, 3 or 4 as the fifth card, you get 800 coins, as big as the jackpot on four Aces in Double Bonus Poker.

Other fours of a kind pay the same as in Double Bonus—250 coins for five played for four 5s through Kings, 400 for four 2s, 3s or 4s and 800 for four Aces without the fifth-card bonus.

The full-pay version, returning 98.9 percent in the long run, pays 9-for-1 on full houses and 6-for-1 on flushes. Unlike Double Bonus, it does not enhance straight paybacks—they're 4-for-1 as in Jacks or Better. It does reduce two pair to 1-for-1.

This game is extremely popular, but'll have your bankroll doing bungee jumps.

5. C. Double Double Jackpot is Sigma Games' answer to IGT's Double Double Bonus. Instead of having the bonus on four Aces kick in when the fifth card is a 2, 3 or 4, Double Double Bonus ups the payoff to 1,600 coins when four Aces are joined by a Jack, Queen or King. Not only that, payoffs are enhanced on four Jacks, Queens and Kings instead of 2s, 3s or 4s. Hit four Jacks, Queens or Kings with an Ace, Jack, Queen or King as the fifth card, and you take away 800 coins.

Because we hold Jacks, Queens or Kings more often than 2s, 3s or 4s, that magnifies the effect of the bonuses. We hit the bonus four of a kinds more often in Double Double Jackpot than in Double Double Bonus.

The rest of the pay table is the same as in Double Double Bonus. However, the switch in four-of-a-kind bonuses makes Double Double Jackpot a higher-paying game whenever the remainder of the pay tables are equal. The full-pay, 9-6 version of Double Double Jackpot pays 100.3 percent in the long run, compared with 98.9 percent on 9-6 Double Double Bonus.

6. I. Aces and Faces is basically Bonus Poker, except that four-of-a-kind bonuses are paid on four Jacks, Queens or Kings instead of 2s, 3s and 4s. Both games pay 400 coins on four Aces with five coins wagered, but Aces and Faces pays 200 coins on four Jacks Queens and Kings, where Bonus Poker pays that amount on four 2s, 3s or 4s.

That means the bonuses occur more frequently in Aces and Faces, since we will hold a single face card but will never hold a single 2, 3 or 4. That makes Aces and Faces, in its 8-5 full-pay version, a 99.5 percent game instead of the 99.2 in 8-5 Bonus Poker.

7. L. At first glance, Multi-Pay Poker looks like a horrendous game. Players see a game that starts the pay table at 7-for-1 on full houses, 20-for-1 on four of a kind. If they don't take the time to investigate more fully, they'll just walk away, or switch to a different game on the Multi-Pay Plus multiple-games machines by Williams that include the game.

But at closer look, we see that this is not a bad game. Players are paid on every type of winner contained in a hand. Hit a full house, and you're not only paid the 7-for-1, you also get 3-for-1 on three of a kind and 2-for-1 on two pair, and you might also get 1-for-1 if your hand includes Kings or Aces. That makes the full house worth not 7-for-1, but 12-for-1 or 13-for-1.

Hit two pair, including Kings or Aces, and you don't get 2-for-1; you get a total of 3-for-1. And since we save single Kings or Aces, a disproportionate share of our two-pair hands pay 3-for-1.

At the Tropicana in Las Vegas, I once hit a royal flush on quarter Multi-Pay Poker. I was paid $1,137 in cash that broke down as follows: 4,000 coins for the royal flush, 500 coins for a straight flush, 25 coins for a flush and 20 coins for a straight. Total: 4,545 coins, or $1,136.25, which the Trop rounded up to $1,137.

8. T. Big E Poker is kind of an odd duck in the video poker world. Players arrange the cards in the shape of a big E. (And you thought that name was just some marketing ploy!) There has been no real strategy developed for Big E yet, and the best I can tell you is to place royal flush cards out on the points, where they can be used both in the vertical column and in the horizontal lines.

Testing out the Big E at The Reserve in Henderson, Nevada, I did manage to arrange a straight flush for myself. But as often as not, late in the game you're groaning that you wish you'd placed this card here and that one there. Play this one for entertainment value if you have a couple of rolls of nickels burning a hole in your pocket, but save your serious play for stronger opportunities.

9. R. Money Fever also is called Bonus Flush Poker on some Williams Multi-Pay Play units. The pay table on the basic game starts at two pair, but the basic game is not where you make your money. When you hit a flush, for the next seven hands you're paid for every card in your flush suit. For example, if you're betting five coins at a time and you hit a flush in spades, and your next hand is 10 of spades, 10 of clubs, 2 of spades, 2 of hearts and Jack of spades, you're paid 20 coins—five for the two pair, and five for each of the three spades.

Better yet, if you hit another flush during the bonus hands, you get another seven hands in Fever mode after you've completed the first seven bonus hands.

There's some question about the long-term payback on this machine. Early reports suggested that the full-pay version, which pays 9-for-1 on full houses and 6-for-1 on flushes, paid in excess of 100 percent with expert play. But TomSki, who devised the Video Poker Strategy Master software, says he comes up with less than 98 percent.

10. B. Triple Play Poker has revolutionized video poker. Every major manufacturer now is showing multiple-hand games. Players can bet three, four, five, 10 or 50 hands at a time. During a stay at The Reserve, I noted that the Ten Play Poker machines were constantly busy. Who knows where this will stop?

At Triple Play, you see one five card hand, and you choose which cards to hold. Those cards then appear face up in your second and third hands. Hit draw, and the remaining 47 cards in the electronic deck are shuffled three times, and you get three different draws.

A variety of games are available on the multigame Triple Play units. You can play three hands at a time on Jacks or Better, Bonus Poker, Double Bonus Poker, Deuces Wild, Double Double Bonus Poker—just about anything.

In 1999, fellow gambling author Frank Scoblete and I were giving seminars together at the Golden Nugget in Las Vegas. One fellow who attended every gathering decided to play Triple Play Poker, and discovered the video poker definition of Nirvana when he was dealt a royal flush off the top of the deck. On Triple Play, that's *three* royals!

11. G. Triple Bonus Poker is a single-hand game, not to be confused with Triple Play Poker. Payoffs are huge on all fours of a kind—375 coins for five wagered for four 5s through Kings, 600 on four 2s, 3s or 4s or 1,200 on four Aces.

Full houses are enhanced to 11-for-1 and flushes to 7-for-1 on the full-pay version, which in the long run returns 99.6 percent with expert play. But the game takes away plenty at the bottom of the pay table, with two pair reduced to 1-for-1, the same payoff as a pair of Kings or Aces. Pairs of Jacks or Queens pay nothing. If you don't hit a four of a kind or two, you won't play for long. But if you do, you should walk away with a nice win.

12. N. Lucky Draw is Silicon Gaming's answer to IGT's Triple Play Poker. The games play exactly the same, except that in Lucky Draw your first hand is a start to four final hands instead of three. Lucky Draw is found on Silicon's high-tech Odyssey machines, with elongated video screens and enhanced sound, computer graphics and special effects.

IGT and Action Gaming, which developed Triple Play Poker and licensed it to IGT, thought Lucky Draw was a little too close to their game. They claimed copyright infringement and stopped distribution of the Silicon games until a licensing agreement was worked out.

13. M. All-American Poker, sometimes called Gator Poker, is an odd little game, found mostly in Bally's Game Maker multi-game machines, with sightings in the late 1990s at the Las Vegas Hilton and at Bally's in Las Vegas. Its distinguishing characteristic is that it has the same payoff, 8-for-1, on full houses, flushes and straights. All fours of a kind pay 40-for-1, and straight flushes are enhanced to 200-for-1. Two pair pays only 1-for-1 as does a pair of Jacks or better.

In the long run, with expert play, this is a 100.7 percent game, one of the best around. With the reduced pay on two pair, long losing streaks are possible. But if you get a larger than normal share of the 8-for-1 hands, you'll do quite nicely on this game.

14. K. Reel Deal introduces an uncertainty factor into video poker. There are different versions of the game, and different pay tables, but all offer low returns on the basic game.

I came across one that was basically 8-5 Jacks or Better, with some drastic differences. Three of a kind paid only 2-for-1, and two pair only 1-for-1, cutting the overall payback by about 20 percent from the 97.3 on basic 8-5 Jacks.

However, any three of a kind or better was worth a spin of the video reels. Each of the three reels had a wild symbol, a red 7, a blue 7 and three blanks. Payoffs were multiplied by 10 for three wilds, five for three red 7s, or two for three blue 7s or mixed 7s. If every stop had an equal chance of occurring, per 216 trials, we'd multiply our payoffs by 10 an average of once, by five seven times and by two 19 times. Of every 216 trials, 189 would leave our payoff the same.

What would that do to our payoff? In this case, it would take it up only to 88.5 percent, making this an incredibly weak game for video poker. Is it possible that we get more than that? Only if the winning reel symbols occur more often than the blanks, and that's an uncertainty most video poker players won't want to tackle.

15. A. Super Bonus Poker is Bally Gaming's entry into the multihand derby. It's designed for Bally's Game Magic platform, a high-tech machine similar to Silicon Gaming's Odyssey machines.

Each hand on Super Bonus Poker has a higher pay table than the one before. Bally's rates the long-term payback on the fourth hand at 103 percent, but you have to play the other three hands to get the fourth one.

Because the pay tables are all different, Super Bonus Poker allows you to hold different cards from the base hand for each draw. That's good for the player—I wouldn't want to be stuck with the same draw on four different games—but the extra decision time means the game is slower than other multihand games, so casinos will think twice about offering it.

16. D. A new game from Action Gaming, the same company that designed Triple Play Poker, Spin Poker combines video poker skill with the nine-line format that has proved popular on video reel slots. You start with a five card hand, choose which cards to hold, then spin the video reels to draw cards on the nine pay lines.

Spin Poker will be available for different games and different pay tables—you'll be able to play Spin Poker Jacks or Better or Spin Poker Bonus Poker. Odds are the same as they would be for a single-hand machine. As with any video poker game, scout the pay tables before you play.

17. J. Double Down Stud started its life as a table game, and was adapted as a video poker game. It's five-card stud poker instead of the usual five card draw, with a pay table that starts at a pair of 6s.

Strategy is easy: Double your bet whenever you have a winning hand in the first four cards, or whenever you have a four-card flush or open-ended straight.

The long-term payback of 97.8 percent isn't as strong as on the best draw-poker based games, and Double Down Stud has never carved out a large share of the market. It remains a specialty game available only in a few Nevada casinos.

18. E. Pick 'Em Poker is available on both single-game machines and Bally's Game Maker multigame machines. In Nevada, it appears mostly on multigame machines, while there are single-game machines in New Jersey.

Payoffs start at a pair of 9s or better, but even the lowest winner at the game pays 2-for-1. A royal with five coins bet pays 6,000 coins, instead of the 4,000 common on draw poker variations.

The player must decide which three-card stack to hold based on a look at the top card in each stack plus two cards that must be kept. Since a return of 99.95 percent with expert play makes this the best game widely available in an Atlantic City market not known for strong video poker, we'll focus on several strategy answers later in this book.

19. O. Five Deck Frenzy uses five decks. They're color-coded—the backs of the electronic decks are different colors. You receive one card from each deck, and when you draw, your replacement cards come from the same decks as the discards.

That makes a big progressive jackpot possible since a sufficiently rare hand—five Aces of spades—is available. There's not a lot of Five Deck Frenzy about. It never really penetrated the Strip tourist market. It's mainly available in limited quantities at off-Strip casinos.

20. Q. Pick Five Poker is a specialty game that has largely withered after a short burst of interest. Players build their own hand, choosing one of each two cards they see at a time until they complete a five-card hand. Game developers claimed a 103 percent payback was possible with expert play, but that expert strategy practically took a *War and Peace*-sized computer printout to detail.

On top of that, it is a very slow game, since players have five separate card decisions to make. That alone would have meant limited space in casinos that like fast decisions and more opportunities for profit per hour. Response from players has largely been lukewarm, so the game seems destined for the dark corners of a limited number of casinos.

Shuffle No. 3:
The Match Game, Part II

In the strategy sections of this book, we'll be referring to different types of hands. No doubt everyone knows what three of a kind is, but I sometimes get letters from readers wondering just what in the world I'm on about when I write about double-inside straight flushes. So let's match the hands below with their descriptions:

1. **8 of clubs, Jack of diamonds, 5 of hearts, 2 of spades, Jack of clubs.**

2. **9 of hearts, 2 of spades, 3 of diamonds, 2 of clubs, 9 of spades.**

3. **Queen of clubs, Queen of hearts, 10 of diamonds, Queen of spades, 7 of clubs.**

4. **8 of hearts, 9 of hearts, 10 of clubs, Jack of spades, Queen of diamonds.**

5. **2 of spades, 3 of spades, 7 of spades, 9 of spades, Ace of spades.**

6. **Ace of hearts, Ace of spades, Ace of clubs, King of diamonds, King of clubs.**

7. **5 of diamonds, 5 of clubs, 2 of clubs, 5 of spades, 5 of hearts.**

8. 3 of diamonds, 4 of diamonds, 5 of diamonds, 6 of diamonds, 7 of diamonds.

9. Ace of clubs, King of clubs, Queen of clubs, Jack of clubs, 10 of clubs.

10. 8 of spades, 7 of hearts, 8 of diamonds, 6 of clubs, 2 of clubs.

11. 4 of spades, 5 of clubs, 6 of clubs, 7 of spades, Jack of diamonds.

12. 4 of spades, 5 of clubs, 7 of spades, 8 of hearts, Jack of diamonds.

13. 2 of hearts, 5 of hearts, 9 of hearts, Jack of hearts, 8 of spades.

14. 4 of clubs, 5 of clubs, 6 of clubs, 7 of clubs, 10 of spades.

15. 4 of clubs, 5 of clubs, 7 of clubs, 8 of clubs, 10 of spades.

16. 2 of diamonds, 5 of hearts, 6 of hearts, 7 of hearts, 10 of diamonds.

17. 2 of diamonds, 5 of hearts, 7 of hearts, 8 of hearts, 10 of diamonds.

18. 3 of clubs, 5 of diamonds, 6 of hearts, 7 of hearts, 10 of hearts.

19. Queen of spades, Jack of spades, 8 of spades, 6 of hearts, 3 of clubs.

20. Jack of spades, 8 of hearts, 5 of diamonds, Ace of spades, Queen of spades.

A. Straight.

B. Three-card inside straight flush.

C. Four-card flush.

D. Full house.

E. High pair.

F. Four-card inside straight flush.

G. Four-card open-ended straight.

H. Three of a kind.

I. Three-card royal.

J. Four-card open-ended straight flush.

K. Four of a kind.

L. Three-card open-ended straight flush.

M. Royal flush.

N. Three-card double-inside straight flush with two high cards.

O. Two pair.

P. Three-card double-inside straight flush with no high cards.

Q. Low pair.

R. Four-card inside straight.

S. Flush.

T. Straight flush.

Shuffle No. 3:
The Match Game, Part II
Answers

1. E. 8 of clubs, Jack of diamonds, 5 of hearts, 2 of spades, Jack of clubs: high pair.

If two cards of the same denomination bring us a payoff, that's a high pair. In most of the games we'll be exploring, pairs of Jacks, Queens, Kings or Aces are considered high pairs. Get two Jacks, and the machine gives you back one coin for every coin wagered. In a few games, notably Triple Bonus Poker and Joker's Wild Kings or Better, the pay table starts with a pair of Kings. In those cases, Queens and Jacks are not high pairs since they bring us no payoffs. In Deuces Wild and Joker's Wild Two Pair or Better, we get no payoff on any pair, so in those games we won't talk about high pairs.

2. O. 9 of hearts, 2 of spades, 3 of diamonds, 2 of clubs, 9 of spades: two pair.

Two of one kind and two of another—in this case two 9s and two 2s—will bring a payoff in most games. The major exception is Deuces Wild, where most pay tables start at three of a kind.

3. H. Queen of clubs, Queen of hearts, 10 of diamonds, Queen of spades, 7 of clubs: three of a kind.

Three cards of the same denomination always bring some payoff—3-for-1 in most games, although it's as low as 1-for-1 in Deuces Wild and as high as 6-for-1 on Aces in Nevada Bonus Poker. In some games, the biggest share of our long-term payback comes from three of a kind, as we'll see when we get to Double Bonus Poker.

4. A. 8 of hearts, 9 of hearts, 10 of clubs, Jack of spades, Queen of diamonds: straight.

Five cards of consecutive rank make up a straight. In many video poker games, they occur about as often as flushes and full houses, but they usually don't pay as much. An exception: All-American Poker, in which flushes, full houses and straights all pay 8-for-1.

5. S. 2 of spades, 3 of spades, 7 of spades, 9 of spades, Ace of spades: flush.

Five cards of the same suit make up a flush. In Jacks or Better–based games, flushes are one of the two main hands in which casinos and manufacturers vary the pay table to change the payback percentage. Full houses are the other.

6. D. Ace of hearts, Ace of spades, Ace of clubs, King of diamonds, King of clubs: full house.

Three cards of one denomination and two of another denomination make up a full house. In most games, when we're dealt a full house in our first five cards, we wouldn't think of doing anything but accepting our payoff gladly. For an exception, see the chapter on Double Bonus Poker.

7. K. 5 of diamonds, 5 of clubs, 2 of clubs, 5 of spades, 5 of hearts: four of a kind.

Four cards of the same denomination = four of a kind. When you see the word "Bonus" in the name of a game, you can be sure there's an enhanced payback on at least some fours of a kind. Bonus Poker, Double Bonus Poker, Double Double Bonus Poker, Nevada Bonus Poker, Triple Bonus Poker—they all give the player a chance at a good payday on four of a kind.

8. T. 3 of diamonds, 4 of diamonds, 5 of diamonds, 6 of diamonds, 7 of diamonds: straight flush.

It's just like the name sounds: Five cards of consecutive denominations, as in a straight, and all of the same suit, as in a flush. Straight flushes are rare, and don't pay off in proportion to their rarity. In most Jacks or Better–based games, we derive only half percent or so of our total payback on straight flushes.

One night at the Tropicana in Las Vegas, I was playing Double Bonus Poker, and the fellow at the next machine started ranting. "Look at this. A straight flush only pays 250 (for five coins bet), and four Aces pay 800. It should be just the opposite. A straight flush is a lot harder to get."

I just let him rant. Putting the big payoff on more frequently occurring hands is nothing to complain about. Heck, given my choice, I'd like to have the 800-coin payoff on a pair of Jacks or better. But then the casinos would lose money, close down and where would we be?

9. M. Ace of clubs, King of clubs, Queen of clubs, Jack of clubs, 10 of clubs: royal flush.

A royal flush is just an Ace-high straight flush—Ace-King-Queen-Jack-10 of the same suit. It's also the one hand in most games on which there's a bonus for betting maximum coins. Typically, a royal flush pays 250 coins for one bet, 500 for two, 750 for three, 1,000 for four... but jumps all the way to 4,000 when that fifth coin is bet.

Occasionally, the payoff is enhanced even further. Some machines, notably in downtown Las Vegas, pay 4,750 coins on a royal when five coins are wagered. Why such an odd figure? On a quarter machine, that's $1,187.50, just a tad below the $1,200 at which the casino and the player are required to file paperwork with the IRS.

Other machines pay 5,000 coins on a royal, and still others pay a progressive jackpot, in which a portion of the coins wagered are added to the royal flush jackpot until somebody wins.

10. Q. 8 of spades, 7 of hearts, 8 of diamonds, 6 of clubs, 2 of clubs: low pair.

A low pair is two cards of the same denomination that do not bring a payoff. On a Jacks or Better game, a pair of 10s or lower is a low pair. On a Kings or Better game, pairs of Queens or Jacks also are low pairs.

11. G. 4 of spades, 5 of clubs, 6 of clubs, 7 of spades, Jack of diamonds: four-card open-ended straight.

Four cards of consecutive denominations are a four-card open-ended straight. Why do we care that it's open-ended? Because a straight can be completed for a paying hand by drawing a card at either end. In this case, with 4-5-6-7, we can complete a straight by drawing any of the deck's four 3s or four 8s.

12. R. 4 of spades, 5 of clubs, 7 of spades, 8 of hearts, Jack of diamonds: four-card inside straight.

Here we have four cards that would be consecutive except for a gap in the middle—4-5-7-8. To complete a straight, we need to fill that gap in the middle. In this case, it takes one of the four 6s in the deck to complete the straight. With only four cards available to give us our winner, we have only half the chance of completing an inside straight as we would to complete an open-ended straight.

A couple of other hands are considered inside straights even though you don't see the gap in the middle. With Ace-King-Queen-Jack, you can't go higher than the Ace, so only the four 10s could complete the straight. With Ace-2-3-4, you can't go lower than the Ace, so only the four 5s could complete the straight. Those are inside straights as surely as if the gap were in the middle of the hand.

13. C. 2 of hearts, 5 of hearts, 9 of hearts, Jack of hearts, 8 of spades: four-card flush.

Four cards of the same suit are four-card flushes. Since there are 13 cards of each suit, we have nine chances in the remaining cards to finish a four-card flush. That makes it more likely to complete a four-card flush than a four-card open-ended straight, which has eight ways to finish it off. Keep that in mind when you're dealt a hand that includes both, such as 2 of hearts, 3 of hearts, 4 of clubs, 5 of hearts, 9 of hearts.

14. J. 4 of clubs, 5 of clubs, 6 of clubs, 7 of clubs, 10 of spades: four-card open-ended straight flush.

Four consecutive cards, all of the same suit, are a four-card open-ended straight flush. That gives us two chances to complete the straight flush—one on each end.

15. F. 4 of clubs, 5 of clubs, 7 of clubs, 8 of clubs, 10 of spades: four-card inside straight flush.

With a four-card inside straight flush, we have only one shot to complete it, by filling the gap in the middle.

16. L. 2 of diamonds, 5 of hearts, 6 of hearts, 7 of hearts, 10 of diamonds: three-card open-ended straight flush.

Three consecutive cards, all of the same suit, are a three-card open-ended straight flush. That leaves us three possible two-card draws that would give us a straight flush. In this hand, with 5, 6 and 7 of hearts, we can complete a straight flush with the 3 and 4 of hearts, 4 and 8 of hearts or 8 and 9 of hearts.

17. B. 2 of diamonds, 5 of hearts, 7 of hearts, 8 of hearts, 10 of diamonds: three-card inside straight flush.

With one gap in the middle, we're left with only two ways to complete a straight flush. Here, with 5, 7 and 8 of hearts, the 6 of hearts must be part of any draw that completes a straight flush. We make it with either 4 and 6 or 6 and 9.

18. P. 3 of clubs, 5 of diamonds, 6 of hearts, 7 of hearts, 10 of hearts: three-card double-inside straight flush with no high cards.

With two gaps, we have only one draw that will complete a straight flush—both gaps must be filled. With 6, 7 and 10 of hearts, we must draw the 8 and 9 to complete a straight flush.

19. N. Queen of spades, Jack of spades, 8 of spades, 6 of hearts, 3 of clubs: three-card double-inside straight flush with two high cards.

Our double-inside straight flushes—indeed, any of our partial straight flushes—are more valuable if they include high cards. That way, if we fail to draw a straight flush, flush or straight, we still could get a winner at the bottom of the pay table by pairing one of the high cards.

20. I. Jack of spades, 8 of hearts, 5 of diamonds, Ace of spades, Queen of spades: three-card royal.

Any three cards of the same suit from among Ace, King, Queen, Jack and 10 make up a three-card royal. Not all three-card royals are created equal. If there's an Ace involved, it limits all straight draws to Ace high, and means we can hit no straight flushes other than royals. If there's a 10, that's one less high card that could be paired for a low-end payoff. In expert strategies, we will sometimes split hairs about the value of three-card royals. For example, in 10-7 Double Bonus Poker, most three-card royals are more valuable than four-card flushes, but what about something like Ace-Queen-10-4 of the same suit? Then we keep all four parts of the flush. Most players will be better off just remembering to keep three-card royals, but for those who want every drop a game has to give, you'll have to split the hairs.

Shuffle No. 4: Definitions

Any game of chance has its own terminology, and video poker is no exception. When we get to strategy problems in coming chapters, we'll be using terms such as "penalty card" and "expected value" over and over again. See if you can define the following video poker terms:

1. **9-6 Jacks or Better**
2. **Penalty card**
3. **Four-card inside straight**
4. **Expert strategy**
5. **Payback percentage**
6. **Shadow hand**
7. **High cards**
8. **Slot club**
9. **Expected value**
10. **Full-pay machine**
11. **100-percent game**
12. **2-for-1 payoff**
13. **Progressive jackpot**
14. **Wild card**
15. **Bonus four-of-a-kind**

Shuffle No. 4: Definitions Answers

1. A 9-6 Jacks or Better game is one that pays 9-for-1 on full houses and 6-for-1 on flushes.

More important than simply knowing "9-6 Jacks or Better" is understanding that the biggest difference on most Jacks or Better–based games is the payoff on full houses and flushes. Throughout this book, we'll use two hyphenated numbers to refer to the full house and flush payoffs that make the difference between two otherwise similar machines.

When you see a reference to 8-5 Jacks or Better, you'll know it's a game that pays 8-for-1 on full houses and 5-for-1 on flushes. If it's 10-7 Double Bonus Poker, it pays 10-for-1 on full houses and 7-for-1 on flushes. If any other payoffs are varied from the standard for that game, it'll be noted.

Referring to Deuces Wild games by numbers would get a little unwieldy, so let's just not do it, okay? There's no sense trying to compare 25-15-9-5-3-2 Deuces Wild to 25-15-9-4-4-3 to 25-16-13-4-3-2. Instead, there will be a little explanatory note with each game. That ought to make it easier on everyone.

2. A penalty card is one received on the initial deal that, if discarded, would decrease the odds of drawing flushes or straights.

For example, if you keep King and Queen of diamonds and discard the 2 of diamonds, the 2 is a penalty card because it is a potential piece of a diamond flush that is no longer available to you. If you keep King and Queen of diamonds and discard a 9 of spades, the 9 is a penalty card because it is no longer available to you as a piece of a straight.

Penalty cards sometimes make a difference in the way an expert plays a hand. If you're playing 9-6 Jacks or Better and you're dealt Ace of hearts, King of diamonds, Queen of spades, Jack of spades and 4 of clubs, your best play is to hold Queen-Jack of spades, keeping alive possibilities for any type of winning hand, including a royal flush. However, if that 4 is in spades instead of clubs, an expert holds Ace-King-Queen-Jack instead, hoping either for a 10 to complete a straight or a high card for a pair of Jacks or better. The 4 of spades is a flush penalty card, decreasing chances of hitting a flush just enough that holding Queen-Jack is not quite as good a play as holding all four high cards.

The concept of penalty cards is for serious players who really want to get every last thousandth of a percent from a video poker game. When quiz answers in this book mention penalty cards, they also will point out a simplified stategy for those who want to play well, but aren't quite ready to turn their lives over to studying video poker.

3. When talking about video poker strategy, we have to differentiate between inside straight draws and open-ended straight draws.

The draw is "inside" if the needed card is between two other cards in the hand. So 5-6-8-9, along with a fifth card too high or low for the straight, is a four-card inside straight. The card needed to complete the straight is a 7, between the 6 and the 8.

On the other hand, if we start with 5-6-7-8, along with a card too high or low for the straight, we have a four-card open, or open-ended, straight. It can be completed with either a 4 or a 9.

If you grew up playing poker on the kitchen table, and your granddaddy told you never to draw to an inside straight, he had sound logic behind him. If there are no wild cards, it's twice as difficult to fill an inside straight as an open-ended straight. In the first example above, there are only four cards that can complete the straight—the four 7s. In the second example, any of eight cards—the four 4s or the four 9s—will give us a straight.

When we play video poker, do we defy granddaddy and draw to inside straights? Sometimes. It depends on the game and the specific cards.

4. Expert strategy is the method of deciding which cards to hold and which to discard in order to give ourselves the best chance of winning in the long run.

Let's go back to the example in Answer No. 2, on penalty cards. If we're playing 9-6 Jacks or Better, and we're dealt Ace of hearts, King of diamonds, Queen of spades, Jack of spades and 4 of spades, an expert would automatically hold Ace-King-Queen-Jack. The mathematics of the game tell him that in the long run, for every five coins he bets, that play will bring 2.98 back to him. A good player, a shade below expert level, might just hold King-Jack of spades and hope for the long-shot royal. It's a very close call—that play will bring a five-coin bettor an average return of 2.92 coins in the long run.

Neither play is guaranteed to work every time, or even most of the time. But either will bring better long-run returns than other possible plays, such as holding only the Jack or holding all three spades. There are no gut feelings or hunches involved. If an expert play doesn't work this time, it doesn't work. The expert player moves on to the next hand, knowing he's taken the best shot the math of the game will allow.

5. Listings of payback percentages are different for video poker than for slot machines. On the slots, payback percentages commonly reported are taken after the fact, and are a measure of how much was actually paid out. If I tell you quarter slots in downtown Las Vegas paid a shade more than 95 percent in 1999—and they did—it means that of every $100 wagered, a little more than $95 was returned to players.

In video poker, the percentages are theoretical, a measure of how much a game will give back to the player in the long run given expert strategy.

When 9-6 Jacks or Better is listed as a 99.5 percent game, it means that if you make expert plays from here to eternity, the most likely result is that you will get back $995 of every $1,000 you wager.

That doesn't mean you are guaranteed 99.5 percent every time you sit down. Anyone who has ever seen a $100 bill disappear down a dollar machine in 10 minutes flat can testify to that. The fast losses are balanced off by the occasional big return. Hit the four Aces on Double Bonus Poker for 800 coins with five played, or the four 2s on Deuces Wild for 1,000 coins, or the ultimate, a royal flush for a big 4,000, and it makes up for a lot of losing sessions.

Every video poker game has its own payback percentage, and none of them are hard and fast. They depend on player skill.

6. When video poker was new, machines "dealt" two electronic hands at a time. The first five cards were those you saw on the screen. The next five were a "shadow hand" of potential draws. In effect, the shadow hand was beneath the cards on the screen, forming five two-card stacks. If you discarded the second card from the left on the screen, the replacement you draw was the second card from the left in the shadow hand. If you discarded the last card on the right, you'd get the last shadow card on the right.

That was changed in the early 1990s. Today, video poker is dealt sequentially. Discard any card, regardless of position on the screen, and you get the next card at the top of the electronic deck. It's just as if you were playing with a regular deck of cards.

Over the years, this has been the most frequent video poker question I've been asked whether by post, e-mail or at seminars. Most seem surprised that shadow hands no longer are dealt. The switch doesn't affect the odds of the game. As long as every electronic card has an equal chance of turning up, it doesn't matter if it's in a shadow hand or from a sequential deal.

7. For our purposes, a high card is a Jack, Queen, King or Ace. (Some video poker aficionados call these "honor cards.") Why? Because on Jacks or Better–based games, the pay table starts with a pair of any of those cards. Two Jacks, or any higher pair, will get us our money back. Lower pairs do not.

If I suggest it's a better play to hold four parts of a flush—four cards in the same suit—instead of a single high card, the high cards I mean are Jacks, Queens, Kings or Aces.

If I were to say "high card" in a Kings or better game such as Triple Play Poker, I'd mean only Kings or Aces. But why confuse the issue? I'll just say "King or Ace" instead of "high card" on such games.

The issue doesn't come up in Deuces Wild at all. With pay tables that start at three of a kind, card denomination matters only if we're talking about wild 2s or cards in a royal flush.

8. Slot clubs are the main tools casinos use to rate players of electronic games for comps—everything from discounted or complimentary rooms to free meals to cash back to invitations to parties and tournaments. Clubs issue players plastic cards the size of credit cards, and players insert the cards into electronic readers at the machines while they play. That enables the casino to track how much you play. Comps are issued accordingly.

My *Slot Machine Answer Book* includes a full chapter on slot clubs and how to get the most bang for your buck. Here, let's just note that video poker players are uniquely positioned to make slot club membership pay off.

That's because the house has a much narrower edge on video poker than on slot machines. One of my regular haunts has 9-6 Jacks or Better, which as we have noted returns 99.5 percent with expert play. It also returns 0.25 percent of wagers on electronic games as cash back to players who use slot club cards. Here's how it does it: For every $4 wagered, the player receives one point. For every 100 points, the player receives $1. That means the player gets $1 back of every $400 wagered, or 0.25 percent.

That alone would raise the effective return on 9-6 Jacks or Better to 99.75 percent. But on Tuesdays, the slot club offers triple points. Then, for every $4 wagered, the player receives three points. You get to the 100 points needed to get $1 back three times as fast, and the cash back rate rises to 0.75 percent. Add that to the 99.5 percent return on 9-6 Jacks or Better, and suddenly you have a 100.25 percent game.

Slot players can't begin to approach that. Get 0.75 percent in cash back while playing slots that return 92, 94, even 96 percent, and you get a nice little bonus. Slot players can't begin to close the gap all the way to 100 percent.

Casinos know this, and some have gone so far as to pay less cash back on video poker than on reel slots. That's something for players to investigate. Check out both the quality of video poker games offered and the slot club rules before you play.

Regardless of what you find, sign up for the slot club in any casino in which you play. In addition to cash back, you'll be eligible for other freebies. Sometimes you'll be offered comps whether you've played recently or not. As I write this, I'm looking at an offer I received from Caesars Palace in last week's mail. Caesars is offering a free room for one night, a discounted rate on another night and a free meal. What did I have to do to bring such an offer? Not much. I haven't played at Caesars in nearly two years. The last time I did, I joined the slot club to take advantage of an offer of $20 in cash back after $50 in play. I played less than 15 minutes, and left with a profit. Still, the offers come.

That's not an isolated case. You won't receive direct mail offers from every slot club, but you will get enough to make it worth your while to join everywhere you play.

9. The expected value, or EV, of a hand is the average return we can expect given a specific playing strategy. To use a simple example, let's say we're playing 9-6 Jacks or Better. Flushes pay 6-for-1 and straights pay 4-for-1. We're dealt 2 of hearts, 6 of hearts, 7 of clubs, 8 of hearts and 9 of hearts.

With that start, we have two viable one-card draws. Either we keep 6-7-8-9 and hope for either a 5 or 10 to complete a straight, or we keep 2-6-8-9 and hope for another heart to complete a flush.

There are 47 possible draws—the 52 cards in the deck minus the five in our initial hand. So let's imagine we bet five coins per hand and start with those cards in a perfect sequence of 47 hands in which each possible draw turns up once. If we hold the four-card open-end straight, eight of those possible 47 draws will complete our straight, because we make it with any of the four 5s and any of the four 10s. On each of those eight hands, we get a 20-coin return for our five-coin bet. No other draws give us a winning hand, so our total return is 160 coins. Divide that by our 47 trials, and we see that on the average, when we make this play we expect to get back 3.4 coins. That is the expected value in this game of holding a four-card open-ended straight with no high cards—3.4 coins per five played.

Now repeat the exercise, holding four cards to a flush instead. The deck includes 13 cards in each suit, so there are nine cards left that will complete our flush. In our perfect sequence of 47 hands in which we see each possible draw once, that means we will hit nine flushes. Each flush in 9-6 Jacks or Better pays 30 coins for five played, so our nine winners return a total of 270 coins. No other draws will give us winning hands. Divide that 270-coin return by 47 hands, and you get an expected value of 5.7 coins per five played.

The possible draw with the highest expected value is the expert play for the hand. Here, we obviously want to hold four cards to a flush instead of four to a straight. Many video poker decisions are much closer calls, as we'll find when we start comparing strategies a little later.

10. A full-pay machine is one with a pay table usually considered the top-of-the line. In basic Jacks or Better, a 9-6 machine is full-pay and worth seeking out over the 8-5, 7-5 and even 6-5 versions that dot casinos.

That doesn't mean a full-pay machine is always the absolute best pay table on the game.

Some Jacks or Better machines, especially in downtown Las Vegas, kick it up a notch by paying 4,700 coins on a royal flush instead of the standard 4,000 for five wagered. Stratosphere Tower in Las Vegas is known for its "super full-pay" machines, including 9-7 and 10-6 Jacks or Better. Such pay tables are rare treasures. But it would seem unreasonable to designate the 9-7 game as the full-pay version of Jacks or Better when its availability is so limited.

11. If the long-term theoretical payback percentage of a video poker machine is 100 percent or more, then it is said to be a 100-percent game. That is not the same thing as a full-pay game. Full-pay Deuces Wild is a 100-percent game, with theoretical return of 100.8 percent. So is full-pay Double Bonus Poker, at 100.2 percent. But full-pay Jacks or Better clocks in at 99.5 percent, full-pay Bonus Poker at 99.2 and full-pay Double Double Bonus Poker at 98.8.

12. A 2-for-1 payoff means that for every coin wagered, a winning hand brings you two coins back.

That differs from a 2-*to*-1 payoff. In roulette, column bets pay 2-to-1. If you bet a chip on the first column and it wins, you keep your one-chip bet and get two chips in winnings. Now you have a total of three chips.

If you're playing Jacks or Better video poker, two pair pays 2-for-1. If you bet one coin, it's gone. It's not on the "table" for you to keep in the event you win. Hit two pair, and the machine pays you two coins for the one you wagered. You wind up with a total of two coins.

That's the way all video poker payoffs work. They're paid in odds-for-1, not odds-to-1. Bet one coin, hit a hand that pays 5-for-1, and you wind up with a total of five coins. If it paid 5-*to*-1, you'd wind up with six coins—the five in winnings plus your original bet.

One consequence of all that is that the bottom of most video poker pay tables is an equivalent to a push on table games. At Jacks or Better, hit a pair of Jacks and you get a 1-for-1 payoff. Bet one coin, and you wind up with one coin. Play blackjack instead, bet one chip and if you tie the dealer, you simply keep your chip. You started with one chip and ended up with one chip—exactly the same as a 1-for-1 video poker hit.

13. Some casinos add progressive jackpots to video poker games. A percentage of all coins played is added to the progressive jackpot until someone wins it. Usually, the progressive jackpot is on a royal flush, but some machines will have multiple progressives that may include straight flushes and fours of a kind.

The higher the jackpots get, the better for the player. An 8-5 Jacks or Better machine, which pays 97.3 percent in the long run with expert play, accounts for a little more than 2 percent of its total payback with royal flushes. The overall payback percentage rises about 1 percent for each 2,000 coins in a progressive jackpot above the base payoff of 4,000 coins for a royal with five coins wagered. As a progressive royal on this 8-5 game approaches 8,800 coins, the overall payback percentage on the machine approaches 100 percent. That doesn't mean you'd always expect to break even when you played 8-5 Jacks with an 8,800-coin royal. You'd still have more losing sessions than winners. But if you never played 8-5 Jacks or Better except when the royal was worth 8,800 coins or more, and you played long enough to have your fair share of royals, you would expect your overall return to be somewhere near 100 percent.

14. A wild card is one that can be used as any card in the deck to form a winning hand. In Deuces Wild, for instance, all four 2s are wild. If you have three Queens and a deuce, the deuce will be used as a Queen to give you four of a kind.

The most common wild cards are the 2s in Deuces Wild and the Joker in Joker's Wild. Sometimes you'll see specialty machines with other wild cards, especially if you hang out in Las Vegas casinos that cater to video poker players.

The Frontier—now the New Frontier—toward the north end of the Strip has had 7s Wild machines for many years. The pay tables look exactly like full-pay Deuces Wild, except that the 200-for-1 jackpot for four wild cards is on 7s instead of 2s. Despite the similar pay tables and four wild cards in each, Deuces Wild is a 100-percent-plus game and 7s Wild is not. Why? Because 7s, with their position in the middle of the deck, are integral parts of more natural straight draws. If you start with 4-5-6-8, 5-6-8-9 or 6-8-9-10, you can fill the inside straight in Deuces Wild by drawing either a 7 or a 2. In 7s Wild, you fill the straight only with a 7, and you would discard the hand instead of drawing to an inside straight. The only similar situation in Deuces Wild is with Ace-3-4-5.

The opposite of a wild card is a "natural." The big jackpot on wild card games usually is for a natural royal flush—a royal that includes no wild cards. Bet five coins in full-pay Kings or Better Joker's Wild, and a natural royal will bring you 4,000 coins. If there's a Joker in your royal, it brings only 100 coins. Similarly, in full-pay Deuces Wild, bet five coins and you'll get 4,000 for your natural royal, but only 125 for a royal with wild cards.

15. A bonus four-of-a-kind is one that pays more than the standard payback for other quads on the machine. In Bonus Poker, most fours of a kind pay 25-for-1, or 125 coins for five wagered. Hit four 2s, 3s and 4s, and you have a bonus four of a kind. It pays 40-for-1, or 200 coins for five wagered. Better yet is four Aces, paying 80-for-1, or 400 for a five-coin bet.

When Bonus Poker proved popular in early 1990s, manufacturer IGT quickly moved to expand on the concept, and developed Double Bonus Poker, Double Double Bonus Poker, Triple Bonus Poker, Super Double Bonus Poker, Nevada Bonus Poker—on and on and on, all offering bigger payoffs on certain fours of a kind.

Shuffle No. 5: Jacks or Better

Jacks or Better five-card draw poker is the base upon which most other video poker games are built. If you can play Jacks or Better well, you have a head start on playing all the Bonus Poker variations.

The pay table on the full-pay 9-6 version of Jacks or Better, which in the long run pays 99.5 percent with expert play, is as follows: Royal flush 250-for-1 (jumps to 4,000 with five coins wagered); straight flush 50-for-1; four of a kind 25-for-1; full house 9-for-1; flush 6-for-1; straight 4-for-1; three of a kind 3-for-1; two pair 2-for-1; pair of Jacks or better 1-for-1.

Let's start with some general questions about the game, along with some strategy questions designed for the 9-6 game but applicable to other pay tables, too. Then we'll move on to strategy adjustments needed to get the most out of pay tables other than the 9-6 version.

JACKS OR BETTER BASICS

1. **When a casino wants to change the payback percentage on a basic Jacks or Better game, it usually changes:**

    A. The payoff on full houses and flushes.
    B. The payoff on three of a kind and straights.
    C. The frequency with which high cards appear.
    D. The frequency of royal flushes.

2. **For each unit that the payoff on a full house or flush is decreased, the player loses:**

    A. 4.4 percent of the total payback.
    B. 3.3 percent of the total payback
    C. 2.2 percent of the total payback.
    D. 1.1 percent of the total payback.

3. **More strategy changes are required to get the most out of a machine when:**

    A. The royal flush payback is increased to 4,700 coins for five played.
    B. The full house payback is decreased.
    C. The flush payback is increased or decreased.
    D. Any of the above; all make major differences in strategy.

4. **Winning hands make up about:**

    A. 45 percent of the total.
    B. 40 percent of the total.
    C. 35 percent of the total.
    D. 30 percent of the total.

5. **The biggest portion of the overall payback percentage comes from:**

    A. Pairs of Jacks or better.
    B. Two pairs.
    C. Full houses.
    D. Royal flushes.

9-6 JACKS OR BETTER STRATEGY

Choose the best play for each of the following hands:

6. **Jack of hearts, 2 of clubs, 2 of diamonds, 4 of clubs, 7 of clubs:**

    A. Hold the Jack.
    B. Hold the pair of 2s.
    C. Hold 2-4-7 of clubs.

7. **5 of clubs, 5 of diamonds, 6 of spades, 7 of hearts, 8 of clubs:**

    A. Hold the pair of 5s.
    B. Hold 5-6-7-8.

8. **5 of clubs, 5 of diamonds, 7 of diamonds, 9 of diamonds, Queen of diamonds:**

    A. Hold the Queen.
    B. Hold the pair of 5s.
    C. Hold 5-7-9-Queen of diamonds.

9. **Ace of hearts, King of hearts, Queen of hearts, Jack of hearts, 4 of hearts:**

    A. Hold the flush.
    B. Hold Ace-King-Queen-Jack

10. **King of spades, Queen of clubs, Jack of hearts, 6 of spades, 3 of clubs:**

    A. Hold King-Queen-Jack.
    B. Hold Queen-Jack.
    C. Hold Jack.

8-5 OR 7-5 JACKS OR BETTER STRATEGY

Hold/discard strategy for 8-5 Jacks or Better is very close to that of the 9-6 game. If you simply apply 9-6 strategy to an 8-5 machine, you won't lose much from the 97.3 percent long-term return you can expect with expert play. A few minor switches will help you get the most bang for your buck.

With a further reduction in the pay table to 7-5, the long-term payback drops to 96.1 percent. Some would say that real experts wouldn't be caught dead playing 7-5 Jacks or Better, but if it's the best game in town, somebody's going to play.

Strategy differences are negligible between 8-5 and 7-5 Jacks or Better. Apply the same adjustments when dropping from 9-6 to either 8-5 or 7-5.

See if you know what to do with these hands if you find yourself at an 8-5 or 7-5 Jacks or Better game:

11. 4 of spades, 5 of spades, 6 of spades, Queen of hearts, Jack of hearts

    A. Hold 4-5-6.

    B. Hold Queen-Jack.

12. King of hearts, Queen of clubs, Jack of spades, 8 of spades, 7 of spades.

    A. Hold King-Queen-Jack.

    B. Hold Queen-Jack.

    C. Hold Jack.

    D. Hold Jack-8-7 of spades.

13. Ace of spades, King of spades, Queen of clubs, 10 of spades, 5 of spades:

    A. Hold Ace-King-10-5.

    B. Hold Ace-King-10.

    C. Hold Ace-King-Queen-10.

14. Ace of diamonds, King of clubs, Queen of clubs, Jack of hearts, 9 of clubs

    A. Hold Ace-King-Queen-Jack

    B. Hold King-Queen-9

    C. Hold King-Queen

15. King of clubs, 10 of clubs, 8 of spades, 6 of diamonds, 3 of clubs:

    A. Hold King.

    B. Hold King-10.

    C. Hold King-10-3.

SUPER–FULL-PAY JACKS OR BETTER STRATEGY

Jacks or Better with 10-6 and 9-7 pay tables made their debut at Vegas World, which stood on the site that now holds the Stratosphere Tower. Stratosphere has carried the torch, offering both among its super–full-pay games.

The 9-7 game is potentially the higher-paying game, with a 100.8 percent return with expert play compared to 100.7 percent on the 10-6 game. But the 10-6 version is the easier to play—applying strategy for 9-6 Jacks or Better will do nicely.

That 7-for-1 payoff on flushes makes a bigger strategy difference. See if you know what to do with these hands in 9-7 Jacks or Better:

16. **Ace of spades, Ace of hearts, King of diamonds, Queen of diamonds, Jack of diamonds.**

    A. Hold the pair of Aces.
    B. Hold King-Queen-Jack.

17. **Ace of clubs, King of clubs, Jack of clubs, 7 of clubs, 3 of spades.**

    A. Hold Ace-King-Jack-7.
    B. Hold Ace-King-Jack.

18. **King of diamonds, Queen of diamonds, Jack of spades, 10 of diamonds, 4 of diamonds.**

    A. Hold King-Queen-Jack-10.
    B. Hold King-Queen-10-4.
    C. Hold King-Queen-10.
    D. Hold King-Queen.

19. **King of spades, Jack of spades, 10 of clubs, 9 of clubs, 6 of spades.**

    A. Hold King-Jack.
    B. Hold King-Jack-10-9.
    C. Hold King-Jack-6.

20. 10 of clubs, 8 of clubs, 7 of diamonds, 6 of diamonds, 2 of clubs.

      A. Hold 10-8-7-6.

      B. Hold 10-8-2.

      C. Discard all five cards.

Shuffle No. 5:
Jacks or Better
Answers

JACKS OR BETTER BASICS

1. A. When a casino wants to change the payback percentage on a basic Jacks or Better game, it usually changes the payoff on full houses and flushes.

That has been important for players to recognize almost as long as there has been video poker. The 9-6 version of Jacks or Better exploded to popularity in the early 1980s. When casinos understood, first, that the game was extremely popular, and second, that they were keeping much less out of each wager than they were on reel-spinning slots, they took action and rolled out the 8-5 version of Jacks or Better.

Operators were banking on players not knowing the difference. Slot machines had different pay tables on the same game, but a lower slot pay table didn't necessarily mean less payback. The hit frequency could be higher to make up for the lower payoffs.

Who knew that video poker was different, that you could actually tell by looking at the pay table which was higher-paying machine? Many players didn't.

All that's taken on added importance with the rise of Native American and riverboat gambling throughout the country. Now we see not only 9-6 and 8-5 Jacks or Better, but 7-5 and 6-5 versions. I once found myself on a riverboat that had 6-5 Jacks or Better, with no other video poker games. What was I to do? The nearest competing casino was eight miles away, and I wasn't a strong enough swimmer to get there.

Actually, what I did was play blackjack, but many players choose to play the weak video poker pay tables. For the most part, they still offer better returns than you'll find on the slots. The 96.2 percent return on 7-5 Jacks or Better beats quarter slots just about anywhere in the country, including Las Vegas, with the possible exception of some Las Vegas locals-oriented casinos. A slot pro looking for games with 100-percent payback may turn his nose up, but tens of thousands of players are on these reduced-payback machines every day.

If your casino offers only reduced-payback games, pay attention to the strategy differences below.

2. D. For each unit that the payoff on a full house or flush is decreased, the player loses about 1.1 percent of the total payback.

Play 9-6 Jacks or Better well, and your expected long-term payback average is 99.5 percent. At an 8-5 pay table, you lose a unit off the full house and a unit off the flush, so you drop a total of 2.2 percent to 97.3. At 7-5, you drop another 1.1 percent to 96.2 It's not an exact 1.1 percent, and at 6-5 Jacks or Better you drop to 95.0. At that level, you might want to think about blackjack or craps instead.

3. C. More strategy changes are required to get the most out of a machine when the flush payback is increased or decreased.

In video poker strategy for any pay table, we already do all we can to enhance our royal flush opportunities, and there are relatively few strategy adjustments available to us when the top jackpot rises. There's also not much more we can do in chasing full houses—we're going to save two pair whether full houses pay 10-for-1, 9-for-1, 8-for-1, 7-for-1 or 6-for-1.

Flush paybacks, however, affect not only draws for flushes themselves, but also how aggresively we go after straight flushes. Do we hold two cards to a royal or three low cards to a straight flush? Do we hold three low cards of the same suit or toss them away? That depends on the pay table. Check out the examples below.

4. A. Winning hands make up about 45 percent of the total.

I'm going to use figures for 9-6 Jacks or Better here, but percentages are close on other pay tables.

About 54.5 percent of hands are garbage hands that will bring us no return. We'll hit a pair of Jacks or better about 21.5 percent of the time, two pair 12.9 percent and three of a kind 7.4 percent.

Even though full houses pay 9-for-1, flushes 6-for-1 and straights 4-for-1, we hit them with about equal frequency. In fact, we hit slightly more full houses than flushes or straights—1.15 percent of our hands are full houses, 1.10 percent are flushes and 1.12 percent are straights.

The big hands, the ones that give us winning sessions, are relatively rare. We hit four of a kind on about a quarter of 1 percent of our hands, straight flushes on about a tenth of a percent and royal flushes on about 25 ten-thousandths of a percent.

5. B. The biggest portion of the overall payback percentage comes from two pairs.

In fact, the lion's share of our overall payback comes on the most common hands at the bottom of the pay table. We get 25.9 percent of our payback on two pairs, 22.3 percent on three of a kind and 21.5 percent on Jacks or better.

The only other hand that gives us more than 10 percent of our payback is the full house, worth 10.4 percent of our return. We get 6.6 percent from flushes, 5.9 percent from fours of a kind, 4.5 percent from straights.

Royal flushes may be our hearts' desire— our spades', clubs' and diamonds' desire, too—but they contribute only 2 percent to our overall return. That's nearly four times as much as straight flushes, which give us only 0.55 percent of our payback. If there's an undervalued hand in Jacks or Better video poker, it's the straight flush.

Keep in mind how much of our payback comes from two pairs. That'll be important when we get to games such as Double Bonus Poker that pay only 1-for-1 on two pairs.

9-6 JACKS OR BETTER STRATEGY:

6. B. Dealt Jack of hearts, 2 of clubs, 2 of diamonds, 4 of clubs, 7 of clubs, hold the pair of 2s.

Many of the hands in this book will be hair-splitters, either because the situation occurs infrequently or because the difference between two possible draws is so small a mistake just won't cost you very much.

This hand is no hair-splitter. It's one of the key basics of Jacks or Better strategy. A low pair is worth more than a single high card.

Many players reason that if they hold a single high card, they have three chances to pair it up for a winning hand. That much is true. Hold just the Jack in this hand, and you'll draw a winner 33.8 percent of the time, while holding the pair of 2s will yield a winner only 28.7 percent of the time.

However, when you hold the Jack, 75 percent of your winners will be nothing more than a high pair with a 1-for-1 payoff—it just returns your bet. Hold the low pair, and all of your winners, every one of them, will be at least two pair, and you'll get at least a 2-for-1 payoff.

Hold the single Jack, and you'll have more winning hands. But hold the pair of 2s, and you'll win more money.

The bottom line is that in the 9-6 game, holding the pair of 2s has an expected value (EV) of 4.12—for every five coins you bet, your average expected return is 4.12 coins when you make this play. Hold the Jack instead, and your EV plummets to 2.46 coins per five played.

This is one of the most frequent plays a video poker player will have to make, and it's not a close call. If you want to maximize your chances of winning, you'll hold the low pair and discard the single high card.

7. A. Dealt 5 of clubs, 5 of diamonds, 6 of spades, 7 of hearts, 8 of clubs, hold the pair of 5s.

There is a line to be drawn. How good do other potential winners have to be before we discard a low pair?

This is not where we draw the line. In the 9-6 game, our EV remains 4.12 on the low pair, while it's 3.40 for the four-card straight open on both ends. Even with full houses reduced to 8-, 7- or 6-for-1, holding the low pair remains the better play.

8. C. Dealt 5 of clubs, 5 of diamonds, 7 of diamonds, 9 of diamonds, Queen of diamonds, hold 5-7-9-Queen of diamonds.

This is where we draw the line. The 6-for-1 payoff on a flush lifts the four diamonds not only past the low pair, but into positive territory for the hand. With that start, on the average, we'll get more money back than we bet.

On the 9-6 game, the EV for holding the four diamonds is 6.06 coins for a five-coin bet, while that low pair is at our familiar 4.12. Even if we drop the flush payback to 5-for-1, this remains a plus-hand for us, with an EV of 5.11 on the four-card flush. On the 8-5 game, the low pair drops to an EV of 4.07.

9. B. Dealt Ace of hearts, King of hearts, Queen of hearts, Jack of hearts, 4 of hearts, hold Ace-King-Queen-Jack

It may be difficult to throw away a 30-coin payoff for five coins bet when flushes pay 6-for-1—or to break up a 25-coin payoff when flushes pay 5-for-1 or 35 coins when the payoff is 7-for-1. But it's a far better play to go for the royal. Our expected value of 92.13 in the 9-6 game far exceeds the certain payoff on the flush.

How do we arrive at that EV? When we discard one card, we leave 47 possible draws—the 47 cards we have not yet seen in the 52-card deck. In this hand, one of those possible draws is the 10 of hearts that will give us a royal flush and a 4,000-coin jackpot, assuming five coins wagered. Any of the seven other hearts remaining in the deck will take us right back to a flush. Multiply those seven flush possibilities by a 30-coin payoff per flush, and we have an average of 210 coins in flush payoffs per 47 trials. The 10s of diamonds, clubs or spades give us straights worth 20 coins a pop, or a total of 60 for all three. Twelve cards—the remaining Aces, Kings, Queens and Jacks—will give us high pairs for five-coin payoffs, or a total of 60 coins per 47 hands.

That's 4,000 coins on the royal flush, 210 on other flushes, 60 on straights and 60 on high pairs. Add that all up, and it's 4,330 coins in paybacks per 47 hands, or an average of 92.13 coins per hand. That's our expected value.

Breaking up the flush turns a sure winner into a loser on 24 of 47 hands, and reduces our payback on 15 of our 23 winners. But when the royal comes, it's all worth it, and then some.

10. A. Dealt King of spades, Queen of clubs, Jack of hearts, 6 of spades, 3 of clubs, hold King-Queen-Jack.

The difference isn't enormous, but the situation of deciding whether to keep just one or more high cards occurs so frequently that this is another of the basic plays every video poker player should know.

When video poker was new, before sophisticated computer analyses were available to players and when the first, seat-of-the-pants strategies were published, the word among those in the know was that the best play was to keep one high card, and the best one to keep was the lowest. Why the lowest? Because it leaves open more straight possibilities. Whereas a straight including a King can be only King high or Ace high, a straight including a Jack can be Ace, King, Queen or Jack high.

That's pretty good reasoning, but it's the wrong strategy. Most of the time, we're better off holding two high cards than one, and better three than two. (An exception: in Jacks or Better, if three high cards of mixed suits include an Ace, we're better off holding only the two lower high cards.)

One of the big reasons is that when we discard high cards, we decrease our chances of hitting high pairs and salvaging a break-even hand. In Answer No. 6 in this section, we saw that when we hold a single Jack and none of the discards are high cards, we wind up with a winning hand 33.8 percent of the time. But here, where holding a single Jack would mean discarding two high cards, we would draw a winning hand only 31.3 percent of the time. Hold all three high cards instead, and we draw a winner 38.5 percent of the time.

Most of our winners will be high pairs, and we can't draw anything higher than a straight when we start with three high cards of mixed suits, but the difference in frequency of winners is high enough that our EV for holding King-Queen-Jack is 2.58, better than the 2.48 on Queen-Jack, which is better than the 2.30 on the Jack alone.

That's a rule you can carry into most non–wild card games. Two high cards are better than one, and three are better than two, unless one of the three is an Ace.

8-5 OR 7-5 JACKS OR BETTER

11. B. Dealt 4 of spades, 5 of spades, 6 of spades, Queen of hearts, Jack of hearts, hold Queen-Jack.

The flush paybacks make the big difference in determining playing strategy. In this case, lowering the flush payback decreases the expected value of a three-card straight flush enough that we're better off holding Queen-Jack of the same suit. With Queen-Jack, the lion's share of our paying hands will be high pairs, but we also leave open a possible royal flush as well as other straight flushes, flushes and straights, and also have possibilities for full houses, two pair and three of a kind.

In 8-5 Jacks or Better, the expected value for holding the suited Queen-Jack is 3.07, compared with 2.96 for holding the suited 4-5-6. That means for every five coins we get, we can expect an average of 3.07 back when we hold Queen-Jack, and 2.96 when we hold 4-5-6.

With a 9-6 pay table, we would make the opposite play, holding 4-5-6. That's because we hit many more flushes starting with three cards of the same suit than with two. With the bigger payoff on flushes on the 9-6 game, that swings the narrow difference, to the tune of an expected value of 3.15 coins per five played for holding 4-5-6 to an EV of 3.12 on Queen-Jack.

12. A. Dealt King of hearts, Queen of clubs, Jack of spades, 8 of spades, 7 of spades, hold King-Queen-Jack.

It's close, but our best play in the 8-5 game is to hold King-Queen-Jack of mixed suits. The EV is 2.58, compared with 2.48 on holding Jack-8-7 of spades and 2.45 for Queen-Jack. Drawing to the single Jack lags behind at 2.22.

If we were playing 9-6 Jacks or Better, we'd hold Jack-8-7, the three-card double-inside straight flush. Again, the flush payoff makes the difference in the 9-6 game, so that the EV on the three-card double-inside straight flush is 2.69 compared to 2.58 on holding all three high cards.

13. B. Dealt Ace of spades, King of spades, Queen of clubs, 10 of spades, 5 of spades, hold Ace-King-10.

In 8-5 Jacks or Better, we hold Ace-King-10 of spades, leaving open the possibility of a royal flush. We do this even though discarding the 5 decreases our chances of hitting a flush. The EV is 6.18 for Ace-King-10, and 5.43 for Ace-King-10-5. The other choice, drawing for an inside straight with Ace-King-Queen-10, is not a serious possibility here. The EV is only 2.66.

On the 9-6 game, we'd want to hold four parts of a flush and hope a one-card draw will give us the 6-for-1 payback. The better payback on a flush increases our EV to 6.38 on all four spades, just nudging out the 6.35 on the three-card royal.

Remember back in definitions, we mentioned penalty cards? In this hand, the 5 of spades is a flush penalty card to consider as we decide whether to go for the royal. The expected value of the three-card royal would increase if that 5 of spades were still in the deck remaining to be played, giving us another possible flush card on the draw. If our initial hand had a 5 of diamonds instead of a 5 of spades, there would be no question. We'd hold the three-card royal. Instead, discarding the extra spade lowers our EV just enough in the 9-6 game that we hold four cards to a flush instead. In the 8-5 game, where the flush payoff is smaller, the penalty for discarding a flush card isn't as big, so we hold just Ace-King-10.

14. A. Dealt Ace of diamonds, King of clubs, Queen of clubs, Jack of hearts, 9 of clubs, hold Ace-King-Queen-Jack.

Ace-King-Queen-Jack is an inside straight, just like 6-7-9-10. That's because only four cards in the deck will complete the straight—the four 10s if we start with Ace-King-Queen-Jack, and the four 8s if we start with 6-7-9-10. For a straight to be considered open-ended, there must be eight possible cards that will complete it. If we held King-Queen-Jack-10, we would complete a straight with any of the four Aces and any of the four 9s.

In Jacks or Better, we do not hold inside straights unless they include at least three high cards, meaning we could draw high pairs if we miss our straights. That goes for 9-6 Jacks or Better, as well as the 8-5 version.

The complicating factor here is that the King, Queen and 9 all are of the same suit, and represent a possible straight flush. In 9-6 Jacks or Better, the higher flush payback dictates that the expert play is to hold a three-card inside straight flush, provided it includes at least one high card, instead of Ace-King-Queen-10 of mixed suits.

When our flush payback is depressed to 5-for-1, we make the opposite play. Any of the four 10s would give us a straight, and any of the remaining high cards would pair us up for a 1-for-1 payoff on a pair of Jacks or Better. The EV is 2.98, compared with 2.91 for King-Queen-9 and 2.76 for King-Queen.

On the 9-6 game, the three-card inside straight flush rises to an EV of 3.11, while the four high cards remain at 2.98.

15. A. Dealt King of clubs, 10 of clubs, 8 of spades, 6 of diamonds, 3 of clubs, hold the King.

We're really nitpicking on this one, getting down into differences of hundredths of a coin. Holding just the King on the 8-5 game gives us an EV of 2.29, no great shakes but still better than the 2.26 for King-10 or 2.03 for King-10-3.

If we're playing the 9-6 game, we'll hold King-10 and keep our fingers crossed. That keeps open the possibility of a royal flush and other straight flushes, and gives us a better chance to hit a flush at the cost of fewer high pairs, threes of a kind and fours of a kind.

That little flip-flop applies only when we're talking about King-10 suited, not Ace-10, Queen-10 or Jack-10. With Ace-10, we'd hold only the Ace on either pay table, and with Queen-10 or Jack-10 we'd hold both cards on either pay table. Why? Because Ace-10 has fewer straight possibilities than King-10, while Queen-10 and Jack-10 have more.

SUPER–FULL-PAY JACKS OR BETTER STRATEGY

16. B. Dealt Ace of spades, Ace of hearts, King of diamonds, Queen of diamonds, Jack of diamonds, hold King-Queen-Jack.

When the return on flushes rises to 7-for-1, we keep open more flush opportunities than we would in the 9-6 game—just the opposite of 8-5 Jacks or Better, where we go for flushes less often. In this example, we go so far as to break up a winning hand to keep a three-card flush with royal flush and straight flush possibilities.

In this example, we go so far as to break up a winning hand to keep a possible flush. Holding the pair of Aces gives us a certain return of five coins, and an average return of 7.68 coins per time we make this play. Holding King-Queen-Jack doesn't guarantee us any return at all, but the average return is 7.69 coins, ever so slightly higher than keeping the pair. That difference is narrow enough that a short-bankrolled player might want to take the sure thing with the pair of Aces. Nevertheless, holding King-Queen-Jack will bring a marginally higher return in the long run.

We would hold the high pair in 9-6 Jacks or Better. A five-coin payoff is certain, and the expected value of 7.68 beats the 7.49 on King-Queen-Jack.

17. A. Dealt Ace of clubs, King of clubs, Jack of clubs, 7 of clubs, 3 of spades, hold Ace-King-Jack-7.

The extra unit payback on the flush makes all the difference. In the 9-7 game, we hold Ace-King-Jack-7, a one-card draw for a flush with an EV of 7.66. That easily beats the 7.09 on Ace-King-Jack, even though we throw away a chance at a royal. In 9-6

Jacks or Better, we'd hold Ace-King-Jack, with an EV of 6.93 that beats the 6.70 on the one-card flush draw.

Eagle-eyed readers might wonder why the 9-6 play here differs from No. 13, in which players hold Ace-King-10-5 and go for the flush instead of holding only three cards to the royal. Having the Jack instead of the 10 in the hand makes the narrow difference, giving the player one more high card that could be paired for a 1-for-1 payback.

18. B. Dealt King of diamonds, Queen of diamonds, Jack of spades, 10 of diamonds, 4 of diamonds, hold King-Queen-10-4.

The four diamonds give us an average return of 7.34 coins for five played, a little better than the 6.91 on King-Queen-10 and quite a lot better than the 4.36 on the four-card open-ended straight, King-Queen-Jack-10.

Without the enhanced flush payback, we go for the three-card royal instead. Even with only two high cards in the three-card royal, instead of three high cards as in No. 17, the three-card royal has an EV of 6.75 that beats the 6.38 on the four-card flush in the 9-6 version.

19. C. Dealt King of spades, Jack of spades, 10 of clubs, 9 of clubs, 6 of spades, hold King-Jack-6.

Even three-card flushes with no straight-flush possibilities are fair game when the flush payback rises to 7-for-1. Here the EV of 2.94 on King-Jack-6 suited squeezes past King-Jack, at 2.93. In the 9-6 game, we'd just hold King-Jack, with an EV of 2.89 that beats the 2.73 for King-Jack-6.

20. B. Dealt 10 of clubs, 8 of clubs, 7 of diamonds, 6 of diamonds, 2 of clubs, hold 10-8-2.

The other hands in this section are refinements; this one represents a whole new way of thinking for most video poker players. Usually, when we see a hand with no high cards, no pairs, no four-card flushes, no four-card straights, no straight flush possibilities, we dump the whole hand.

But when the flush payoff rises to 7-for-1, we're not so quick to hit the draw button. In 9-7 Jacks or Better, we hold three-card flushes, even with no high cards and no straight-flush possibilities. We also hold three-card flushes in 10-7 or 9-7 Double Bonus Poker—that 7-for-1 payoff on flushes is the key.

This hand is not a big winner, but it's better than chucking it all and starting over. The EV of 1.94 is better than the 1.81 for discarding all five cards and the 1.70 for the inside straight. At 9-6 Jacks or Better, we'd discard the entire hand, with EVs of 1.80 for a full discard, 1.73 on 10-8-2 and 1.70 for 10-8-7-6.

Shuffle No. 6:
Bonus Poker

After the initial rush of popularity of Jacks or Better, video poker pioneer IGT started to roll out games that increased the volatility. Increased volatility gave players a better chance to walk away with a big win, with the tradeoff that a greater percentage of sessions would be losers.

One way to increase volatility was to introduce games with wild cards, such as Deuces Wild and Joker's Wild, with lower payoffs at the bottom of the pay table and large secondary jackpots on certain wild-card hands—four 2s in Deuces Wild or five of a kind in Joker's Wild.

Another way to increase volatility was to increase the payoffs high on the pay table and decrease some lower down. That's what Bonus Poker does. It increases the payoff on four of a kind, while decreasing full houses and flushes.

The pay table on the full-pay version is as follows: Royal flush 250-for-1 (jumps to 4,000 with five coins wagered); straight flush 50-for-1; four Aces 80-for-1; four 2s, 3s or 4s 40-for-1; four 5s through Kings 25-for-1; full house 8-for-1; flush 5-for-1; straight 4-for-1; three of a kind 3-for-1; two pair 2-for-1; pair of Jacks or better 1-for-1. With expert strategy, it returns 99.2 percent in the long run.

There are versions of Bonus Poker that reduce the full house paybacks to 7-for-1 or 6-for-1. Rarer is the super–full-pay version, which pays 8-for-1 on full houses but 6-for-1 on flushes. I've seen that version only at the Stratosphere in Las Vegas. It's a terrific game, paying 100.3 percent with expert play.

Bonus Poker was the game that launched a thousand variations—or so it seems. The popularity of this game led to Double Bonus Poker, Double Double Bonus Poker, Bonus Poker Deluxe, Triple Bonus Poker and many other descendants.

1. **Provided there are no odd variations in the pay tables, Bonus Poker has a higher payback percentage than Jacks or Better:**

   A. Always.
   B. Whenever the Bonus Poker's total of the full house and flush paybacks are no more than one unit less than those on Jacks or Better.
   C. Whenever the Bonus Poker's total of the full house and flush paybacks are no more than two units less than those on Jacks or Better.
   D. Never.

2. **In Bonus Poker, four Aces occur:**

   A. More frequently than in Jacks or Better.
   B. Less frequently than in Jacks or Better.
   C. About as frequently as in Jacks or Better.

3. **The biggest strategy difference between 8-5 Jacks or Better and 8-5 Bonus Poker is:**

   A. We sometimes hold single 2s, 3s or 4s in Bonus Poker.
   B. We sometimes break up two pair to go for four 2s, 3s or 4s in Bonus Poker.
   C. There are no major strategy differences between 8-5 Jacks or Better and 8-5 Bonus Poker.

4. **The biggest strategy differences between 8-5 Bonus Poker and super–full-pay 8-6 Bonus are:**

   A. The same as in going from 8-5 Jacks or Better to 9-6 Jacks or Better.
   B. We hold three-card flushes in the 8-6 version.

C. There are no strategy differences.

5. **If the 40-for-1 payoff is on four Kings, Queens or Jacks instead of four 2s, 3s or 4s:**

A. The overall payback percentage is not affected.
B. The overall payback percentage rises.
C. The overall payback percentage drops.

Shuffle No. 6: Bonus Poker Answers

1. B. Provided there are no odd variations in the pay tables, Bonus Poker has a higher payback percentage than Jacks or Better whenever the Bonus Poker's total of the full house and flush paybacks are no more than one unit less than those on Jacks or Better.

If your local casino has 6-5 Bonus Poker (full house plus flush equals 11), and 7-5 Jacks or Better (full house plus flush equals 12), then Bonus Poker is the higher-paying game. However, if the difference is two units or more, Jacks or Better is the stronger play—8-5 Jacks or Better (full house plus flush equals 13) is a better game than 6-5 Bonus Poker.

If the Bonus Poker payoffs are equal to or greater than those on available Jacks or Better machines, it's no contest: take the bonuses. I once had a reader complain to me that his local casino had dropped Jacks or Better pay tables from 8-5 to 6-5. (Yuck!!) But I had just been in that casino and knew that it also had 8-5 Bonus Poker. It was a no-brainer—the Bonus Poker was a better game even before the reduction in the Jacks or Better pay table.

If there's something quirky on the low end of the pay table, all bets are off. I've seen Bonus Poker machines that pay only 2-for-1 on three of a kind, making it a much weaker game than Jacks or Better. Likewise, if two pair is lowered to 1-for-1 without big increases higher in the pay table, it's a game to avoid.

For some reason, many Triple Play Poker machines offer a game called Triple Play Bonus Poker that is really Bonus Poker

Deluxe in disguise. It enhances all fours of a kind to 80-for-1, but pays only 1-for-1 on two pair. You may like Bonus Poker Deluxe, but if you were expecting Bonus Poker and its 2-for-1 payoff on two pair, this isn't it.

The bottom line is, even though we're paying special attention to the full house and flush pays since they're the most common variations, we should read the entire pay table before we play.

2. C. In Bonus Poker, four Aces occur about as frequently as in Jacks or Better.

With five coins wagered, the 400-coin payoff on four Aces is a nice little jackpot, but we don't really do anything special to try to force it to come more often. We don't break up full houses that include three Aces or hold a single Ace instead of an unsuited Ace-King, as we do in Double Bonus Poker.

Without any special strategies to force the pace, four-Ace hands occur just as often in Bonus Poker as in Jacks or Better.

3. C. There are no major strategy differences between 8-5 Jacks or Better and 8-5 Bonus Poker.

If you learn to play Jacks or Better well, you'll also be able to play Bonus Poker well. If you can answer the questions about strategy changes from 9-6 to 8-5 Jacks or Better in the last chapter, you're ready for 8-5, 7-5 or 6-5 Bonus Poker.

4. A. The biggest strategy differences between 8-5 Bonus Poker and super–full-pay 8-6 Bonus are the same as in going from 8-5 Jacks or Better to 9-6 Jacks or Better.

As we discussed in the last chapter on Jacks or Better, the major differences in strategy are made by the flush paybacks, especially as they impact three-card straight flushes. If you can play 9-6 Jacks or Better, you can play 8-6 Bonus Poker.

5. B. If the 40-for-1 payoff is on four Kings, Queens or Jacks instead of four 2s, 3s or 4s, the overall payback percentage rises.

This game exists. It's called Aces and Faces, and you'll mainly find it at Binion's Horseshoe in downtown Las Vegas. With an 8-5 pay table on full houses and flushes, the payback rises to 99.5 percent from the 99.2 on full-pay Bonus Poker. That's because we hold single Jacks, Queens or Kings and will occasionally luck into four of a kind, but we do not hold unpaired 2s, 3s or 4s except as parts of potential flushes and straights.

Strategy differences are negligible from regular old Bonus Poker. Here's an example of a difference: Dealt Queen, 10 and 2 of diamonds, 9 of hearts and 8 of spades, in regular Bonus Poker, we'd hold the Queen and the 10, leaving open the long shot at a royal flush as well as other potential winners. We do that even though there are three penalty cards in the hand. Discarding the 9 and the 8 decreases our chances of drawing a straight, while discarding the 2 of diamonds decreases our chances of drawing a flush.

When we switch to Aces and Faces, the 10 becomes kind of a reverse penalty card—if we keep it, we have a smaller chance into lucking into a four Queens bonus. So we keep just the Queen.

How much difference does it make? Not much. In Aces and Faces, the expected value of holding just the Queen is 2.32, compared with 2.31 on Queen-10. In 8-5 Bonus Poker, holding Queen-10 has an EV of 2.31, ever so slightly better than the 2.30 on holding the lone Queen.

That's such a tiny difference that most players shouldn't concern themselves with it. The majority of the time that you see Queen-10 suited, they won't be accompanied by all those penalty cards, and you'll want to hold Queen-10. Better that you should remember that play than to worry too much about the exception.

Shuffle No. 7: Bonus Poker Deluxe

Think of Bonus Poker Deluxe as the midpoint between Bonus Poker and the more popular Double Bonus Poker. It steps up the bonuses by paying 80-for-1 on any four of a kind. That leaves a nice 400-coin payoff for five coins played—a quarter player walks away with a cool $100 when the quads hit. We don't start rearranging strategies to chase quads as we do in Double Bonus, when four Aces pay 800 coins for one played, but four of a kind is what we're after when we play Bonus Deluxe.

Higher returns on four of a kind mean something has to be taken out elsewhere on the pay table. That elsewhere is on two pair, which pay only 1-for-1 instead of the 2-for-1 we find on Jacks or Better and Bonus Poker. So it goes with most of the big bonusing games. In Double Bonus, Double Double Bonus, Double Double Jackpot, Triple Bonus Poker and All-American Poker, we get only 1-for-1 on two pair.

That's a drastic change, and raising the payoff on fours of a kind to 80-for-1 doesn't make up all of the shortfall. In the full-pay version of Bonus Poker Deluxe, a little more is given back to the player by raising the flush paybacks to 6-for-1. That leaves the following pay table: Royal flush 250-for-1 (jumps to 4,000 with five coins wagered); straight flush 50-for-1; four of a kind 80-for-1; full house 8-for-1; flush 6-for-1; straight 4-for-1; three of a kind 3-for-1; two pair 1-for-1; pair of Jacks or better 1-for-1.

Often, casinos will decrease the payoff on flushes to 5-for-1, and some will also decrease full house payoffs to 7-for-1. That leaves 8-6, 8-5 and 7-5 Bonus Poker Deluxe as the most common variations.

For the most part, the same strategy you play on 8-5 Bonus Poker will serve you well. In the following questions, we'll look at some differences.

BONUS POKER DELUXE BASICS

1. The full-pay 8-6 version of Bonus Poker Deluxe has:

> A. A higher payback percentage than 8-5 Bonus Poker.
>
> B. A lower payback percentage than 8-5 Bonus Poker.
>
> C. About the same payback percentage as 8-5 Bonus Poker.

2. In Bonus Poker Deluxe, winning hands make up about:

> A. 45 percent of the total.
>
> B. 40 percent of the total.
>
> C. 35 percent of the total.
>
> D. 30 percent of the total.

3. The largest share of our payback in Bonus Poker Deluxe comes from:

> A. Fours of a kind.
>
> B. Threes of a kind
>
> C. Two pairs.
>
> D. Jacks or better.

4. The most important strategy differences between 8-6 Bonus Poker Deluxe and 8-5 Bonus Poker are driven by the payoff changes on:

> A. Fours of a kind
>
> B. Flushes.
>
> C. Two pairs.

8-6 BONUS POKER DELUXE STRATEGY

5. **Queen of spades, Jack of diamonds, 8 of diamonds, 7 of diamonds, 3 of clubs.**

    A. Hold Queen-Jack.
    B. Hold Jack.
    C. Hold Jack-8-7.

6. **Ace of clubs, Queen of diamonds, 10 of diamonds, 9 of hearts, 3 of spades**

    A. Hold Ace-Queen.
    B. Hold Queen-10.
    C. Hold Queen.

7. **Queen of diamonds, Jack of hearts, 9 of hearts, 8 of spades, 6 of spades:**

    A. Hold Jack.
    B. Hold Queen-Jack.
    C. Hold Queen-Jack-9-8.

8. **5 of clubs, 6 of diamonds, 7 of hearts, 9 of spades, 2 of spades.**

    A. Hold 5-6-7-9.
    B. Discard all five cards.

8-5 BONUS POKER DELUXE STRATEGY

9. **Ace of spades, King of hearts, Jack of spades, 10 of diamonds, 4 of hearts.**

    A. Hold Ace-Jack.
    B. Hold King-Jack.
    C. Hold Ace-King-Jack-10.

10. Ace of diamonds, King of hearts, Queen of hearts, 9 of hearts, Jack of spades.

    A. Hold Ace-King-Queen-Jack.

    B. Hold King-Queen.

    C. Hold King-Queen-9.

Shuffle No. 7:
Bonus Poker Deluxe
Answers

BONUS POKER DELUXE BASICS

1. B. The full-pay 8-6 version of Bonus Poker Deluxe has a lower payback percentage than 8-5 Bonus Poker.

8-6 Bonus Poker Deluxe returns 98.5 percent in the long run with expert play, not quite as good as the 99.2 percent on 8-5 Bonus Poker. At 8-5, Bonus Poker Deluxe drops to 97.4 percent and at 7-5 it drops to 96.3 percent.

I've found that casinos that have 8-6 Bonus Poker Deluxe usually also will have full-pay versions of other games, such as 9-6 Jacks or Better, 8-5 Bonus Poker or 10-7 Double Bonus Poker, that have higher payback percentages.

Not only that, but casinos that reduce the pay tables on Bonus Poker Deluxe also usually will have games that pay more, even if they're not full-pay games. For that reason, I rarely play this game.

Nevertheless, I know players who swear by it because they like getting the bonus on any four of a kind instead of a specified few.

2. A. In Bonus Poker Deluxe, winning hands make up about 45 percent of the total.

Even though the pay table has changed a great deal from Jacks or Better, the proportion of winning hands is similar. Of all hands, 54.8 percent are losers, 21.1 percent are pairs of Jacks or better, 12.8 percent are two pairs and 7.4 percent are threes of a kind. Full houses (1.15 percent), flushes (1.11 percent) and straights (1.28 percent) still occur with close to equal frequency, although now straights are the most common of the three instead of full houses. Four of a kind still occurs in about a quarter of a percent of all hands, straight flushes in one-hundredth of a percent and royal flushes in 25 ten-thousandths of a percent.

3. B. The largest share of our payback in Bonus Poker Deluxe comes from threes of a kind.

Even though winning hands occur with a similar relative frequency in Bonus Poker Deluxe and Jacks or Better, what they do for us has been turned topsy-turvy by the decreased payback in two pairs. In Jacks or Better and Bonus Poker, two pairs contribute about a quarter of our total payback. In 8-6 Double Bonus Deluxe, that plummets to 12.8 percent.

Threes of a kind now make up the biggest portion of our payback, 22.2 percent of the total, followed by pairs of Jacks or better at 21.1 percent. The big jump that offsets the drop at two pair is the contribution by four of a kind, now 18.9 percent of our total. That's a huge increase from the 5.9 percent contribution that four of a kind makes to our Jacks or Better total.

In 8-6 Bonus Deluxe, full houses make up 9.2 percent of our payback, compared to 6.7 percent for flushes, 5.1 percent for straights, 1.9 percent for royal flushes and 0.5 percent for straight flushes.

4. B and C. The most important strategy differences between Bonus Poker Deluxe and Bonus Poker are driven by the payoff changes on: flushes and two pairs.

As we saw in the chapter on Jacks or Better, a change in the payback on flushes has a big impact on our strategy, especially as it relates to playing three-card inside straight flushes.

Lowering the two pair payback to 1-for-1 has an enormous impact on the volatility of the game, and also affects a few strategy decisions. We'll check out some below.

8-6 BONUS POKER DELUXE STRATEGY

5. C. Dealt Queen of spades, Jack of diamonds, 8 of diamonds, 7 of diamonds, 3 of clubs, hold Jack-8-7.

The higher-paying flush and lower-paying two pair work together to make it an easy choice to hold the three-card double-inside straight flush in 8-6 Bonus Poker Deluxe. For every five coins we wager, we'll get back 2.58 by holding Jack-8-7, a three-card double-inside straight flush. We'll get back only 2.30 by holding Queen-Jack.

The bigger flush payoff makes it a runaway decision, but the smaller two-pair return would be enough by itself to push the decision in favor of Jack-8-7. If we hold Queen-Jack instead, we'll hit more two-pair hands than if we hold Jack-8-7. But that doesn't matter as much in Bonus Deluxe, where two pairs pay only 1-for-1. In 8-5 Bonus Deluxe, the play is a closer call, but we still hold Jack-8-7, with an EV of 2.37, instead of Queen-Jack, at 2.34.

In 8-5 Bonus Poker, which pays 2-for-1 on two pair, Queen-Jack wins out by a narrow margin, with an expected value of 2.52 coins per five wagered compared to 2.50 for Jack-8-7.

6. B. Dealt Ace of clubs, Queen of diamonds, 10 of diamonds, 9 of hearts, 3 of spades, hold Queen-10.

By the tiniest of margins, the higher flush payback pushes this one in favor of holding Queen-10 and keeping open our flush, straight flush and royal flush possibilities. Keep Queen-10, and we have an expected value of 2.17, compared to 2.16 on Ace-Queen.

In 8-5 Bonus Poker, we'd make the opposite play, holding Ace-Queen with an EV of 2.37 instead of Queen-10 with an EV of 2.34.

You'll note that the EV on either of these plays is higher in Bonus Poker than in Bonus Poker Deluxe. That's because two pair is a fairly common outcome when you hold two cards, and two pair pays twice as much in Bonus Poker.

7. C. Dealt Queen of diamonds, Jack of hearts, 9 of hearts, 8 of spades, 6 of spades, Queen-Jack-9-8.

Here's a switch for Jacks or Better or Bonus Poker players, who are used to holding four-card inside straights only if they include at least three high cards. In Bonus Poker Deluxe, we hold lesser inside straights, too. Here, Queen-Jack-9-8 has an expected value of 2.34, beating the 2.30 on Queen-Jack.

In 8-5 Bonus Poker, we'd hold only Queen-Jack, with an EV of 2.49 compared to 2.34 on Queen-Jack-9-8.

Why the switch? It has to do with Bonus Poker Deluxe's lower payback on two pairs, as we'll see in the next answer.

8. A. Dealt 5 of clubs, 6 of diamonds, 7 of hearts, 9 of spades, 2 of spades, hold 5-6-7-9

It's hard to think of a more basic tenet at the poker table than "Never draw to inside straights." It's an adjustment for most of us when we take up video poker, where in Jacks or Better and Bonus Poker we do draw to inside straights, provided they include at least three high cards that could be paired to make a winner even if we miss our straight.

Bonus Poker Deluxe takes drawing to inside straights to another level. Here, we draw to inside straights even if they have no high cards. Why? Decreasing the value of two pairs to 1-for-1 lowers the value of a full five-card redraw enough that drawing to an inside straight is better than simply discarding the whole hand.

The expected value for holding the inside straight is 1.70, while a full redraw is at 1.58. In 8-5 Bonus Poker, holding the inside straight still would have an EV of 1.70, but a redraw would rise to 1.78.

Drawing to the inside straight is a long shot; we'll make it only once per 11.75 times we try it. But when two pairs pay only 1-for-1, it's better than nothing.

8-5 BONUS POKER DELUXE STRATEGY

9. C. Dealt Ace of spades, King of hearts, Jack of spades, 10 of diamonds, 4 of hearts, hold Ace-King-Jack-10.

Depressing the value of a flush to 5-for-1 makes holding Ace-Jack of the same suit drop below going for the four-card inside straight with three high cards. Our EVs on the 8-5 version of

Bonus Poker Deluxe are 2.66 on Ace-King-Jack-10, and 2.61 on Ace-Jack.

On the full-pay 8-6 version, we'd hold Ace-Jack and leave open our flush possibilities. It's an incredibly slim margin, with an EV of 2.6645 on Ace-Jack and 2.6596 on Ace-King-Jack-10.

We make that strategy flip-flop only if an Ace is involved in our two-card royal, because the Ace limits straight possibilities. If in the hand above, the Ace were in hearts and the King in spades, so that our two-card royal was King-Jack, we'd hold just King-Jack on either pay table.

10. A. Dealt Ace of diamonds, King of hearts, Queen of hearts, 9 of hearts, Jack of spades, hold Ace-King-Queen-Jack.

This is the same kind of adjustment we saw quite a bit of when going from 9-6 Jacks or Better to the 8-5 version. In 8-5 Bonus Poker Deluxe, the lower flush payback means we don't put quite the same emphasis on three-card inside straight flushes as we do in the full-pay 8-6 game. For the 8-5 game, our EV is 2.98 on Ace-King-Queen-Jack, better than the 2.79 on King-Queen-9.

When flushes pay 6-for-1, the play is reversed by a narrow margin. Then, the EV rises to 2.99 on King-Queen-9, nosing out Ace-King-Queen-Jack, which remains at 2.98.

Shuffle No. 8: All-American Poker

We've noted in earlier chapters that in many video poker games, full houses, flushes and straights occur with about the same frequency. Nevertheless, full houses pay about twice as much as straights—a little more or less, depending on the game—and flush paybacks are in between.

All-American Poker is different. Full houses, flushes and straights all pay the same 8-for-1. Not only that, but straight flush paybacks are quadrupled to 200-for-1 from the usual 50-for-1. That's a major change, one that necessitates a strategy for this game that's all its own.

These pay table changes work together to skew the value of partial flushes and partial straights. Ever been tempted to keep a three-card straight, or a two-card straight flush with a gap on the inside and no high cards? Those are both viable hands in All-American Poker.

All fours of a kind pay 40-for-1 here. That's better than the 25-for-1 in Jacks or Better but without the bigger jackpots on four Aces common in Bonus Poker and its descendants. As in Bonus Poker Deluxe, two pair pays only 1-for-1.

The full pay table is as follows: Royal flush 250-for-1 (jumps to 4,000 with five coins wagered); straight flush 200-for-1; four of a kind 40-for-1; full house 8-for-1; flush 8-for-1; straight 8-for-1; three of a kind 3-for-1; two pair 1-for-1; pair of Jacks or better 1-for-1.

If you can make the strategy adjustments, that's a great game. With expert play, it returns 100.72 percent. But you'd better know your three-card open-ended straights from your two-card inside straight flushes.

ALL-AMERICAN POKER BASICS

1. In All-American Poker, straights occur:

    A. About as often as full houses.

    B. More than half again as often as full houses.

    C. Twice as often as full houses.

2. The biggest share of our return comes from:

    A. Threes of a kind.

    B. Straights.

    C. Flushes.

    D. Full houses.

3. Straight flushes in All-American Poker occur:

    A. About as often as in 9-6 Jacks or Better.

    B. About a third again as often as in 9-6 Jacks or Better.

    C. Twice as often as in 9-6 Jacks or Better.

4. All-American Poker is sometimes known as:

    A. Uncle Sam Poker.

    B. Straight Arrow Poker.

    C. Gator Poker.

5. All-American Poker usually is found:

    A. On Triple Play Poker machines.

    B. On Bally's Game Maker multiple-game machines.

    C. At convenience stores and gas stations.

ALL-AMERICAN POKER STRATEGY

6. Queen of diamonds, Jack of diamonds, 10 of diamonds, Jack of spades, 6 of clubs.

    A. Hold the pair of Jacks.

    B. Hold Queen-Jack-10 of diamonds.

7. **King of diamonds, Queen of diamonds, Jack of diamonds, Queen of hearts, 5 of spades.**

    A. Hold the pair of Queens.

    B. Hold King-Queen-Jack of diamonds.

8. **King of hearts, Queen of spades, Queen of hearts, Jack of diamonds, Jack of hearts,**

    A. Hold the Jacks and Queens.

    B. Hold King-Queen-Jack of hearts.

9. **9 of hearts, 9 of spades, 10 of clubs, Jack of diamonds, Queen of hearts.**

    A. Hold 10-Jack-Queen and one of the 9s.

    B. Hold Jack-Queen.

    C. Hold the pair of 9s.

10. **3 of hearts, 3 of spades, 4 of spades, 5 of spades, 7 of diamonds.**

    A. Hold the pair of 3s.

    B. Hold 3-4-5 of spades.

11. **5 of clubs, 5 of spades, 7 of hearts, 10 of hearts, Jack of hearts.**

    A. Hold the pair of 5s.

    B. Hold Jack-10.

    C. Hold Jack-10-7.

12. **4 of spades, 7 of diamonds, 8 of spades, 9 of clubs, Jack of clubs.**

    A. Hold 7-8-9-Jack.

    B. Hold the Jack.

13. **Ace of diamonds, King of hearts, Queen of spades, 5 of clubs, 6 of hearts.**

    A. Hold Ace-King-Queen.

    B. Hold King-Queen.

    C. Hold the Queen.

14. 3 of hearts, 5 of hearts, 6 of spades, 7 of hearts, 8 of hearts.

    A. Hold 5-6-7-8.

    B. Hold the four hearts.

    C. Hold either A or B; flushes and straights have the same payoff.

15. 4 of spades, 7 of spades, 8 of spades, Queen of hearts, Jack of hearts.

    A. Hold 4-7-8.

    B. Hold Queen-Jack.

16. King of diamonds, Queen of diamonds, 7 of diamonds, 6 of clubs, 4 of spades.

    A. Hold King-Queen.

    B. Hold King-Queen-7.

17. Jack of clubs, 8 of clubs, 6 of spades, 4 of hearts, 2 of diamonds.

    A. Hold Jack-8.

    B. Hold the Jack.

18. Ace of hearts, 10 of hearts, 8 of clubs, 6 of spades, 4 of diamonds.

    A. Hold the Ace.

    B. Hold Ace-10.

19. 8 of clubs, 9 of spades, 10 of hearts, 3 of diamonds, 5 of clubs.

    A. Hold 8-9-10.

    B. Hold 5-8 of clubs.

    C. Discard all five cards.

20. 7 of diamonds, 9 of diamonds, 5 of clubs, 4 of spades, 2 of hearts.

    A. Hold 2-4-5.

    B. Hold 4-5-7.

    C. Hold 7-9 of diamonds.

    D. Discard all five cards.

Shuffle No. 8: All-American Poker Answers

ALL-AMERICAN POKER BASICS

1. B. In All-American Poker, straights occur more than half again as often as full houses.

We'll catch a straight about once every 54 hands in All-American Poker, compared with once every 91 hands for a full house. That's a big change from 9-6 Jacks or Better, where we have a full house about once per 87 hands and a straight once per 89.

Flushes also increase in All-American Poker, at once per 64 hands instead of once per 91, as in Jacks or Better.

Why the difference? The 8-for-1 payoffs mean we emphasize straights and flushes more in our strategy, holding hands we'd break up in Jacks or Better.

2. A. The biggest share of our return comes from threes of a kind.

That shouldn't be surprising. Three of a kind is the most frequently occurring hand that pays more than 1-for-1. We get 20.6 percent of our payback from threes of a kind. High pairs are next at 18.3 percent, followed by straights (14.7), flushes (12.6), two pairs (12.0), full houses (8.8), fours of a kind (9.0), straight flushes (2.8) and royal flushes (1.8).

3. B. Straight flushes in All-American Poker occur about a third again as often as in 9-6 Jacks or Better.

Here, we get a straight flush about once per 7,053 hands, while in Jacks or Better they come up about once per 9,148 hands. Factor in the 200-for-1 payback on straight flushes, and the 2.8 percent of our return attributable to straight flushes is about five times as great a share of our return as we get from straight flushes in 9-6 Jacks or Better.

4. C. All-American Poker is sometimes known as Gator Poker, although I've not seen a machine labeled "Gator Poker" in several years. It's the same game with the same pay table.

5. B. All-American Poker usually is found on Bally's Game Maker multiple-game machines.

Although introduced on single-game machines, your best chance to find it nowadays is on multiple-game machines. While the others around you are choosing video keno or a slot game, you can choose All-American Poker and have the best of it.

Las Vegas' Park Place properties seem to like the game; in recent years, I've found All-American Poker at both Bally's and the Las Vegas Hilton. Readers have reported to me that the game has filtered into the South and onto Midwestern riverboats, although I have yet to see it outside Las Vegas.

ALL-AMERICAN POKER STRATEGY

6. B. Dealt Queen of diamonds, Jack of diamonds, 10 of diamonds, Jack of spades, 6 of clubs, hold Queen-Jack-10 of diamonds.

All-American Poker players have to get used to being on the lookout for three-card royals, three-card straight flushes, three-card flushes, even three-card straights. You won't necessarily break up winning hands for all of these, as we'll see below. But we will break up a pair of Jacks or better for a three-card royal.

In 9-6 Jacks or Better, we'd need a four-card royal or four-card straight flush before we'd break up a high pair. In All-American Poker, with flushes, straights and straight flushes all enhanced, we break up the high pair even for three-card royals. The expected values here are 9.92 on Queen-Jack-10, and 7.04 on the pair of Jacks.

7. B. Dealt King of diamonds, Queen of diamonds, Jack of diamonds, Queen of hearts, 5 of spades, hold King-Queen-Jack of diamonds.

This is similar to No. 6, except that our three-card royal is King high instead of Queen high. That restricts possible straights to King high or Ace high. Does the lower probability of hitting a straight mean we should turn to the high pair? Nope. The EV on the suited King-Queen-Jack, 8.99, is down almost a full coin from Queen-Jack-10, but it still beats the 7.04 on the high pair.

We'd keep the three-card royal over a high pair even if it were Ace high, and even if it included a 10. Potential straights and flushes are that powerful in this game.

8. B. Dealt King of hearts, Queen of spades, Queen of hearts, Jack of diamonds, Jack of hearts, hold King-Queen-Jack of hearts.

Most three-card royals have higher expected values than two pair, even though drawing to two pair gives us a 1 in 11.75 shot at a full house. In fact, we'll hold two pair instead of a three-card royal only if the three-card royal includes an Ace. Here, with King-Queen-Jack, we have an EV of 8.79 that beats the 7.98 on the Queens and Jacks.

9. A. Dealt 9 of hearts, 9 of spades, 10 of clubs, Jack of diamonds, Queen of hearts, hold 10-Jack-Queen and one of the 9s.

In regular Jacks or Better, the only four-card straight that gives us a better start than a low pair is 10-Jack-Queen-King. Not in All-American Poker. Any four-card straight will bring us more return in the long run than a low pair. Here, with two high cards in the four-card straight, the EV is more than double that of the low pair. We expect an average return of 7.45 coins per five wagered on the four-card straight, and 3.48 on the low pair.

10. B. 3 of hearts, 3 of spades, 4 of spades, 5 of spades, 7 of diamonds, hold 3-4-5 of spades.

Even with no high cards, three-card straight flushes are better than low pairs in this game, as long as the three-card straight flushes are open-ended or have only one gap on the inside. Here, with no gaps, 3-4-5 of spades, with an EV of 6.15, beats the pair of 3s, at 3.48. Make it a hand with one gap, such as 3-4-6, and it would still beat the pair. With 3-4-7, we switch and play the pair.

11. C. Dealt 5 of clubs, 5 of spades, 7 of hearts, 10 of hearts, Jack of hearts, hold Jack-10-7.

Here we have a double-inside three-card straight flush, a hand that would rank below the pair of 5s if there were no high cards to pair up for a possible payoff at the bottom of the pay table. The Jack makes the difference. With that high card in the hand, our expected values are 3.97 coins per five bet on Jack-10-7, and 3.48 on the pair.

12. A. Dealt 4 of spades, 7 of diamonds, 8 of spades, 9 of clubs, Jack of clubs, hold 7-8-9-Jack.

This play wouldn't cut it in Jacks or Better, where we hold four-card inside straights only if they include at least three high cards. In All-American Poker, with a straight payoff twice that of Jacks or Better, we love inside straights. The expected values are 3.72 on the inside straight and 2.24 on the single Jack. As it happens, the single Jack isn't even the second-best play in this hand. Jack-9 of clubs—that's right, a two-card inside straight flush—has an EV of 2.40.

13. A. Dealt Ace of diamonds, King of hearts, Queen of spades, 5 of clubs, 6 of hearts, hold Ace-King-Queen.

We look at this hand as All-American Poker players and we see three parts of a straight. We're visualizing a Jack and a 10 and an 8-for-1 payoff. OK, so we'll see a high pair far more often than we see the straight. But when the straights come, it's all worthwhile. This hand is not a big winner, but we'll get 2.45 coins back per five wagered on Ace-King-Queen and only 2.34 on King-Queen.

As Jacks or Better players, we'd see the hand differently. We'd be seeking 2-for-1 payoffs on two pairs, instead of the 1-for-1 on All-American. We wouldn't be worrying so much about straights, which pay only 4-for-1. High pairs and two pairs would be our bread and butter on this hand, but we'd have visions of

full houses and fours of a kind. And we'd hold King-Queen instead.

14. B. Dealt 3 of hearts, 5 of hearts, 6 of spades, 7 of hearts,
8 of hearts, hold the four hearts.

Flushes and straights have the same payoff in All-American,
but given a four-card start they don't hit with the same frequency.
There are only eight cards here that will complete our straight—
the four 4s and the four 9s. But there are nine hearts remaining in
the deck that will complete the flush. Our EVs are 7.66 on the
four-card flush, and 6.80 on the four-card straight.

15. A. Dealt 4 of spades, 7 of spades, 8 of spades, Queen of
hearts, Jack of hearts, hold 4-7-8.

We've already seen that three-card inside straight flushes
with fewer than two gaps and no high cards are better plays than
low pairs. Here we have a three-card straight flush with no high
cards, but two gaps. It's not as good as a low pair, but it's better
than a two-card royal. EVs are 3.44 on 4-7-8, 3.29 on Queen-
Jack.

16. B. Dealt King of diamonds, Queen of diamonds, 7 of diamonds, 6 of clubs, 4 of spades, hold King-Queen-7.

It's a close call, but we hold a third card of the same suit
with a two-card royal flush unless the two-card royal consists of
Queen-Jack. Here, we expect a return of 3.02 coins per five
played on King-Queen-7, barely beating the 3.01 on King-
Queen.

17. A. Dealt Jack of clubs, 8 of clubs, 6 of spades, 4 of
hearts, 2 of diamonds, hold Jack-8.

What's this? A two-card double-inside straight flush? And we
keep it?

Yep. And we'd do the same with Queen-9. On this pay table,
both are stronger plays than keeping a single high card. Here, we
have an EV of 2.30 on Jack-8, and 2.29 on the Jack.

18. B. Dealt Ace of hearts, 10 of hearts, 8 of clubs, 6 of
spades, 4 of diamonds, hold Ace-10.

In Jacks or Better, we don't hold a suited Ace-10. Here we do, to the tune of an expected value of 2.27 on Ace-10 compared to 2.16 on the Ace.

19. A. Dealt 8 of clubs, 9 of spades, 10 of hearts, 3 of diamonds, 5 of clubs, hold 8-9-10.

Even three-card open-ended straights are worthwhile in All-American. With no high cards, they rank low on the totem pole, beneath single high cards but above three-card flushes with no high cards and two-card straight flushes with no high cards.

In Jacks or Better, we'd discard this entire hand and start again, but here we have an EV of 2.14 on the three-card straight that's much better than the 1.66 on a total redraw.

20. C. Dealt 7 of diamonds, 9 of diamonds, 5 of clubs, 4 of spades, 2 of hearts, hold 7-9 of diamonds.

This is the lowest ranking playable hand on our strategy table, a two-card inside straight flush with one gap. With two gaps, such as 7-10 of diamonds, we'd toss the whole hand. With only one gap, the 7 and 9 have an expected value of 1.83. Not great, but better than the 1.69 on starting over.

Shuffle No. 9:
Double Bonus Poker

There are a lot of reasons to like Double Bonus Poker. First of all, in its full-pay version that pays 10-for-1 on full houses, 7-for-1 on flushes and 5-for-1 on straights, it's a high-paying game, with a potential 100.17 percent return with expert play. Second, it offers the chance at a big win even if you don't hit a royal flush. Many's the time I've turned a so-so day at the casino into a good one—or a losing day into a winner—by hitting four Aces for an 800-coin payoff. Okay, it doesn't compare to the 4,000-coin jackpot on a royal flush, but the Aces come up about 10 times as often.

That 800-coin secondary jackpot for five coins wagered even made converts of some slot players—my mother, for one. (Hi Mom!) She'd found Jacks or Better boring, but once there was the real possibility of winning $200 on a quarter machine on a four-Ace hand that would pay only $31.25 on Jacks or Better, she left the reels for the higher hit frequency and higher payback percentage of video poker.

I also like Double Bonus Poker because the full-pay version is very widespread. Unlike full-pay Deuces Wild, which is confined to Nevada, you can walk into some casinos in newer gaming states and play 10-7 Double Bonus. In many gaming jurisdictions, full-pay Double Bonus Poker is the only available video poker game with a potential payback of more than 100 percent.

Why? It seems that when the game was approved in jurisdictions that prohibit games with theoretical paybacks in excess of 100 percent, the software available to regulators couldn't accurately rate the game. In one riverboat state, I was invited to speak at a conference on gaming hosted by the economics department of a local university. I mentioned that the casino whose meeting space we were using was the first in the area to offer a 100-percent-plus video poker game —10-7 Double Bonus Poker.

At the lunch break, a gaming board agent approached to assure me there was no 100 percent–plus game there. The laboratory that licensed the game had run millions of trials using a video poker strategy, and had come up with a theoretical payback that was under the legal limit of 100 percent return.

I asked if video poker in that state was required to be dealt from a randomly shuffled 52-card electronic deck, with each card having an equal chance of being dealt. He assured me that was the case. I shook his hand, thanked him for the information and went to lunch, knowing that the machines in that casino were potential 100.17 percent games. The gaming lab no doubt used a video poker strategy in testing the game, but it didn't use *the* strategy for 10-7 Double Bonus.

Years later, an industry source told me that leading video poker manufacturer IGT along with independent testing laboratories had upgraded software and were now better able to calculate the potential payback percentages on video poker games. It may well be that if 10-7 Double Bonus had gone to riverboat states for approval in 2000 instead of 1992 and 1993, it would not have been licensed.

However, Double Bonus is now firmly entrenched. The 10-7 version is still used in that same casino that hosted the conference. Licensing has never been called into question, because even though the theoretical payback potential is in excess of 100 percent, the actual payback is less. That's because Double Bonus is a tricky game, with many special cases and strategy differences from Jacks or Better. Players make enough mistakes that the machines make a profit for the casino. The casino is happy, the gaming board is happy and players are happy, too, because they're getting a great game.

The 10-7 version of Double Bonus Poker has the following pay table: Royal flush 250-for-1 (jumps to 4,000 with five coins wagered); straight flush 50-for-1; four Aces 160-for-1; four 2s, 3s or 4s 80-for-1; four 5s through Kings 50-for-1; full house 10-for-1; flush 7-for-1; straight 5-for-1; three of a kind 3-for-1; two pair 1-for-1; pair of Jacks or better 1-for-1.

With expert play, that's a 100.17 percent game, but even if you just play Jacks or Better strategy, it's a 99.8 percent game. Results are volatile because so much of the payback is concentrated in the less common hands, and the 1-for-1 payback on two pair won't take you far in a cold streak. On quarter machines, I've won several hundred dollars in an hour, and I've also given up after dumping my fifth $20 bill in 20 minutes. Dollar machines—well, they're either very rewarding or very expensive.

In the hands that follow, we're going to look at some of the basic changes from Jacks or Better to Double Bonus—plays that will help you get over the 100 percent hump in the 10-7 game. Then we'll check out some of the strategy changes to get the most out of lower pay tables.

DOUBLE BONUS POKER BASICS

1. **To change the payback percentage, Double Bonus Poker payoffs commonly are changed on:**

    A. Full houses.
    B. Flushes.
    C. Straights.
    D. All of the above.

2. **In full-pay Double Bonus Poker, royal flushes occur:**

    A. More often than in Jacks or Better.
    B. Less often than in Jacks or Better.
    C. About as often as in Jacks or Better.

3. **In 10-7 Double Bonus Poker, the three types of hands that combine to make up more than 56 percent of our payback are:**

    A. Jacks or better, two pair and three of a kind.

    B. Jacks or better, three of a kind and full house.

    C. Jacks or better, three of a kind and four of a kind.

10-7 DOUBLE BONUS POKER STRATEGY

4. Queen of clubs, Queen of diamonds, 7 of spades, 7 of hearts, 3 of diamonds:

    A. Hold the Queens.

    B. Hold the Queens and 7s.

5. Ace of spades, Ace of hearts, Ace of clubs, 6 of spades, 6 of diamonds:

    A. Hold only the Aces.

    B. Hold the full house.

6. 8 of hearts, 7 of spades, 6 of spades, 4 of clubs, 2 of diamonds:

    A. Hold 8-7-6-4.

    B. Discard all five cards.

7. 8 of clubs, 7 of clubs, 2 of clubs, 3 of diamonds, 10 of spades:

    A. Discard all five cards.

    B. Hold the three-card flush

8: King of hearts, Queen of hearts, 8 of hearts, 5 of clubs, 2 of spades:

    A. Hold King-Queen.

    B. Hold the three-card flush.

9. 10 of hearts, 10 of diamonds, 9 of hearts, 8 of clubs, 7 of spades:

    A. Hold the pair of 10s.

    B. Hold 9-8-7 and one of the 10s.

10. Ace of hearts, King of hearts, Jack of hearts, 8 of hearts, Jack of clubs:

    A. Hold the three-card royal.
    B. Hold all four hearts.
    C. Hold the pair of Jacks.

9-7 DOUBLE BONUS POKER STRATEGY

As we saw in the section on Jacks or Better, lowering the full house payback has a smaller effect on strategy than lowering the flush payback. The 9-7 version of Double Bonus Poker, which pays 99.1 percent in the long run, plays much like the 10-7 game, but there is one important difference. Let's check it out:

11. Ace of hearts, Ace of diamonds, 2 of hearts, 2 of diamonds, 6 of spades:

    A. Hold the pair of Aces.
    B. Hold both pairs.

9-6 DOUBLE BONUS POKER STRATEGY

When we lower the full house and flush paybacks by a unit each, we have a game that's significantly different from 10-7 or 9-7 Double Bonus Poker. It's a 97.8 percent game, although in some casinos you can find a 9-6 Double Bonus game that pays 200-for-1 on four Aces instead of the standard 160-for-1. That brings the payback percentage back up to 99.0 percent.

Remember that dropping the pay table on flushes has a big impact on how we regard four-card flushes and three-card straight flushes as we check out the following hands:

12. King of diamonds, Queen of diamonds, Jack of diamonds, 4 of diamonds, 7 of spades:

    A. Hold all four diamonds.
    B. Hold King-Queen-Jack.

13. King of diamonds, Queen of diamonds, 9 of diamonds, Jack of spades, 6 of hearts:

    A: Hold King-Queen.

    B. Hold King-Queen-9

    C. Hold King-Queen-Jack.

    D. Hold King-Queen-Jack-9.

14. Jack of spades, Jack of clubs, King of clubs, Ace of clubs, 7 of clubs:

    A. Hold the pair of Jacks.

    B. Hold Ace-King-Jack of clubs.

    C. Hold Ace-King-Jack-7 of clubs.

15. Ace of clubs, 9 of hearts, 7 of hearts, 5 of hearts, 2 of spades:

    A. Hold the Ace.

    B. Hold 9-7-5.

16. King of hearts, 7 of hearts, 5 of hearts, 8 of spades, 3 of diamonds:

    A. Hold the King.

    B. Hold King-7-5.

17. 9 of hearts, 8 of hearts, 2 of hearts, 3 of clubs, 4 of spades:

    A. Hold 9-8-2.

    B. Discard all five cards.

8-5-4 DOUBLE BONUS POKER STRATEGY

This is a game that really puts the squeeze on a player. I'll specify 8-5-4 here because unlike most Double Bonus machines, this one pays only 4-for-1 on straights. The combination of losing two units on the full house payback, two on the flush payback and another one on the straight drops the payback all the way to 94.2 percent, and that's with expert play.

In a word: yuck. My fondest wish is that you never find yourself playing 8-5-4 Bonus Poker. But in the event it's the best game your local casino has to offer, check out these few strategy switches:

18. **Queen of clubs, Jack of clubs, 10 of clubs, Jack of spades, 6 of hearts.**

    A. Hold the pair of Jacks.
    B. Hold Queen-Jack-10.

19. **2 of hearts, 2 of diamonds, 3 of clubs, 4 of spades, 5 of hearts.**

    A. Hold one of the 2s and the 3, 4 and 5.
    B. Hold the pair of 2s.

20. **Ace of hearts, Queen of spades, 10 of spades, 7 of clubs, 4 of diamonds.**

    A. Hold the Ace.
    B. Hold Ace-Queen.
    C. Hold Queen-10.

Shuffle No. 9:
Double Bonus Poker
Answers

DOUBLE BONUS POKER BASICS

1. D. To change the payback percentage, Double Bonus Poker payoffs commonly are changed on full houses, flushes and straights.

If you've learned to check out full house and flush payoffs while comparing Jacks or Better machines, you already know most of what you need to know to compare Double Bonus pay tables. The most common Double Bonus variations simply change the 10-7 full house-flush payoffs to 9-7, leaving a 99.1 percent game, or 9-6, leaving a 97.8 percenter.

However, Double Bonus players also should check payoffs on straights. One of the attractions of Double Bonus Poker is that on most machines, straights pay 5-for-1, one unit better than the 4-for-1 on Jacks or Better. Sometimes, however, you'll find a Double Bonus machine that pays only 4-for-1 on straights. I've seen 9-6-4 and 9-5-4 Double Bonus machines, but the most common version with the straight cut also trims full houses to 8-for-1 and flushes to 5-for-1.

That leaves an 8-5-4 game that pays only 94.2 percent. And that's with expert play. That's not a video poker game. That's a shakedown of the unwary.

I highly recommend that you not play Double Bonus Poker if the payoff on straights is below 5-for-1. However, knowing that some players will find themselves in a casino with no decent

video poker and will decide to give this low-payer a go, I've included some strategy questions for the 8-5-4 game at the end of
this chapter.

There also are a couple of rare variations that give the player
a little extra. A few 10-7 Double Bonus machines raise the
straight flush payback to 80-for-1, increasing the overall payback
percentage to 100.5 percent. (I've never seen one of these outside
Nevada.) And some 9-6 Double Bonus games raise the payoff on
four Aces to 200-for-1, leaving a potential 1,000-coin jackpot for
five coins played. These elevate the 9-6 game from 97.8 to 99.0
percent. Look for them on Bally's Game Maker multiple-game
machines.

2. B. In full-pay Double Bonus Poker, royal flushes occur less
often than in Jacks or Better.

It might seem odd that royal flushes occur less often in the
higher-paying game, but they do. That's mostly because of the 7-
for-1 flush payback in the full-pay version of Double Bonus. We
adjust our strategy to hold partial flushes more often, even if they
cost us a chance at going for a royal. Given Ace-Jack-9 of the
same suit, we hold all three in full-pay Double Bonus, but only
Ace-Jack in full-pay Jacks or Better. Given Jack-6-3 of the same
suit, we hold all three in full-pay Double Bonus, but only the Jack
in Jacks or Better.

The bottom line is that we see royal flushes only about once
per 48,000 hands in full-pay Double Bonus, while we see them
once per 40,400 hands in Jacks or Better.

If we drop down to the awful 8-5-4 Double Bonus game, our
royal flush frequency goes back up to once per 40,445 hands,
proving that it takes more than royal flushes to make a good
video poker game.

3. C. In 10-7 Double Bonus Poker, the three types of hands
that combine to make up more than 56 percent of our payback
are Jacks or better, three of a kind and four of a kind.

The biggest share comes from three of a kind, which accounts for 21.7 percent of our payback. Pairs of Jacks or better
are next at 19.2 percent. Four of a kind makes up 15.4 percent of

our return, a little more than 2.5 times what it does for us in Jacks or Better.

Two pairs account for 12.5 percent of our return, followed by full houses at 11.2, flushes at 10.5, straights at 7.5, royal flushes at 1.7 and straight flushes at 0.57.

10-7 DOUBLE BONUS POKER STRATEGY

4. B. Dealt Queen of clubs, Queen of diamonds, 7 of spades, 7 of hearts, 3 of diamonds, hold the Queens and 7s.

Players approaching Double Bonus Poker, Bonus Poker Deluxe, Double Double Bonus Poker or any game in which two pair pays only 1-for-1 think this play is obvious. Two pair pays only 1-for-1, you'd get the 1-for-1 on the pair of Queens alone, so why not discard the second pair and go for three of a kind, or even four of a kind?

Not so fast, folks. If we hold both pairs, we have four chances in the remaining 47 cards to draw a full house. That's a good enough chance that our expected value of 8.83 coins returned per five coins wagered is far better than the 7.29 on the Queens alone. As the payoff on full houses drops, the gap narrows, but even on the lowly 8-5-4 version of Double Bonus, we're still better off holding both pairs.

5. A. Dealt Ace of spades, Ace of hearts, Ace of clubs, 6 of spades, 6 of diamonds, hold only the Aces.

In the 10-7 version, if you bet five coins, you'll get 50 back every time you hold the full house. It's something you can count on, and the reluctance to break that up is understandable. However, if you discard the low pair and hold only the Aces, you're still assured of no worse than a 15-coin payoff for three of a kind, and your long-term average return will be 50.57 coins per trial.

Here's the breakdown: There are 1,081 possible two-card draws among the remaining 47 cards. Of those, 968 will fail to improve our hand, and we'll settle for three of a kind. However, 67 draws will be pairs that will get us back to a full house, and 46 times per 1,081 hands we'll draw the fourth Ace for the 800-coin jackpot.

More often than not, we're going to wind up with less than we could have. But in the long run, we'll wind up with more. That's true on every version of Double Bonus. In fact, as the full-house payback drops, the gap between expected value of holding just the Aces and holding the full house widens.

6. A. 8 of hearts, 7 of spades, 6 of spades, 4 of clubs, 2 of diamonds, hold 8-7-6-4.

Those who have fully soaked in the last chapter on Bonus Poker Deluxe know that when the payoff on two pair is dropped to 1-for-1, the value of a complete redraw falls enough that we're better off holding inside straights instead of discarding all five cards. In Double Bonus, we add the fact that the payoff on straights is raised to 5-for-1. That makes this hand a no-brainer. Our expected value on a five-coin wager is 2.13 when we hold the inside straight, easily better than the 1.65 for a full redraw.

7. B. Dealt 8 of clubs, 7 of clubs, 2 of clubs, 3 of diamonds, 10 of spades, hold the three-card flush.

We can pick up a hint here from the section on super–full-pay 9-7 Jacks or Better in Shuffle No. 4. When the payoff on flushes rises to 7-for-1, it makes holding three cards of the same suit worthwhile, provided we don't have anything better in the hand. Here we have no pairs, no four-card straights, no high cards—if straights paid 6-for-1 or less, we'd chuck it all and start over. Not here. We expect a return on the three card flush of 1.82 coins for every five we wager, compared with 1.65 on a total redraw.

8. A. Dealt King of hearts, Queen of hearts, 8 of hearts, 5 of clubs, 2 of spades, hold King-Queen.

As we saw in No. 7, we often hold three-card flushes in Double Bonus Poker, provided flushes pay 7-for-1. That usually applies when we have high cards, even though we're giving up the long shot at a royal flush. If, for example, we had Jack-8-5 of the same suit, along with two junk cards, we would hold Jack-8-5.

It's a little trickier when we have *two* high cards. If our three cards of the same suit were Ace-King-8, Ace-Queen-8 or Ace-

Jack-8, we'd still hold all three suited cards. But with King-Queen-8, King-Jack-8 or Queen-Jack-8, we just hold the two cards to the royal.

Why the difference? The Ace limits the number of possible straight draws, so we give up much in holding a non-straight card such as an 8 in order to maximize flush opportunities. If our hand includes an Ace and another high card, our only straight possibilities are Ace high. With a King, we can be either Ace high or King high, or with Queen-Jack we could be Ace, King or Queen high.

The difference is narrow, but if you're trying to squeeze everything out of the game, hold three card flushes with two high cards when they include an Ace, but just hold the two high cards if they're King or Queen high.

In this hand, our expected value is 2.825 compared with 2.817 for King-Queen-8. If we'd been dealt an Ace instead of a King, the EV would remain 2.817 on Ace-Queen-8, but drop to 2.749 on Ace-Queen.

9. B. Dealt 10 of hearts, 10 of diamonds, 9 of hearts, 8 of clubs, 7 of spades, hold 9-8-7 and one of the 10s.

In Jacks or Better we'd make the opposite play and hold the pair of 10s, but this isn't plain old Jacks or Better. Two major differences impact this hand. Most important is that straights pay 5-for-1 in Double Bonus instead of the 4-for-1 in Jacks or Better, raising the value of holding the four-card straight. In addition, the value of holding the pair is diminished because Double Bonus pays only 1-for-1 instead of 2-for-1 on two pair. That one-two punch leaves us with a decision that isn't even a particularly close call. The EVs here are 4.26 on the four-card straight, and 3.72 on the pair of 6s.

10. B. Dealt Ace of hearts, King of hearts, Jack of hearts, 8 of hearts, Jack of clubs, hold all four hearts.

The heightened value of flushes leads us to break up a sure winner in the pair of Jacks in order to chase something better. When we make this play, we expect an average return of 7.55 coins per five wagered by holding the four-card flush, compared with 7.28 on the pair of Jacks and 6.85 on the three-card royal. When the flush pays less than 7-for-1, we hold the Jacks instead.

(Aside to budding experts who want to milk every last drop out of the 10-7 game: we don't break up high pairs for any three-card royal that includes both an Ace and a 10, for any three-card royal that includes an Ace in which we'd be discarding a penalty card, nor for King-Queen-10 or King-Jack-10 if there are penalty cards involved.)

9-7 DOUBLE BONUS POKER STRATEGY

11. A. Dealt Ace of hearts, Ace of diamonds, 2 of hearts, 2 of diamonds, 6 of spades, hold the pair of Aces.

When full houses pay 10-for-1, that's enough for us to forgo our slim chance at drawing Aces nos. 3 and 4 to take the 1-in-11.75 shot at a full house instead. But when the full house payoff drops to 9-for-1, the percentages swing the other way.

Even in 10-7 Double Bonus, it's a close call. Our expected value is 8.83 for holding both pairs, compared with 8.82 on holding just the Aces. Here, in 9-7 Double Bonus, the value of holding just the Aces drops a bit, to an average return of 8.77 coins per five wagered, but the EV of holding both pairs plummets to 8.40.

The gap widens as the full-house payoff drops. Holding both pairs is a play strictly for the 10-7 game; in 9-7, 9-6, 8-5 or (God forbid!) lower pay tables, hold just the Aces.

This applies only when we have a pair of Aces. With Kings, Queens or Jacks, we'd hold both pairs and hope for the full house on any available pay table, even though pairs of face cards assure us a 1-for-1 payoff, just as Aces do.

What's the difference? The 160-for-1 payoff on four Aces. Four Kings, Queens or Jacks would bring us just 250 coins for five wagered, not the 800-coin bonanza that comes with four Aces.

9-6 DOUBLE BONUS POKER STRATEGY

12. B. King of diamonds, Queen of diamonds, Jack of diamonds, 4 of diamonds, 7 of spades, hold King-Queen-Jack.

This is a very similar problem to No. 10. There, we held four parts of a flush instead of three parts to a royal. The difference is that here, flushes pay only 6-for-1, decreasing the value of the four-card flush. The EV of the four-card flush in 9-6 Double Bonus is 6.70, no match for the 7.43 on the three-card royal. On the 10-7 game, the four card royal, at 7.66, noses out the four-card flush, at 7.59.

13. D. Dealt King of diamonds, Queen of diamonds, 9 of diamonds, Jack of spades, 6 of hearts, hold King-Queen-Jack-9.

As in most versions of Double Bonus, the payoff on straights is elevated to 5-for-1, which moves inside straights higher on our list of hands to play than in most games. Together with the flush payoff depressed to 6-for-1, that tilts us in favor of holding the four-card inside straight, with an EV of 3.09, slightly better than the 3.05 on the three-card inside straight flush.

If we were playing 10-7 Double Bonus instead, we'd hold the three-card inside straight flush, King-Queen-9, with an EV that jumps to 3.26 while that of King-Queen-Jack-9 remains at 3.09.

14. A. Dealt Jack of spades, Jack of clubs, King of clubs, Ace of clubs, 7 of clubs, hold the pair of Jacks.

When should we break up a high pair? In most Jacks or Better versions, we break one up only to pursue a four-card royal flush or four-card straight flush. In 10-7 Double Bonus Poker, we also break up pairs of Kings, Queens or Jacks for most three-card royals and for four-card flushes that include at least two high cards.

But this answer isn't about 10-7 Double Bonus Poker, it's about the 9-6 version. Here, the value of the flush isn't high enough for us to be worrying about many three-card royals or four-card flushes. We'll take our chances with the high pair, and an EV of 7.23, instead of pursuing the three-card royal (6.68) or four-card flush (6.60). In the 10-7 game, we'd hold the four-card flush (7.55) over the pair (7.28) or the three-card royal (6.85).

Compared with Jacks or Better, even 9-6 Double Bonus does expand slightly on the number of hands for which it's worth breaking up a high pair. Hold Queen-Jack-10 of the same suit instead of a high pair. Advanced players would break up the high pair for King-Queen-Jack suited provided there was no more than one penalty card.

15. A. Dealt Ace of clubs, 9 of hearts, 7 of hearts, 5 of hearts, 2 of spades, hold the Ace.

This might seem like the obvious play to some players, but in the 10-7 game we play the opposite way. There, the heightened payback on flushes means we hold more three-card double-inside straight flushes. We push those hands farther down the list in 9-6 Double Bonus, where the lone Ace has an EV of 2.31 compared to 2.15 for 9-7-5. In the 10-7 game, the 9-7-5 leaps to 2.35, just nosing out the 2.34 on the single Ace.

16. A. Dealt King of hearts, 7 of hearts, 5 of hearts, 8 of spades, 3 of diamonds, hold the King.

Basically, we like three-card flushes when they pay 7-for-1, and we don't like them when they pay less. Here, where flushes pay 6-for-1, the single King has an expected value of 2.15 coins in return for every five wagered, a little better than the 2.11 on holding King-7-5. In the 10-7 game, King-7-5 has an EV of 2.32, bettering the 2.16 on the lone King.

17. B. Dealt 9 of hearts, 8 of hearts, 2 of hearts, 3 of clubs, 4 of spades, discard all five cards.

Discarding three-card flushes isn't just a matter of a single high card being a better play, as in No. 16. With no straight flush possibilities, three-card flushes just aren't worth our time when the payoffs are 6-for-1 or less. In 9-6 Double Bonus, the EV of discarding all five cards is 1.64, compared to 1.61 on 9-8-2. In 10-7 Double Bonus, the EV of 1.82 on the three-card flush beats the 1.65 on a complete redraw.

8-5-4 DOUBLE BONUS POKER STRATEGY

18. A. Dealt Queen of clubs, Jack of clubs, 10 of clubs, Jack of spades, 6 of hearts, hold the pair of Jacks.

Check back in No. 14, and you'll see that in higher-paying versions of Double Bonus, we break up the pair of Jacks to hold Queen-Jack-10 of the same suit. Here, with flushes paying only 5-for-1, we don't. The expected values are 7.18 on the pair of Jacks and 7.12 on Queen-Jack-10. On the 9-6 version of Double Bonus, Queen-Jack-10 has an EV of 7.52 to 7.23 on the pair of Jacks. The gap in favor of Queen-Jack-10 gets wider as the flush payoff increases.

19. B. Dealt 2 of hearts, 2 of diamonds, 3 of clubs, 4 of spades, 5 of hearts, hold the pair of 2s.

On most Double Bonus pay tables, we'd hold 2-3-4-5 and hope for a straight. Not in 8-5-4 Double Bonus. Remember, the "4" stands for a 4-for-1 payoff on straights, one unit less than the 5-for-1 that we get on most Double Bonus machines. That one unit makes all the difference.

In 8-5-4 Double Bonus, the pair of 2s has an EV of 4.03, while the four-card open-ended straight is at 3.40. In the more common 9-6 Double Bonus with straights paying 5-for-1, the value of the four-card straight leaps to 4.26, better than the 4.08 on the pair of 2s.

20. A. Dealt Ace of hearts, Queen of spades, 10 of spades, 7 of clubs, 4 of diamonds, hold the Ace.

Our flush paybacks are reduced, our straight paybacks are reduced—we're in a sad state when we're forced to play 8-5-4 Double Bonus. Might as well take a long shot with the lone Ace, which has an expected value of 2.22 compared with the 2.20 on Ace-Queen and 2.17 on Queen-10.

On 9-6 Double Bonus, the hand that's third best on the 8-5-4 list jumps to the top. Queen-10 gives us the best opportunities for flushes, straights, straight flushes and even the odd royal, and it has an EV of 2.28, compared to 2.25 on the Ace and 2.22 on Ace-Queen. Queen-10 remains the best play in 9-7 and 10-7 versions of Double Bonus.

Shuffle No. 10: Double Bonus Variations

The popularity of Double Bonus Poker has led to many similar games. All use the Double Bonus formula of dropping the two-pair payoff to 1-for-1 and enhancing the four-of-a-kind payoff, but each has its own wrinkle. Want a bigger bonus on four Kings, Queens and Aces? Try Super Double Bonus Poker. Maybe you'd like a shot at a 2,000-coin jackpot on four Aces. Then Super Aces might be your game. (So might Double Double Bonus Poker, but that's the next chapter.) Willing to settle for 1,000 coins on four Aces, and like the idea of double pay on three Aces? That's Nevada Bonus Poker. There are others—when casinos want custom pay tables, they frequently start with a Double Bonus base.

None of these variations are exactly casino standards. Nearly every casino has Double Bonus Poker and lots of it, but its variants are change of pace games, machines that individual casinos can use in small banks to set themselves apart from the crowd a bit.

Let's take a look at how rearranging these pay tables affects the way we play:

SUPER DOUBLE BONUS POKER

Bigger bonuses on four Kings, Queens or Jacks are nice for the player, because we often hold single face cards, whereas we never hold single 2s, 3s or 4s. So a big part of the attraction is that

Super Double Bonus Poker pays 120-for-1 on four Kings, Queens or Jacks, meaning a 600-coin bonanza for five wagered. Straight flushes also are enhanced to 80-for-1, or 400 coins for five wagered.

That jackpot is offset by decreases in full house, flush and straight paybacks. That leaves the following Super Double Bonus pay table: Royal flush 250-for-1 (jumps to 4,000 with five coins wagered); straight flush 80-for-1; four Aces 160-for-1; four Kings, Queens or Jacks 120-for-1; four 2s, 3s or 4s 80-for-1; four 5s through 10s 50-for-1; full house 9-for-1; flush 5-for-1; straight 4-for-1; three of a kind 3-for-1; two pair 1-for-1; pair of Jacks or better 1-for-1.

It's a 99.7 percent game, and I've been in casinos where it's the best game in the house. At the same time, it's a roller-coaster, with volatility higher than the already high Double Bonus Poker.

1. **9 of hearts, 8 of hearts, 7 of hearts, 6 of hearts, 5 of spades.**

    A. Hold the straight.
    B. Hold 9-8-7-6.

2. **Ace of hearts, Ace of spades, 7 of diamonds, 7 of hearts, 5 of spades.**

    A. Hold the pair of Aces.
    B. Hold Ace-Ace-7-7.

3. **King of clubs, King of diamonds, 7 of clubs, 7 of spades, 5 of diamonds.**

    A. Hold the pair of Kings.
    B. Hold King-King-7-7.

4. **King of hearts, King of clubs, King of spades, 9 of spades, 9 of diamonds.**

    A. Hold the full house.
    B. Hold the three Kings.

5. **Queen of spades, Jack of spades, 10 of spades, Jack of diamonds, 5 of clubs.**

    A. Hold the pair of Jacks.

    B. Hold Queen-Jack-10 of spades.

6. **King of clubs, Queen of clubs, Jack of clubs, 7 of clubs, 4 of hearts.**

    A. Hold King-Queen-Jack-7.

    B. Hold King-Queen-Jack.

7. **2 of hearts, 2 of spades, 3 of diamonds, 4 of clubs, 5 of spades.**

    A. Hold 2-3-4-5.

    B. Hold the pair of 2s.

8. **Queen of diamonds, Jack of diamonds, 9 of diamonds, 5 of hearts, 5 of spades.**

    A. Hold Queen-Jack.

    B. Hold Queen-Jack-9.

    C. Hold the pair of 5s.

9. **Ace of diamonds, Queen of hearts, Jack of hearts, 9 of spades, 8 of clubs.**

    A. Hold Queen-Jack.

    B. Hold Queen-Jack-9-8.

    C. Hold Ace-Queen-Jack.

10. **King of diamonds, 10 of hearts, 8 of spades, 7 of spades, 4 of spades.**

    A. Hold the King.

    B. Hold 8-7-4.

SUPER ACES

The 800-coin jackpot for four Aces on Double Bonus Poker was so popular, why not make it even bigger?

In the case of Super Aces, bigger is 2,000 coins—and we don't need a specific fifth card kicker, as in Double Double Bonus Poker, where we need a 2, 3 or 4 as the fifth card in order to get a 2,000-coin payoff. With five coins bet on Super Aces, all four-Ace hands are worth 2,000 coins, regardless of the fifth card.

That leaves a bonanza on four Aces that's half the size of the jackpot for a royal flush, and it's on a hand that occurs nearly 10 times as often. We'll hit a royal flush in this game about once per 40,000 hands, and four Aces about once per 4,250.

On other quads, the payoffs are the same as in Double Bonus Poker—50-for-1 on four 5s through Kings, and 80-for-1 on four 2s, 3s and 4s.

To make up for the payday on Aces, the pay table is reduced on full houses, flushes and straights to 8-5-4.

Here's the pay table: Royal flush 250-for-1 (jumps to 4,000 with five coins wagered); straight flush 50-for-1; four Aces 400-for-1; four 2s, 3s or 4s 80-for-1; four 5s through Kings 50-for-1; full house 8-for-1; flush 5-for-1; straight 4-for-1; three of a kind 3-for-1; two pair 1-for-1; pair of Jacks or better 1-for-1.

That leaves a game that plays more like 8-5-4 Double Bonus Poker than like the 10-7 version, even though Super Aces returns 99.8 percent with expert play, much closer to the 100.2 percent on 10-7 Double Bonus than the 94.2 on 8-5-4 Double Bonus.

11. Ace of spades, Ace of diamonds, 2 of diamonds, 3 of diamonds, 4 of diamonds:

    A. Hold Ace-2-3-4.

    B. Hold the pair of Aces.

12. Ace of spades, King of spades, Queen of spades, 8 of spades, 7 of hearts.

    A. Hold Ace-King-Queen-8.

    B. Hold Ace-King-Queen.

13. 5 of hearts, 5 of spades, 6 of clubs, 7 of hearts, 8 of diamonds.

    A. Hold the pair of 5s.

    B. Hold 5-6-7-8.

14. Ace of clubs, King of hearts, Queen of diamonds, Jack of diamonds, 9 of diamonds.

    A. Hold Ace-King-Queen-Jack.

    B. Hold Queen-Jack-9.

    C. Hold Queen-Jack.

15. Ace of spades, King of hearts, 7 of diamonds, 5 of hearts, 2 of spades.

    A. Hold the Ace.

    B. Hold the King.

    C. Hold Ace-King.

16. Ace of spades, King of spades, 7 of diamonds, 5 of hearts, 2 of hearts.

    A. Hold the Ace.

    B. Hold the King.

    C. Hold Ace-King.

17. Ace of spades, King of spades, Queen of hearts, Jack of hearts, 9 of hearts.

    A. Hold the Ace.

    B. Hold Ace-King.

    C. Hold Queen-Jack.

    D. Hold Queen-Jack-9.

    E. Hold Ace-King-Queen-Jack.

18. King of hearts, 10 of hearts, 7 of diamonds, 6 of clubs, 3 of spades.

    A. Hold the King.

    B. Hold King-10.

19. Ace of hearts, Jack of spades, 10 of spades, 7 of spades, 2 of clubs.

    A. Hold the Ace.

    B. Hold Ace-Jack.

    C. Hold Jack-10-7.

20. 9 of hearts, 5 of hearts, 3 of hearts, 10 of spades, 8 of clubs.

    A. Hold 9-5-3.
    B. Discard all five cards.

NEVADA BONUS POKER

We have a rarity in Nevada Bonus Poker—a game with a variable pay table on three of a kind. Most threes of a kind pay the standard 3-for-1, but three Aces pay 6-for-1. Combine that with a 200-for-1 payoff on four Aces, and Aces become by far the most valuable denomination in the deck.

That's not always the case in video poker. In Jacks or Better, in which all fours of a kind pay the same 25-for-1, the Ace is the least valuable high card because it gives us the fewest straight possibilities. Tack on enough bonuses, however, and the value of the Ace overwhelms that little problem.

Unlike Double Bonus Poker and the variations listed above, four Aces are the only quads with a bonus payoff. Other fours of a kind pay the same 25-for-1 as on Jacks or Better. However, like all Double Bonus variations, Nevada Bonus Poker drops the two-pair payoff to 1-for-1. And like full-pay Double Bonus, it enhances full houses (10-for-1 in full-pay Nevada Bonus Poker), flushes (8-for-1) and straights (7-for-1). Straight flushes also are raised—to 100-for-1.

The first time I ever played Nevada Bonus Poker, I hit a straight flush on my fifth hand. That I've never hit another on this game doesn't stop me from liking that particular enhancement, even as rarely as it comes into play.

The full pay-table is as follows: Royal flush 250-for-1 (jumps to 4,000 with five coins wagered); straight flush 100-for-1; four Aces 200-for-1; four 2s through Kings 25-for-1; full house 10-for-1; flush 8-for-1; straight 5-for-1; three Aces 6-for-1; three 2s through Kings 3-for-1; two pair 1-for-1; pair of Jacks or better 1-for-1.

That leaves a 98.8 percent game. I've been in many riverboat and Native American casinos with no 100-percent games, but several hovering around 99 percent. If that's the case in your local casino, then this game is both playable and fun. Watch out for reduced pay tables—I have seen a 10-7 version of this game that returns only 97.6 percent.

21. 8 of clubs, 9 of hearts, 10 of hearts, Jack of hearts, Queen of hearts.

    A. Hold the straight.
    B. Hold 9-10-Jack-Queen.

22. Ace of spades, Ace of diamonds, Jack of spades, Jack of diamonds, 10 of hearts.

    A. Hold the pair of Aces.
    B. Hold Ace-Ace-Jack-Jack.

23. Ace of hearts, Ace of clubs, 2 of clubs, 3 of clubs, 4 of clubs.

    A. Hold the pair of Aces.
    B. Hold Ace-2-3-4 of clubs.

24. Ace of hearts, 7 of hearts, 5 of hearts, 9 of diamonds, 2 of spades.

    A. Hold the Ace.
    B. Hold Ace-7-5.

25. Jack of hearts, 10 of hearts, 2 of spades, 5 of spades, 6 of spades.

    A. Hold the Jack.
    B. Hold Jack-10.
    C. Hold 2-5-6.

Shuffle No. 10: Double Bonus Variations Answers

SUPER DOUBLE BONUS POKER

1. B. Dealt 9 of hearts, 8 of hearts, 7 of hearts, 6 of hearts, 5 of spades, hold 9-8-7-6.

Several things are at work here. The return on a flush is lower than in the best versions of Double Bonus, but the return on a straight flush is higher. At the same time, the value of the straight is diminished in this game.

The bottom line for Super Double Bonus is that for every five coins we bet, we'll average a return of 22.3 if we go for the straight flush, and that beats settling for a certain payback of 20 coins if we hold the straight.

2. A. Dealt Ace of hearts, Ace of spades, 7 of diamonds, 7 of hearts, 5 of spades, hold the pair of Aces.

We play this hand just like any version of Double Bonus Poker in which the full house pays less than 10-for-1. We'll take our chances chasing the four-Ace jackpot, and if we don't get it, we'll hope for at least three Aces, or even a full house. The expected value is 8.77 on the pair of Aces, and 8.40 on the two pair.

3. B. Dealt King of clubs, King of diamonds, 7 of clubs, 7 of spades, 5 of diamonds, hold King-King-7-7.

This is a similar situation to No. 2, in which we had a two pair that included a high pair. However, on this hand the payoff on four Kings, Queens or Jacks isn't enough to make us stray from the normal play—even at 120-for-1. Keeping both pairs and taking the 1-in-11.75 shot at a full house remains our best play. Holding both pairs has an EV of 8.40, compared to 8.21 on just the Kings.

Break up two pair only if it includes a pair of Aces.

4. A. Dealt King of hearts, King of clubs, King of spades, 9 of spades, 9 of diamonds, hold the full house.

Just as in No. 3, we have to keep in mind that while the big payoff on four of the same faces is good, it's not quite good enough for us to step outside normal play. Hold the full house with five coins wagered, and we'll get 45 coins back. Break it up and hold just the Kings instead, and our expected value is 41.75 coins. Pretty good, but not good enough.

Just as in Double Bonus, we do break up full houses for hands that include three Aces, but not for anything less.

5. A. Dealt Queen of spades, Jack of spades, 10 of spades, Jack of diamonds, 5 of clubs, hold the pair of Jacks.

Holding Queen-Jack-10 leaves open not only a possible royal flush, but also a whole bunch of flush and straight possibilities. In full-pay Double Bonus Poker, where the values of both flushes and straights are higher than in Super Double Bonus, we'd hold Queen-Jack-10 over a pair of Jacks. The enhanced payback on four Jacks in Super Double Bonus means it's not even a close call here, with an EV of 8.20 on the Jacks and 7.40 on the three-card royal.

6. B. Dealt King of clubs, Queen of clubs, Jack of clubs, 7 of clubs, 4 of hearts, hold King-Queen-Jack.

With the flush payoff lowered to 5-for-1, we like three cards to the royal better than four cards to a flush. With King-Queen-Jack, our EV of 7.27 is far better than the 5.74 on all four clubs.

7. B. Dealt 2 of hearts, 2 of spades, 3 of diamonds, 4 of clubs, 5 of spades, hold the pair of 2s.

In good versions of Double Bonus, a straight pays 5-for-1, and we'd hold the four-card straight. In Super Double Bonus, straights pay only 4-for-1, and that drops the expected value of the four-card straight enough that we'll get more in the long run out of the pair of 2s. EVs are 4.08 on the pair of 2s, and 3.40 on the four-card straight.

8. C. Dealt Queen of diamonds, Jack of diamonds, 9 of diamonds, 5 of hearts, 5 of spades, hold the pair of 5s.

When flushes pay only 5-for-1, three-card straight flushes drop down our list, even in a game like Super Double Bonus with an enhanced payoff on straight flushes. We hit a ton more flushes than straight flushes, so the flushes are the bigger factor.

Here, the EV on the pair of 5s is 3.67, a little better than the 3.65 on Queen-Jack-9.

Wondering why the pair of 5s has a lower expected value than the pair of 2s in No. 7? It's because we get only a 250-coin payback on four 5s, compared with 400 on four 2s.

9. A. Dealt Ace of diamonds, Queen of hearts, Jack of hearts, 9 of spades, 8 of clubs, hold Queen-Jack.

No big adjustments are needed here. A Queen and Jack of the same suit remain a pretty good starting point, with an EV of 2.82 that easily beats the 2.34 on Queen-Jack-9-8, a four-card inside straight with two high cards. We'll take a chance on miracle draws for a royal flush, straight flush, four Queens or four Jacks, but settle for a high pair or two pair, with chances at a flush, straight or full house.

10. A. Dealt King of diamonds, 10 of hearts, 8 of spades, 7 of spades, 4 of spades, hold the King.

Which is more important in determining our strategy, a depressed payoff on flushes and straights or an enhanced payoff on straight flushes? Answer: flushes and straights occur far more frequently, and play a much more important role in determining our strategy.

In Super Double Bonus Poker, we have higher straight flush paybacks than in full-pay Double Bonus Poker, but lower flush paybacks. So in Super Double Bonus, we hold the King, with an EV of 2.25, and discard the three-card double-inside straight flush, at 2.01.

In 10-7 Double Bonus, we make the opposite play, and hold the three spades.

SUPER ACES

11. B. Dealt Ace of spades, Ace of diamonds, 2 of diamonds, 3 of diamonds, 4 of diamonds, hold the pair of Aces.

We have to change our mindset a little in Super Aces. In most Jacks or Better–based games, which include all the Bonus Poker variants, we'll hold a four-card straight flush instead of a high pair. That even includes Double Double Bonus Poker, where we get the 2,000-coin jackpot only a little more than a fourth of the time we get four Aces.

In Super Aces, the Ace quads are worth 2,000 coins for five played every time, and that means a strategy adjustment. Here, holding the pair of Aces is worth an average expected return of 12.03 coins for five played, while the four-card straight flush is worth 11.06.

12. B. Dealt Ace of spades, King of spades, Queen of spades, 8 of spades, 7 of hearts, hold Ace-King-Queen.

If you've been following along, you know where we're going with this one. Because the flush is worth only 5-for-1 in this game, we're better off holding the three-card royal than taking a one-card shot at the flush. This maximizes our chances to pair up one of the high cards, and leaves open straight as well as flush opportunities. Our expected values are 6.65 per five coins played on the three-card royal, and 5.74 on the four-card flush.

13. A. Dealt 5 of hearts, 5 of spades, 6 of clubs, 7 of hearts, 8 of diamonds, hold the pair of 5s.

With straights paying only 4-for-1, low pairs are a better play than four-card straights, even when the straights are open on both ends. Here, the expected value is 3.62 on the pair, and 3.40 on the four-card straight.

14. B. Dealt Ace of clubs, King of hearts, Queen of diamonds, Jack of diamonds, 9 of diamonds, hold Queen-Jack-9.

I've had players tell me they *never* hit straight flushes, that they even hit more royals than regular straight flushes. There's probably a little selective memory at work there, but even so, straight flushes are rare. They're even rarer than they need to be, because most average players pass up too many straight flush opportunities.

Here, the three-card inside straight flush is our best play, with an expected value of 3.27 that beats the 2.98 on the four-card inside straight, Ace-King-Queen-Jack.

Note that the three-card inside straight flush would *not* be the stronger play if the potential straight were open on both ends.

15. A. Dealt Ace of spades, King of hearts, 7 of diamonds, 5 of hearts, 2 of spades, hold the Ace.

This is a problem for Double Bonus Poker experts, those well versed in penalty cards. In 10-7 Double Bonus, we'd hold Ace-King here. Why? Partly because the 2 of spades is a penalty card for flushes and straights, diminishing the value of a single Ace just enough that Ace-King is a better play.

Here, when we hold just the Ace, we'll hit four Aces only 44 times out of every 299,360 we make this play. That's not enough that the 2,000-coin payoff in Super Aces makes a huge difference, but it shifts the expected values just enough that we don't worry so much about a flush penalty card. In Super Aces, we hold the single Ace, with an EV of 2.48, instead of Ace-King, at 2.29, despite having to discard the 2 of spades.

16. C. Dealt Ace of spades, King of spades, 7 of diamonds, 5 of hearts, 2 of hearts, hold Ace-King.

Cards here are in the same denomination as in No. 15. The difference is in the suits. Here, the Ace and King are of the same suit, leaving flush and royal flush possibilities as well as possible straights, high pairs, two pairs, threes of a kind, full houses and fours of a kind. That tips the balance so that here Ace-King (EV 2.79) wins out over the lone Ace (2.47).

17. D. Dealt Ace of spades, King of spades, Queen of hearts, Jack of hearts, 9 of hearts, hold Queen-Jack-9.

There are all kinds of possibilities with this hand, but the strongest remains the three-card inside straight flush with two high cards, with an EV of 2.77 compared to 2.72 for Ace-King.

Why does the suited Ace-King have a slightly lower expected value here than in No. 16? Because here, we'd be throwing away a Queen and a Jack, diminishing our chances of hitting high pairs or straights.

18. B. Dealt King of hearts, 10 of hearts, 7 of diamonds, 6 of clubs, 3 of spades, hold King-10.

It's a closer call than in 10-7 Double Bonus, but we still hold King-10 of the same suit when we're not discarding any flush penalty cards. Here, the expected value per five coins bet is 2.13 on King-10, marginally better than the 2.10 on the single King.

If we're throwing away flush cards, we make the opposite call. Imagine this hand with a 6 of hearts instead of a 6 of clubs; in that case, we'd hold the single King instead of King-10. What would we do in 10-7 Double Bonus? With the third heart in the hand, we'd hold King-10-6 because of the 7-for-1 payoff on flushes.

19. A. Dealt Ace of hearts, Jack of spades, 10 of spades, 7 of spades, 2 of clubs, hold the Ace.

Remember that in the introduction to the section on Super Aces, we mentioned that the game plays more like 8-5-4 Double Bonus than like the 10-7 version. Among the prime examples of this fact are double-inside straight flushes such as Jack-10-7 of spades. We love 'em with the 7-for-1 flush payback in full-pay Double Bonus, and don't like 'em quite as much with the drop to 5-for-1 in 8-5-4 Double Bonus and Super Aces. In Super Aces, the Ace comes in at an EV of 2.52 compared to 2.30 on Jack-10-7. In 10-7 Double Bonus, we'd keep Jack-10-7.

20. B. Dealt 9 of hearts, 5 of hearts, 3 of hearts, 10 of spades, 8 of clubs, discard all five cards.

When flushes pay only 5-for-1, forget about three-card flushes with no high cards and no straight-flush opportunities. A complete redraw gives us an expected value of 1.63, bettering the 1.40 on the three-card flush.

NEVADA BONUS POKER

21. B. Dealt 8 of clubs, 9 of hearts, 10 of hearts, Jack of hearts, Queen of hearts, hold 9-10-Jack-Queen.

In most video poker games, this is a no-brainer—we hold the pat straight. We'll break up a pat straight for a four-card royal, but not for lesser four-card straight flushes.

But in Nevada Bonus Poker, a four-card straight flush plays right to the strengths of the game. The flush return is enhanced to 8-for-1, and the straight flush to 100-for-1. We can't afford to pass up the opportunity here. Our EV is 30.53 on the four-card open-ended straight flush, much stronger than the flat 25-coin payoff per five wagered on the straight.

22. A. Dealt Ace of spades, Ace of diamonds, Jack of spades, Jack of diamonds, 10 of hearts, hold the pair of Aces.

In Double Bonus Poker, we found that when full houses paid 10-for-1, we held two pair instead of just a pair of Aces. Here, full houses pay 10-for-1, but we break up two pair to hold just the Aces. Why? We're eyeing that 6-for-1 payoff on three Aces. This is not a close call, with the EV on the Aces checking in at 11.11, compared to 8.83 on the two pair.

23. B. Dealt Ace of hearts, Ace of clubs, 2 of clubs, 3 of clubs, 4 of clubs, hold Ace-2-3-4 of clubs.

This is a similar problem to No. 11, in which we had to decide between a pair of Aces and a four-card inside straight flush in Super Aces. There, the Aces were the better play. In Nevada Bonus Poker, despite the enhanced return on three Aces, we go for the straight flush instead. We have more chances at a flush, worth 8-for-1, than at a third Ace, worth 6-for-1. We'll also hit the straight flush, worth 500 coins with five wagered, an average of once per 47 chances, while if we hold only the Aces we'll draw the other pair for a 2,000-coin jackpot only once per 360.

The EV of 18.94 on the four-card straight flush is nearly double the 11.08 on the pair of Aces.

24. B. Dealt Ace of hearts, 7 of hearts, 5 of hearts, 9 of diamonds, 2 of spades, hold Ace-5-7.

There aren't many closer calls than this one. With the 8-for-1 payoff on flushes, we like three-card flushes in Nevada Bonus Poker. We like them even more than we do in 10-7 Double Bonus. But we also like single Aces, because of the potential for a 6-for-1 payoff on three Aces and, rarely, bigger hands. The bottom line: the bigger flush payback carries the day with an EV of 2.56 compared to 2.54 on the single Ace.

If you find yourself on the 10-7 version of this game, the play reverses itself. The lower flush payback makes holding the single Ace the better play.

25. C. Dealt Jack of hearts, 10 of hearts, 2 of spades, 5 of spades, 6 of spades, hold 2-5-6.

The first time I showed this problem to an e-mail friend, he thought it was a joke. When the game is Jacks or Better, Bonus Poker or Double Bonus Poker, we hold the two-card royal. That includes 10-7 Double Bonus, with a 7-for-1 flush return. But in Nevada Bonus Poker, where that flush kicks up another notch to 8-for-1 and we also have a 100-for-1 payoff on straight flushes, we have to go for the three-card double-inside straight flush, even with no high cards. Our EV is 2.71 on 2-5-6, and only 2.51 on Jack-10.

Shuffle No. 11: Double Double Bonus Poker

If doubling the four-of-a-kind bonuses is good, why not kick them up another notch?

Double Double Bonus Poker does just that, and so it's been extremely popular with players. The biggest payoff remains 4,000 coins on a royal flush provided five are wagered. But now the secondary jackpot leaps to 2,000 coins for four Aces accompanied by a 2, 3 or 4. If the fifth card in the hand is a 5 through King, then four Aces pay the same 160-for-1—800 coins for five wagered—as in Double Bonus Poker.

There's also a 160-for-1 bonanza on four 2s, 3s or 4s, if the fifth card is an Ace, 2, 3 or 4. Other quads pay 50-for-1, as in Double Bonus Poker.

To make up for the extra bonuses, the straight payoff drops back to 4-for-1, instead of the 5-for-1 in Double Bonus. Full house and flush paybacks also drop slightly, so that the full-pay version is a 9-6 game that returns 98.9 percent with expert play. Some casinos take the pay table down to 9-5, 8-5 and 7-5 versions. Even on 9-6 Double Double Bonus, the return is a little lower than on most full-pay games, and dropping the pay table to 8-5 reduces the payback percentage to 96.8 percent. That makes it difficult to recommend Double Double Bonus in anything but its full-pay format.

The pay table for full-pay Double Double Bonus Poker is as follows: Royal flush 250-for-1 (jumps to 4,000 with five coins wagered); straight flush 50-for-1; four Aces with 2, 3 or 4 as kicker

400-for-1; four Aces 160-for-1; four 2s, 3s or 4s with Ace, 2, 3 or 4 kicker 160-for-1; four 2s, 3s or 4s 80-for-1; four 5s through Kings 50-for-1; full house 9-for-1; flush 6-for-1; straight 4-for-1; three of a kind 3-for-1; two pair 1-for-1; pair of Jacks or better 1-for-1.

That leaves a game that plays very much like 9-6 Double Bonus Poker, except for a reduced emphasis on straights and a slightly increased emphasis on Aces. Let's check it out with the following problems:

9-6 DOUBLE DOUBLE BONUS POKER STRATEGY

1. **Ace of hearts, Ace of diamonds, Ace of clubs, King of spades, King of clubs.**

    A. Hold the full house.
    B. Hold the three Aces.

2. **Ace of hearts, Ace of diamonds, Ace of clubs, 5 of spades, 2 of clubs.**

    A. Hold the three Aces.
    B. Hold the three Aces with the 2 as a kicker.

3. **Ace of clubs, Ace of spades, 5 of hearts, 2 of clubs, 2 of spades.**

    A. Hold the pair of Aces.
    B. Hold both pairs.
    C. Hold the Aces and one of the 2s.

4. **Ace of spades, 7 of clubs, 5 of hearts, 3 of diamonds, 2 of diamonds.**

    A. Hold the Ace.
    B. Hold Ace-2-3-5.

5. **Ace of spades, 7 of clubs, 5 of spades, 3 of spades, 2 of spades.**

    A. Hold the Ace.

    B. Hold Ace-2-3-5.

6. 2 of hearts, 2 of spades, 2 of diamonds, King of clubs, King of hearts.

    A. Hold the 2s.

    B. Hold the full house

7. 2 of clubs, 2 of diamonds, 5 of hearts, 5 of spades, Jack of diamonds.

    A. Hold both pairs.

    B. Hold the 2s.

    C. Hold the Jack.

8. 2 of spades, 2 of diamonds, 7 of hearts, 5 of clubs, Ace of clubs.

    A. Hold the 2s.

    B. Hold the 2s and the Ace kicker.

9. Queen of hearts, Jack of diamonds, 9 of clubs, 8 of spades, 4 of hearts.

    A. Hold Queen-Jack.

    B. Hold Queen-Jack-9-8.

10. Queen of hearts, Jack of diamonds, 9 of clubs, 8 of spades, 8 of hearts.

    A. Hold Queen-Jack.

    B. Hold Queen-Jack-9-8.

    C. Hold the pair of 8s.

11. Jack of clubs, 9 of hearts, 8 of hearts, 7 of spades, 4 of diamonds.

    A. Hold the Jack.

    B. Hold Jack-9-8-7.

12. Queen of spades, Jack of spades, 10 of spades, Jack of hearts, 2 of diamonds.

A. Hold the pair of Jacks.

B. Hold Queen-Jack-10 of spades.

13. **Ace of hearts, King of hearts, Queen of hearts, 8 of diamonds, 9 of spades.**

A. Hold the Ace.

B. Hold Ace-King-Queen.

14. **10 of hearts, 10 of spades, Jack of diamonds, Queen of clubs, King of spades:**

A. Hold the pair of 10s.

B. Hold 10-Jack-Queen-King.

15. **10 of hearts, 10 of spades, 9 of diamonds, 8 of clubs, 7 of diamonds.**

A. Hold the pair of 10s.

B. Hold 10-9-8-7.

16. **Ace of spades, King of clubs, Queen of hearts, Jack of hearts, 9 of hearts.**

A. Hold the Ace.

B. Hold Ace-King-Queen-Jack.

C. Hold Queen-Jack.

D. Hold Queen-Jack-9.

17. **Ace of hearts, Jack of spades, 10 of spades, 7 of clubs, 3 of diamonds.**

A. Hold the Ace.

B. Hold Jack-10.

18. **Ace of clubs, King of hearts, Jack of spades, 8 of diamonds, 5 of diamonds.**

A. Hold Ace-King-Jack.

B. Hold King-Jack.

C. Hold the Ace.

8-5 DOUBLE DOUBLE BONUS POKER STRATEGY

This is not a game I recommend, but I see folks playing it every time I go to a casino that has it. As noted above, full house–flush paybacks are lowered to 8-5. That leaves a 96.8 percent game with a strategy that's not wildly different from 9-6 Double Double Bonus, but which needs a little fine tuning. It's similar to the fine-tuning we made when flush paybacks were lowered to 5-for-1 in Jacks or Better or Double Bonus Poker. With that in mind, see how you do with a few strategy problems for 8-5 Double Double Bonus:

19. **Ace of hearts, King of hearts, Queen of hearts, 7 of spades, 5 of hearts.**

    A. Hold Ace-King-Queen.
    B. Hold Ace-King-Queen-5.

20. **Ace of clubs, King of spades, Queen of hearts, Jack of spades, 9 of spades.**

    A. Hold the Ace.
    B. Hold Ace-King-Queen-Jack.
    C. Hold King-Jack.
    D. Hold King-Jack-9.

21. **King of spades, Queen of hearts, Jack of diamonds, 8 of diamonds, 7 of diamonds.**

    A. Hold King-Queen-Jack.
    B. Hold Jack-8-7.

22. **Queen of hearts, Jack of hearts, 10 of hearts, Jack of diamonds, 5 of diamonds.**

    A. Hold the pair of Jacks.
    B. Hold Queen-Jack-10 of hearts.

23. Queen of diamonds, Jack of spades, 7 of clubs, 5 of clubs, 3 of clubs.

    A. Hold Queen-Jack.

    B. Hold 7-5-3.

DOUBLE DOUBLE JACKPOT POKER STRATEGY

Double Double Bonus Poker, like most of the most popular video poker games, is manufactured by IGT. Sigma Games has challenged with Double Double Jackpot Poker. It's similar to Double Double Bonus except that we need a King, Queen or Jack instead of a 2, 3 or 4 to go with four aces in order to receive the secondary jackpot. This jackpot is also slightly smaller— 1,600 coins for five played. We also get 800 coins for four played on four Kings, Queens and Jacks with an Ace, King, Queen or Jack as a kicker.

As in the Bonus Poker game Aces and Faces, that kicks up the frequency of bonus fours of a kind because we often hold a single face card, but we never hold an unpaired 2, 3 or 4 by itself.

Straight payoffs also are increased to the 5-for-1 you get on Double Bonus instead of the 4-for-1 on Double Double Bonus. That leaves a game with 100.3 percent payback, much better than the 98.9 on full-pay Double Double Bonus.

The pay table for full-pay Double Double Jackpot Poker is as follows: Royal flush 250-for-1 (jumps to 4,000 with five coins wagered); straight flush 50-for-1; four Aces with face card as kicker 320-for-1; four Aces 160-for-1; four Kings, Queens or Jacks with Ace or face kicker 160-for-1; four Kings, Queens or Jacks 80-for-1; four 2s through 10s 50-for-1; full house 9-for-1; flush 6-for-1; straight 5-for-1; three of a kind 3-for-1; two pair 1-for-1; pair of Jacks or better 1-for-1.

Of course, there are reduced pay tables available on Double Double Jackpot as in any other game. If straights are reduced to 4-for-1, you can ignore the adjustments called for in the questions that deal with straights. If full houses and flushes are reduced, you'll have to make the same kinds of adjustments you make when paybacks on those hands drop in Double Double Bonus or any other game.

In this section, let's try some strategy problems for full-pay Double Double Jackpot Poker:

24. **Queen of diamonds, Jack of diamonds, 10 of diamonds, Jack of clubs, 5 of spades.**

    A. Hold Queen-Jack-10.
    B. Hold the pair of Jacks.

25. **Ace of hearts, Jack of diamonds, 10 of diamonds, 7 of clubs, 5 of spades.**

    A. Hold the Ace.
    B. Hold Ace-Jack.
    C. Hold Jack-10.

26. **Ace of spades, King of clubs, 9 of hearts, 6 of spades, 4 of diamonds.**

    A. Hold the Ace.
    B. Hold Ace-King.

27. **Queen of diamonds, Jack of clubs, 10 of diamonds, 7 of spades, 6 of spades.**

    A. Hold Queen-10.
    B. Hold Queen-Jack.
    C. Hold Queen-Jack-10.

28. **Ace of hearts, King of diamonds, Queen of diamonds, Jack of spades, 9 of diamonds.**

    A. Hold Ace-King-Queen-Jack.
    B. Hold King-Queen.
    C. Hold King-Queen-9.

29. **Queen of clubs, 10 of spades, 9 of hearts, 8 of diamonds, 5 of spades.**

A. Hold the Queen.
B. Hold Queen-10-9-8.

30. **Queen of hearts, Jack of hearts, 9 of spades, 8 of diamonds, 5 of spades.**

A. Hold the Queen.
B. Hold the Jack.
C. Hold Queen-Jack.
D. Hold Queen-Jack-9-8.

Shuffle No. 11: Double Double Bonus Poker Answers

9-6 DOUBLE DOUBLE BONUS POKER STRATEGY

1. B. Dealt Ace of hearts, Ace of diamonds, Ace of clubs, King of spades, King of clubs, hold the three Aces.

We make the same play in Double Bonus Poker, but it's less of a close call here because of the bigger potential jackpot on four Aces. We can settle for a full house and collect 45 coins for a five-coin bet in the 9-6 version, or we can draw for the fourth Ace, in which our expected average return is 63.58 coins.

I did just that the first time I ever played this game. It was at the Fiesta in northwest Las Vegas. I'd had a good run on a full-pay Deuces Wild game, including hitting the four 2s for 1,000 coins, and was taking a walk to stretch out a bit. Eventually I sat down at a five-game Multi-Poker machine, and one of the options was 9-6 Double Double Bonus. After about 15 minutes, I was dealt a full house with three Aces and two 9s.

I'd never run an analysis on this game, but reasoned that if breaking up the full house was the correct play on Double Bonus, it was here, too. The lady next to me had looked over and was about to congratulate me on the full house, when I reached for the draw button. "Oh, no!" she wailed. "Look what you're doing!"

What I did was to draw the fourth Ace and a 3 for 2,000 coins. That, of course, set off a chorus of "Better lucky than good."

I don't deny the lucky part. I'd just hit an 89-1 long shot. But I'd also made the best play available.

2. A. Dealt Ace of hearts, Ace of diamonds, Ace of clubs, 5 of spades, 2 of clubs, hold the three Aces.

Despite the bigger jackpot for having a 2, 3 or 4 kicker to go with four Aces, we don't hold a kicker along with three Aces. Why? Because holding the kicker diminishes our chances of drawing the fourth Ace. If we hold just the three Aces, there are 1,081 possible draws, and 46 of them will give us the fourth Ace. That means we draw the fourth Ace once out of every 23.5 hands. If we hold a kicker with our three Aces, there are 47 possible draws, and only one of them is the fourth Ace. Better we should double the frequency of four Aces than make sure that when we do get them, they'll pay the big jackpot.

The expected values per five coins bet are 62.45 on the three Aces, 59.15 on the three Aces plus kicker.

3. A. Dealt Ace of clubs, Ace of spades, 5 of hearts, 2 of clubs, 2 of spades, hold the pair of Aces.

In Double Bonus Poker, we hold both pairs in the 10-7 version, but keep just the Aces instead when the full house payoff drops below 10-for-1. Top-of-the-line Double Double Bonus pays just 9-for-1 on full houses, so the Aces are worth more in this game, too. It's not a close call, with EVs of 9.50 on the Aces, 8.40 on both pairs and 7.83 on the Aces plus a deuce kicker.

4. A. Dealt Ace of spades, 7 of clubs, 5 of hearts, 3 of diamonds, 2 of diamonds, hold the Ace.

The payoff on straights isn't high enough for us to worry about inside straights with one high card. We do keep inside straights with two or three high cards unless two of the high cards are of the same suit. Then we'd just keep the suited high cards. With just one high card, we're better off with the high card than the inside straight. In this hand, the EV is 2.37 on the Ace, and 2.02 on the inside straight.

5. B. Dealt Ace of spades, 7 of clubs, 5 of spades, 3 of spades, 2 of spades, hold Ace-2-3-5.

Inside straight flushes, such as Ace-2-3-5 of spades, are a different matter from mere inside straights. We'd even break up a pair of Aces for an inside straight flush. Here, with a single Ace, it's no contest. In the long run, the inside straight flush will bring us back an average return of 12.02 coins per five wagered, while the Ace alone will bring us 2.30.

6. B. Dealt 2 of hearts, 2 of spades, 2 of diamonds, King of clubs, King of hearts, hold the full house.

Here's the problem: In Double Bonus Poker, four Aces pay 800 coins for five bet, and we break up full houses to draw for a fourth Ace. In Double Double Bonus Poker, four 2s, 3s or 4s pay 800 coins for five bet if they come with an Ace, 2, 3 or 4 as a fifth-card kicker. So do we now break up a full house for four 2s, 3s or 4s?

No, we don't. If we draw to three 2s, the necessary fifth card will turn up only 12 of every 46 times we hit the fourth 2. Nearly three-quarters of the time, the four 2s will pay only 400 coins with a five-coin bet. Our average return will be 37.68 coins per five wagered if we hold the 2s, and that doesn't measure up to the flat 45-coin payoff on the full house.

If four 2s always paid 160-for-1, meaning an 800-coin jackpot with a five-coin bet, then we would break up the full house to hold the 2s.

7. A. Dealt 2 of clubs, 2 of diamonds, 5 of hearts, 5 of spades, Jack of diamonds, hold both pairs.

The pair of 2s is more valuable here than in most games, and its EV of 4.40 is not a bad start. But the two pairs give you a sure winner, and once in every 11.75 hands it'll turn into a full house. That gives it an expected value of 8.40 coins per five wagered. The Jack is not really in the running here, with an EV of 2.24.

8. A. Dealt 2 of spades, 2 of diamonds, 7 of hearts, 5 of clubs, Ace of clubs, hold the 2s.

Holding the Ace kicker ensures that whenever we hit four 2s, they'll be worth 800 coins. But that's about the only benefit, and it does a great deal of harm. Instead of hitting the four 2s once per 360 trials if we keep the 2s alone, we'll hit them only once per 1,081 trials if we add the kicker. It also reduces three of a kind to once per 12.93 trials instead of once per 8.75.

The bottom line is an EV of 4.35 on the 2s, and 3.14 on the 2s plus kicker.

9. B. Dealt Queen of hearts, Jack of diamonds, 9 of clubs, 8 of spades, 4 of hearts, hold Queen-Jack-9-8.

In Double Double Bonus, we hold inside straights with two or three high cards of different suits. In Jacks or Better or Bonus Poker, with a 2-for-1 payoff on two pairs, the value of holding Queen-Jack would be elevated. In those games, we need at least three high cards before we hold an inside straight. In Double Double Bonus, our EVs are 2.34 on the inside straight, 2.29 on Queen-Jack.

10. C. Dealt Queen of hearts, Jack of diamonds, 9 of clubs, 8 of spades, 8 of hearts, hold the pair of 8s.

Inside straights with two high cards have some value in this game, but not as much as a low pair that has the potential to become two pairs, three of a kind or even more. The EV of 3.67 on the low pair is far better than the 2.34 on the inside straight or 2.28 on the Queen and Jack.

11. A. Dealt Jack of clubs, 9 of hearts, 8 of hearts, 7 of spades, 4 of diamonds, hold the Jack.

This really isn't much different from the Ace-2-3-5 of mixed suits we explored in No. 4. Given an inside straight with just one high card, we're better off with just the high card. It's a little closer call here than in No. 4 because a Jack isn't as valuable a card as an Ace in Double Double Bonus. Still, with an EV of 2.21, it beats the 2.02 on the inside straight.

12. B. Dealt Queen of spades, Jack of spades, 10 of spades, Jack of hearts, 2 of diamonds, hold Queen-Jack-10 of spades.

This is a special case. Queen-Jack-10 is our most valuable three-card royal, because it leaves open the most possible straights and straight flushes. The EV of 7.31 isn't far above the

7.23 on the pair of Jacks, but it's enough to single out this particular three-card royal. If our three-card royal consisted of, say, Ace-King-Jack instead, we'd hold the pair of Jacks.

13. B. Dealt Ace of hearts, King of hearts, Queen of hearts, 8 of diamonds, 9 of spades, hold Ace-King-Queen.

An Ace is a valuable card in Double Double Bonus Poker but it's no match for a three-card royal. Even just comparing the big jackpot potential is an interesting experiment. Keep Ace-King-Queen of the same suit, and you have 1,081 possible draws, of which one will give you a royal flush and the 4,000-coin jackpot. Hold just the Ace, and there are 178,365 possible draws. Forty-four of those—one in 4,054—will give you four Aces. And of those 44, only 12 will include a 2, 3 or 4 kicker, meaning you hit that 2,000-coin jackpot only once per 14,864 trials.

You have a better chance at hitting the bigger jackpot. Keep all three high hearts, and you have an EV of 7.06 that is more than triple the 2.20 on the single Ace.

14. B. Dealt 10 of hearts, 10 of spades, Jack of diamonds, Queen of clubs, King of spades, hold 10-Jack-Queen-King.

We'd hold a four-card straight with three unsuited high cards even if the draw was on the inside. Here, the straight is open-ended, and has an EV of 4.36 that's much stronger than the 3.67 on the low pair.

15. A. Dealt 10 of hearts, 10 of spades, 9 of diamonds, 8 of clubs, 7 of diamonds, hold the pair of 10s.

Four-card straights are not as strong a play if they include no high cards that can be paired up to give us another potential pay. We keep four-card open-ended straights instead of low pairs only if the straights include at least one high card. The EVs here are 3.67 on the pair of 10s, 3.40 on the four-card straight.

16. D. Dealt Ace of spades, King of clubs, Queen of hearts, Jack of hearts, 9 of hearts, hold Queen-Jack-9.

Don't ignore the opportunity presented by three-card inside straight flushes with high cards. They can become flushes, straights, low pairs, even three of a kind. With an EV of 3.47,

Queen-Jack-9 is much stronger than the next best play, the four-card inside straight Ace-King-Queen-Jack at 2.98.

17. A. Dealt Ace of hearts, Jack of spades, 10 of spades, 7 of clubs, 3 of diamonds, hold the Ace.

Rare as it is with a four-card draw, the potential 2,000-coin jackpot on four Aces with a 2, 3 or 4 kicker makes a difference in this hand. In Double Bonus Poker, and most Jacks or Better–based games, we'd hold Jack-10. Here, we hold the Ace with an EV of 2.31 that barely beats the 2.30 on Jack-10.

At that level of difference, those who play other games most of the time and just dabble a bit in Double Double Bonus might do better to be consistent and keep suited Jack-10 over an Ace of a different suit at any time. Those who want to milk every last drop out of Double Double Bonus will make the adjustment.

18. C. Dealt Ace of clubs, King of hearts, Jack of spades, 8 of diamonds, 5 of diamonds, hold the Ace.

In most games, dealt Ace, King and Jack of mixed suits, we'll hold the King and the Jack and dump the Ace. Not here. Here, Aces are the most valuable cards in the deck. The EV of 2.27 on the Ace is better than the 2.21 on King-Jack or 2.16 on Ace-King-Jack.

8-5 DOUBLE DOUBLE BONUS POKER STRATEGY

19. A. Dealt Ace of hearts, King of hearts, Queen of hearts, 7 of spades, 5 of hearts, hold Ace-King-Queen.

Whether we hold three parts of a royal or four parts of a flush is dependent on the payback on the flush. In 10-7 Double Bonus Poker, we hold four parts of a flush. In any available version of Double Double Bonus, we hold three parts of a royal. It's a close call in 9-6 Double Double Bonus, but not in the 8-5 version. EVs are 6.65 on the three-card royal, and 5.74 on the four-card flush.

20. B. Dealt Ace of clubs, King of spades, Queen of hearts, Jack of spades, 9 of spades hold Ace-King-Queen-Jack.

This is the same problem as in No. 16, only at a lower pay table. With flush paybacks reduced to 5-for-1, the value of inside straight flushes also fall. The expected value of Ace-King-Queen-Jack is the same 2.98 coins per five wagered as in No. 16, but the EV of the inside straight flush drops to 2.78 from the 3.47 above.

It does take all four high cards for the inside straight to be more valuable than the three-card inside straight flush. If instead we had King and 3 of hearts and Queen, Jack and 9 of spades, we would hold Queen-Jack-9.

21. A. Dealt King of spades, Queen of hearts, Jack of diamonds, 8 of diamonds, 7 of diamonds, hold King-Queen-Jack.

The three-card straight flush, Jack-8-7, has only one high card and two gaps on the inside. In 9-6 Double Double Bonus, that wouldn't matter so much to us, and we'd hold Jack-8-7. But here the flush payback is reduced to 5-for-1, limiting the value of Jack-8-7. The EVs in the 8-5 game are 2.45 on King-Queen-Jack, and 2.36 on Jack-8-7.

22. A. Dealt Queen of hearts, Jack of hearts, 10 of hearts, Jack of diamonds, 5 of diamonds, hold the pair of Jacks.

In 9-6 Double Double Bonus, we saw that the only three-card royal we hold at the expense of breaking up a high pair is Queen-Jack-10. In the 8-5 version, the lower flush payback diminishes the value of the three-card royal enough that the pair of Jacks is better even than Queen-Jack-10. Our EVs are 7.18 on the Jacks, 7.12 on Queen-Jack-10.

23. A. Dealt Queen of diamonds, Jack of spades, 7 of clubs, 5 of clubs, 3 of clubs, hold Queen-Jack.

Two unsuited high cards aren't a great start to any hand. It takes a five-coin bet to get an average 2.34 back, so we're not making any money. But it beats the EV of 1.86 on the three-card double-inside straight flush with no high cards. That combination is the second weakest start we'd accept rather than tossing the entire hand. The weakest is a four-card inside straight with no high cards.

DOUBLE DOUBLE JACKPOT POKER STRATEGY

24. B. Dealt Queen of diamonds, Jack of diamonds, 10 of diamonds, Jack of clubs, 5 of spades, hold the pair of Jacks.

Here's a key difference between Double Double Bonus Poker and Double Double Jackpot. We get increased payoffs on four Kings, Queens or Jacks in Double Double Jackpot, and that increases the value of high pairs. In 9-6 Double Double Bonus, we hold the suited Queen-Jack-10, but in Double Double Jackpot the EV of 7.92 on the high pair beats the 7.51 on the three-card royal.

25. C. Dealt Ace of hearts, Jack of diamonds, 10 of diamonds, 7 of clubs, 5 of spades, hold Jack-10.

In 9-6 Double Double Bonus, we hold just the Ace. But this is 9-6 Double Double Jackpot, where we have enhanced payoffs on four faces, and that enhances the value of the two-card royal, Jack-10. EVs are 2.38 on Jack-10 and 2.3003 on the lone Ace and 2.2997 on Ace-Jack.

26. B. Dealt Ace of spades, King of clubs, 9 of hearts, 6 of spades, 4 of diamonds, hold Ace-King.

This is a similar situation to No. 25, only without the two-card royal muddying things. With enhanced jackpots on both Aces and faces, we keep both the Ace and a face card in preference to a lone Ace. The EVs are close, 2.32 on Ace-King and 2.28 on just the Ace.

27. C. Dealt Queen of diamonds, Jack of clubs, 10 of diamonds, 7 of spades, 6 of spades, hold Queen-Jack-10.

Double Double Jackpot pays 5-for-1 on straights, so we leave open a few more possibilities. In Double Double Bonus, we'd just hold Queen-Jack, but here the EV of 2.47 on Queen-Jack-10 beats the 2.40 on Queen-Jack and the 2.21 on Queen-10.

28. A. Dealt Ace of hearts, King of diamonds, Queen of diamonds, Jack of spades, 9 of diamonds, hold Ace-King-Queen-Jack.

The straight payoff makes a difference in this hand, just as in No. 27. We'll get back 3.40 coins for every five we bet on Ace-King-Queen-Jack; 3.04 on King-Queen-9; and 2.69 on King-Queen. In Double Double Bonus, we hold the three-card inside straight flush, King-Queen-9, on the 9-6 game, but switch to the four-card inside straight when the flush payoff is reduced.

29. B. Dealt Queen of clubs, 10 of spades, 9 of hearts, 8 of diamonds, 5 of spades, hold Queen-10-9-8.

Chalk up another difference from Double Double Bonus. With a 5-for-1 payoff on straights, four-card straights with one high card are worth our effort. We get back 2.45 for every five coins we wager on Queen-10-9-8, and only 2.28 on the lone Queen. In Double Double Bonus, we hold only the Queen on any pay table.

30. C. Dealt Queen of hearts, Jack of hearts, 9 of spades, 8 of diamonds, 5 of spades, hold Queen-Jack.

Higher straight paybacks can make up a lot of difference, but not the difference between a two-card royal and an inside straight. The EVs are 2.98 on Queen-Jack, 2.77 on Queen-Jack-9-8. Both expected values are higher than you'd find on Double Double Bonus, which yields 2.86 on the two-card royal and 2.34 on the inside straight. On Double Double Jackpot, the two-card royal is more valuable because of the potential four-face jackpot and the inside straight is more valuable because of the 5-for-1 straight payback.

Shuffle No. 12: Triple Bonus Poker

In Triple Bonus Poker, the four-of-a-kind bonuses get so big that the game can no longer support a Jacks or better pay table. Instead, the pay table starts at a pair of Kings. That dramatically changes the game. We have many fewer winning hands, and much of our return is concentrated in a few big hits.

There are no kickers involved in the bonus hands. All four-Ace hands pay 240-for-1, leaving a 1,200-coin jackpot for five coins wagered. Bet five coins and pull four 2s, 3s or 4s, and you'll get 600 coins, and it's 375 on any other four of a kind.

It's a long way from the 25-for-1, 125-for-5 jackpot on Jacks or Better, but the long-term return is about the same. Full-pay Triple Bonus Poker returns 99.6 percent in the long run, while 9-6 Jacks or Better pays 99.5 percent.

The full-pay table for Triple Bonus Poker is as follows: Royal flush 250-for-1 (jumps to 4,000 with five coins wagered); straight flush 50-for-1; four Aces 240-for-1; four 2s, 3s or 4s 120-for-1; four 5s through Kings 75-for-1; full house 11-for-1; flush 7-for-1; straight 4-for-1; three of a kind 3-for-1; two pair 1-for-1; pair of Jacks or better 1-for-1.

Triple Bonus strategy is not difficult despite the major pay table changes. Check out these questions:

TRIPLE BONUS POKER BASICS

1. **Winning hands make up about:**

A. 45 percent of the total.
B. 40 percent of the total.
C. 35 percent of the total.
D. 30 percent of the total.

2. **Royal flushes occur:**

A. More frequently than in Double Bonus Poker.
B. Less frequently than in Double Bonus Poker.
C. About as frequently as in Double Bonus Poker.

3. **The most frequently occurring winning hands are:**

A. Fours of a kind.
B. Threes of a kind.
C. Two pairs.
D. High pairs.

4. **Flushes occur:**

A. More often than straights or full houses.
B. Less often than straights or full houses.
C. About as often as straights or full houses.

5. **The biggest share of our payoff in Triple Bonus Poker comes from:**

A. Fours of a kind.
B. Threes of a kind.
C. Two pairs.
D. High pairs.

TRIPLE BONUS POKER STRATEGY

6. **Ace of hearts, Ace of spades, Ace of diamonds, 9 of hearts, 9 of clubs.**

A. Hold the full house.
B. Hold the three Aces.

7. **4 of diamonds, 4 of clubs, 4 of spades, 9 of hearts, 9 of clubs.**

    A. Hold the full house.

    B. Hold the three 4s.

8. **Ace of clubs, Ace of diamonds, 9 of spades, 9 of hearts, 5 of spades.**

    A. Hold both pairs.

    B. Hold the pair of Aces.

9. **King of spades, King of clubs, 9 of diamonds, 9 of clubs, 5 of hearts.**

    A. Hold both pairs.

    B. Hold the pair of Kings.

10. **King of hearts, Queen of spades, Jack of diamonds, 8 of clubs, 7 of diamonds.**

    A. Hold King-Queen-Jack.

    B. Hold King-Jack.

    C. Hold the Queen-Jack.

    D. Hold the King.

11. **King of hearts, Queen of hearts, Jack of hearts, 8 of clubs, 7 of hearts.**

    A. Hold King-Queen-Jack.

    B. Hold King-Queen-Jack-7.

    C. Hold the King.

12. **9 of hearts, 9 of spades, Queen of hearts, 7 of hearts, 5 of hearts.**

    A. Hold the pair of 9s.

    B. Hold the Queen.

    C. Hold the four hearts.

13. **9 of hearts, 9 of spades, 8 of clubs, 7 of diamonds, 6 of hearts.**

    A. Hold the pair of 9s.

    B. Hold 9-8-7-6.

14. King of clubs, Queen of clubs, 6 of diamonds, 5 of hearts, 2 of spades.

   A. Hold King-Queen.
   B. Hold the King.

15. Ace of diamonds, King of diamonds, 8 of diamonds, 10 of hearts, 5 of clubs.

   A. Hold the Ace.
   B. Hold Ace-King.
   C. Hold Ace-King-8.

16. Ace of diamonds, King of diamonds, Queen of hearts, Queen of spades, 7 of diamonds.

   A. Hold the Ace.
   B. Hold Ace-King.
   C. Hold Ace-King-7.
   D. Hold the pair of Queens.

17. 7 of hearts, 8 of hearts, 10 of clubs, Jack of spades, King of diamonds.

   A. Hold the King.
   B. Hold King-Jack
   C. Hold 7-8-10-Jack.

18. Ace of hearts, King of spades, 9 of diamonds, 8 of clubs, 5 of clubs.

   A. Hold the Ace.
   B. Hold Ace-King.

19. Ace of hearts, King of hearts, 9 of diamonds, 8 of clubs, 5 of clubs.

   A. Hold the Ace.
   B. Hold Ace-King.

20. Jack of clubs, 9 of spades, 6 of diamonds, 5 of clubs, 2 of diamonds.

    A. Hold the Jack.

    B. Discard all five.

Shuffle No. 12:
Triple Bonus Poker
Answers

TRIPLE BONUS POKER BASICS

1. C. Winning hands make up about 35 percent of the total.

We've looked at this question in several other games, and with small variation the answer has been that we win on about 45 percent of our hands. In Triple Bonus Poker, that changes dramatically. Pairs of Queens and Jacks now are just losing hands, and our share of losing hands climbs to 65.3 percent.

2. B. Royal flushes occur less frequently than in Double Bonus Poker.

In Triple Bonus, we get a royal flush an average of once per 49,817 hands, a little less often than the once in 48,048 we get them in Double Bonus Poker, and considerably less often than the once per 40,400 in 9-6 Jacks or Better.

One big difference is that since we get no payoff on pairs of Queens and Jacks, we don't save single Queens or Jacks. Even suited Queens and Jacks are low on our list of viable plays.

3. C. The most frequently occurring winning hands are two pairs.

In every game we've explored up till now, high pairs were our most frequent winning hands. Not in Triple Bonus Poker. The difference, of course, is that pairs of Queens and Jacks don't pay, so we have only half as many potential high pairs. We wind up with two pair an average of once per 8.3 hands, and a high pair once per 9 hands.

4. A. Flushes occur more often than straights or full houses.

With flushes paying 7-for-1, our drawing strategy often favors holding partial flushes and straight flushes. We'll hold four parts of a flush instead of paring down to three parts of a royal. At the same time, we get only 4-for-1 on straights instead of the 5-for-1 on Double Bonus Poker, so we don't do anything special to force an increase in the frequency of straights.

The bottom line is that we get flushes about once per 60.7 hands, while we get straights once per 80.8 and full houses once per 93.6.

We already explored the frequency of high pairs and two pairs in No. 3, and royal flushes in No. 2. As for other hands, we get three of a kind once per 13.6 hands, four of a kind once per 422.8 and straight flushes once per 8,619.9.

5. A. The biggest share of our payoff in Triple Bonus Poker comes from fours of a kind.

With the big payoffs on every type of four of a kind, a whopping 23.9 percent of our return comes from quads. The only other hand accounting for more than 20 percent is three of a kind, at 22.1, followed by two pairs at 12.0, full houses at 11.8, flushes at 11.5, high pairs at 11.1, straights at 5.0, royal flushes at 1.6 and straight flushes at 0.6.

TRIPLE BONUS POKER STRATEGY

6. B. Dealt Ace of hearts, Ace of spades, Ace of diamonds, 9 of hearts, 9 of clubs, hold the three Aces.

This is just a warmup. Just as in Double Bonus and Double Double Bonus, we break up full houses to hold three Aces and go for the jackpot. With all Ace quads paying 240-for-1, it's not a close call here, even though full houses pay 11-for-1. With five coins bet, we'll get a flat 55-coin return on the full house, but have an expected value of 67.9 on the Aces.

7. A. Dealt 4 of diamonds, 4 of clubs, 4 of spades, 9 of hearts, 9 of clubs, hold the full house.

The 600-coin jackpot on four 4s for five coins wagered can make our night, but it's not as strong as a pat full house. As in No. 6, the pat full house brings a 55-coin payoff, but here that outweighs the expected return of 42.37 coins per five bet when we keep just the 4s.

8. B. Dealt Ace of clubs, Ace of diamonds, 9 of spades, 9 of hearts, 5 of spades, hold the pair of Aces.

You may remember that in Double Bonus Poker, this is a play that reverses itself when the pay table drops. When full houses pay 10-for-1, we keep both pairs; when they pay 9-for-1 or less, we keep just the Aces.

Triple Bonus Poker is different. Yes, full houses pay 11-for-1, even more than the 10-for-1 in full-pay Double Bonus. But even that's not enough to overcome the influence of the big jackpot on four Aces. Our EVs are 9.98 on the Aces, 9.26 on the two pairs.

9. A. Dealt King of spades, King of clubs, 9 of diamonds, 9 of clubs, 5 of hearts, hold both pairs.

We break up two pairs only for Aces. With other high pairs, we're better off taking the 1 in 11.75 shot at a full house. Our EVs are 9.26 on the two pairs, 7.69 on the pair of Kings.

What if one of the pairs consisted of 2s, 3s or 4s, giving us a shot at 600 coins for five wagered on four of a kind instead of the 375 we'd get on the Kings here? We'd still keep both pairs. In fact, breaking up two pairs to keep 2s, 3s or 4s would be an even bigger mistake than keeping just the Kings, because we get no payoff on a low pair.

10. D. Dealt King of hearts, Queen of spades, Jack of diamonds, 8 of clubs, 7 of diamonds, hold the King.

The lone King is really the only viable play here, with an EV of 1.98 that beats the 1.48 on either King-Jack or King-Queen, or the 1.40 on King-Queen-Jack. Queens and Jacks are just low cards in this game; a pair gives no payoff. Keeping them along with our King increases the frequency of straights, but does nothing else positive. At the same time, holding them drastically decreases our number of potential high pairs, and they get in the way of other winning hands.

11. B. Dealt King of hearts, Queen of hearts, Jack of hearts, 8 of clubs, 7 of hearts, hold King-Queen-Jack-7.

The 7-for-1 payoff on flushes dictates that we hold a fourth card of the same suit with a three-card royal. The expected value of King-Queen-Jack-7 is 7.02, better than the 6.39 on King-Queen-Jack. None of the other options are even close—the next best are the three-card flushes, King-Jack-7 and Queen-Jack-7, both with EVs of 1.97.

12. C. Dealt 9 of hearts, 9 of spades, Queen of hearts, 7 of hearts, 5 of hearts, hold the four hearts.

If a four-card flush is better than a three-card royal, as in No. 11, it's certainly going to be better than a low pair. There's no contest, with the four-card flush checking in at 6.70, compared to the 4.11 EV on the 9s.

13. A. Dealt 9 of hearts, 9 of spades, 8 of clubs, 7 of diamonds, 6 of hearts, hold the pair of 9s.

With straights paying only 4-for-1 in this game, four-card open-ended straights aren't as strong as low pairs. Low pairs also have higher expected values here than in other games with 1-for-1 payoffs on two pairs because of the bigger returns on four of a kind. The EVs are 4.11 on the 9s, 3.40 on the inside straight.

14. A. Dealt King of clubs, Queen of clubs, 6 of diamonds, 5 of hearts, 2 of spades, hold King-Queen.

If the King and Queen were of different suits, we'd just hold the Queen, but here we still have to keep one eye on the possible royal flush. Along with the enhanced flush payoff, our slim shot at a royal gives us an EV of 2.13 on King-Queen, much better than 1.94 on the lone King.

15. C. Dealt Ace of diamonds, King of diamonds, 8 of diamonds, 10 of hearts, 5 of clubs, hold Ace-King-8.

Once again, the enhanced flush payoff makes a difference. Three-card flushes that include Ace-King are stronger than the Ace-King alone, by an EV margin of 2.82 to 2.75. However, if the hand included a suited Ace-King plus a three-card flush in a different suit—such as Ace-King of diamonds and 10-8-5 of clubs—the Ace-King would be the better play.

16. D. Dealt Ace of diamonds, King of diamonds, Queen of hearts, Queen of spades, 7 of diamonds, hold the pair of Queens.

Even though the pair of Queens is not a paying hand by itself, a low pair is a more powerful hand than most players think. It can become two pair, three of a kind, a full house, even four of a kind. With full houses paying 11-for-1 and four of a kind payments in the stratosphere, a low pair is a pretty good start. The EV of 4.11 on the low pair outweighs the 2.59 on Ace-King or 2.07 on the lone Ace.

17. A. Dealt 7 of hearts, 8 of hearts, 10 of clubs, Jack of spades, King of diamonds, hold the King.

That Jack is just a low card in this game, so 7-8-10-Jack is just a four-card inside straight with no high cards. We do play that hand if we have nothing better—but a high card is better. EVs are 1.98 on the King, 1.70 on the inside straight.

18. A. Dealt Ace of hearts, King of spades, 9 of diamonds, 8 of clubs, 5 of clubs, hold the Ace.

It's a close call, but the chance at that 240-for-1 jackpot on four Aces leads us to drop the King. On the average, with five coins wagered, we'll get 2.135 back when we hold just the Ace, and 2.128 when we hold Ace-King.

19. B. Dealt Ace of hearts, King of hearts, 9 of diamonds, 8 of clubs, 5 of clubs, hold Ace-King.

This is the same hand as No. 18, with one important difference. The Ace-King are of the same suit, leaving open flush and, yes, royal flush possibilities. EVs are 2.73 on Ace-King, 2.08 on the Ace.

20. B. Dealt Jack of clubs, 9 of spades, 6 of diamonds, 5 of clubs, 2 of diamonds, discard all five.

Except when they appear in combinations that take us a little closer to a royal flush, we treat Jacks and Queens just like any other low card. The EV of a complete redraw is only 1.28, but it's better than the 1.23 on the lone Jack.

If you were going to keep a single card out of this mess, which one would it be? The highest EV is on the 9, at 1.25. Why the 9? It has the full range of straight possibilities, from King high to 5 low. The Jack, on the other hand, is limited by the deck ending at the Ace at the top, and the 2 is limited even further by having only one step to the Ace at the bottom. The 5 and 6 have the full range of straight possibilities like the 9, but are lower in value because to keep either card would mean tossing away one of the same suit, limiting possible flushes.

That's all academic, of course. The best play on the hand is to start over.

Shuffle No. 13: Deuces Wild

Someday, maybe this series will include *The Deuces Wild Answer Book*. To explore every variation on Deuces Wild certainly would require an entire volume.

Deuces are wild—that is, a 2 can be substituted for any card to make a winning combination. If your hand is Jack-Jack-Jack-2-2, you don't have a full house, you have five Jacks. The big jackpot is on a royal flush with no wild cards. Bet five coins and get Ace-King-Queen-Jack-10 and you have a 4,000-coin jackpot. Get Ace-King-Queen-Jack-2, and you have a wild royal worth 125 coins for five wagered instead.

There's a nice secondary jackpot on four deuces. It pays 200-for-1, or 1,000 coins on a five-coin wager, on most versions of Deuces Wild. There are also games called Double Pay Deuces in which those 2s will bring you 2,000 coins instead, Loose Deuces in which you'll get 2,500 coins and Triple Pay Deuces in which the 2s pay 3,000 coins for five wagered.

The original Deuces Wild game is one of the best things going for video poker players. It's so good, in fact, that it's never spread outside Nevada. Full-pay Deuces Wild, which returns 100.8 percent with expert play, remains available in Las Vegas in places as diverse as the Tropicana on the booming south end of the Strip and locals hangouts such as the Fiesta and Reserve.

Most players don't play well enough to get better than 100 percent return on the machines, so the game survives because of its popularity among non-expert players.

The full-pay table is as follows: Natural royal flush 250-for-1 (jumps to 4,000 with five coins wagered); four 2s 200-for-1; royal flush with wild cards 25-for-1; five of a kind 15-for-1; straight flush 9-for-1; four of a kind 5-for-1; full house 3-for-1; flush 2-for-1; straight 2-for-1; three of a kind 1-for-1.

Unlike Jacks or Better, in which most of the pay table variation focuses on flushes and full houses, casinos and manufacturers have changed Deuces Wild all over the pay table in an effort to attract us to lower-paying machines. The most common change is lowering the four-of-a-kind payback to 4-for-1, then making up some of the difference by increasing other payoffs.

Let's focus on full-pay Deuces Wild and two particularly widespread variations: games known to aficionados as Illinois Deuces and Colorado Deuces. They don't have those names on the machine glass. It just says Deuces Wild, so it's up to us to know the difference by looking at the pay tables.

Illinois Deuces got its name because it rose to popularity at the Par-A-Dice Casino in East Peoria, Illinois. (It had actually been introduced in Nevada.) Colorado Deuces made its first impact in the low-limit casinos in Colorado. Both are widely available across the United States, including Nevada casinos.

Both games reduce the four-of-a-kind payback to 4-for-1. Illinois Deuces raises full houses to 4-for-1 and flushes to 3-for-1. Colorado Deuces raises five of a kind to 16-for-1 and straight flushes to 13-for-1.

That leaves the following pay tables:

ILLINOIS DEUCES: Natural royal flush 250-for-1 (jumps to 4,000 with five coins wagered); four 2s 200-for-1; royal flush with wild cards 25-for-1; five of a kind 15-for-1; straight flush 9-for-1; four of a kind 4-for-1; full house 4-for-1; flush 3-for-1; straight 2-for-1; three of a kind 1-for-1.

COLORADO DEUCES: Natural royal flush 250-for-1 (jumps to 4,000 with five coins wagered); four 2s 200-for-1; royal flush with wild cards 25-for-1; five of a kind 16-for-1; straight flush 13-for-1; four of a kind 4-for-1; full house 3-for-1; flush 2-for-1; straight 2-for-1; three of a kind 1-for-1.

See if you can figure out which is the better version. The answer will be in this chapter.

Following are several general questions about full-pay
Deuces Wild video poker. Then we're going to do something a
little different. Because changes between pay tables are so dra-
matic in this game, answers to strategy questions will list *three*
answers: one for full-pay Deuces, one for Illinois Deuces and one
for Colorado Deuces. Sometimes we'll play the hand the same
way in all three games; sometimes there will be three different
answers. See if you know when and why.

Afterward, we'll look at Loose Deuces to explore what happens when the secondary jackpot on four 2s is increased.

We'll not be able to get to every variation of Deuces Wild,
but let's try to make a dent.

DEUCES WILD BASICS

FULL-PAY DEUCES

1. Winning hands make up about:

    A. 45 percent of the total.
    B. 40 percent of the total.
    C. 35 percent of the total.
    D. 30 percent of the total.

2. Royal flushes occur:

    A. More frequently than in Jacks or Better.
    B. Less frequently than in Jacks Better.
    C. About as frequently as in Jacks or Better.

3. The most frequently occurring winning hands are:

    A. Fours of a kind.
    B. Full houses.
    C. Flushes.
    D. Straights.
    E. Threes of a kind

4. **Straights occur:**

    A. More than three times as often as flushes.
    B. About as often as flushes.
    C. Less than one-third as often as flushes.

5. **The biggest share of our payoff in full-pay Deuces Wild comes from:**

    A. Fours of a kind.
    B. Full houses.
    C. Flushes.
    D. Straights.
    E. Threes of a kind.

FULL-PAY, ILLINOIS AND COLORADO DEUCES

6. **The pay table change that affects our return the most is:**

    A. The reduction of fours of a kind in Illinois and Colorado Deuces.
    B. The increase of full houses and flushes on Illinois Deuces.
    C. The increase of fives of a kind and straight flushes on Colorado Deuces.

7. **From highest payback percentage to lowest, the ranking of these three games is:**

    A. Full-pay, Colorado, Illinois.
    B. Full-pay, Illinois, Colorado.
    C. Illinois, Full-pay, Colorado.
    D. Colorado, Full-pay, Illinois.

DEUCES WILD STRATEGY

NO-DEUCE HANDS

8. **8 of hearts, 8 of spades, 5 of hearts, Jack of hearts, Ace of hearts.**

    A. Hold the 8s.

B. Hold Ace-Jack.

C. Hold all four hearts.

9. **9 of clubs, 10 of clubs, Jack of clubs, Queen of clubs, King of clubs.**

A. Hold the straight flush.

B. Hold 10-Jack-Queen-King.

10. **King of diamonds, Jack of diamonds, 10 of diamonds, 9 of diamonds, 5 of diamonds.**

A. Hold the flush.

B. Hold King-Jack-10.

C. Hold King-Jack-10-9.

11. **9 of clubs, 9 of spades, Jack of hearts, Jack of diamonds, Queen of clubs.**

A. Hold the Jacks.

B. Hold the 9s.

C. Hold the Jacks and 9s.

12. **5 of spades, 6 of spades, 7 of spades, 8 of spades, 10 of spades.**

A. Hold the flush.

B. Hold 5-6-7-8.

13. **5 of spades, 6 of spades, 7 of spades, 8 of spades, 9 of clubs.**

A. Hold the straight.

B. Hold 5-6-7-8.

14. **9 of clubs, Jack of clubs, Queen of clubs, King of clubs, 6 of spades.**

A. Hold 9-Jack-Queen-King.

B. Hold Jack-Queen-King.

15. **7 of diamonds, 8 of clubs, 9 of diamonds, 10 of diamonds, King of diamonds.**

A. Hold 7-8-9-10.

    B. Hold 7-9-10-King.

    C. Hold 10-King.

16. Ace of hearts, 3 of hearts, 4 of hearts, 7 of clubs, 9 of spades.

    A. Hold Ace-3-4.

    B. Discard all five.

17. King of spades, 10 of spades, 9 of diamonds, 5 of hearts, 3 of spades.

    A. Hold King-10.

    B. Discard all five.

18. 8 of hearts, 9 of hearts, 10 of hearts, Jack of clubs, 5 of spades.

    A. Hold 8-9-10.

    B. Hold 8-9-10-Jack.

19. Jack of diamonds, 10 of diamonds, 7 of diamonds, 4 of clubs, 3 of spades.

    A. Hold Jack-10.

    B. Hold Jack-10-7.

    C. Discard all five.

20. 5 of hearts, 6 of clubs, 7 of clubs, 8 of clubs, Queen of clubs.

    A. Hold 5-6-7-8.

    B. Hold 6-7-8.

    C. Hold 6-7-8-Queen.

ONE-DEUCE HANDS

21. 2 of hearts, Queen of spades, Jack of spades, 8 of spades, 6 of diamonds.

    A. Hold only the 2.

    B. Hold 2-Queen-Jack.

    C. Hold 2-Queen-Jack-8

22. 2 of hearts, King of hearts, 9 of hearts, 8 of hearts, 3 of diamonds.

    A. Hold only the 2.
    B. Hold the 2 plus the three hearts.
    C. Hold 2-8-9.

23. 4 of hearts, 7 of hearts, 8 of hearts, 9 of hearts, 2 of clubs.

    A. Hold 2-4-7-8-9.
    B. Hold 2-7-8-9.
    C. Hold the 2.

24. 2 of spades, 5 of clubs, 6 of clubs, 9 of hearts, Jack of spades.

    A. Hold the 2.
    B. Hold 2-5-6.

25. 2 of diamonds, King of clubs, 10 of clubs, 6 of diamonds, 7 of diamonds.

    A. Hold the 2.
    B. Hold 2-King-10.
    C. Hold 2-6-7.

TWO-DEUCE HANDS

26. 2 of hearts, 2 of spades, Queen of hearts, 9 of clubs, 4 of spades.

    A. Hold 2-2.
    B. Hold 2-2-Queen.

27. 2 of hearts, 2 of spades, Jack of hearts, 10 of hearts, 5 of hearts.

    A. Hold 2-2.
    B. Hold 2-2-Jack-10.
    C. Hold the flush.

28. 2 of hearts, 2 of spades, 8 of clubs, 7 of clubs, 4 of hearts.

    A. Hold 2-2.

   B. Hold 2-2-7-8.
   C. Hold the straight

29. 2 of hearts, 2 of clubs, 4 of spades, 5 of spades, 9 of clubs.

   A. Hold the 2s.
   B. Hold 2-2-4-5.

30. 2 of spades, 2 of diamonds, 6 of clubs, 8 of clubs, Jack of diamonds.

   A. Hold the 2s.
   B. Hold 2-2-Jack.
   C. Hold 2-2-6-8.

31. 2 of clubs, 2 of diamonds, 3 of hearts, 4 of hearts, 8 of spades.

   A. Hold the 2s.
   B. Hold 2-2-3-4.

32. 2 of hearts, 2 of spades, 7 of diamonds, 10 of diamonds, Queen of clubs.

   A. Hold the 2s.
   B. Hold 2-2-7-10

Three-Deuce Hands

33. 2 of hearts, 2 of spades, 2 of diamonds, 5 of spades, 4 of spades.

   A. Hold 2-2-2.
   B. Hold the straight flush.

34. 2 of hearts, 2 of spades, 2 of diamonds, Queen of diamonds, 10 of clubs.

   A. Hold 2-2-2.
   B. Hold 2-2-2-Queen.
   C. Hold 2-2-2-10.

FOUR-DEUCE HANDS

35. 2 of hearts, 2 of spades, 2 of diamonds, 2 of clubs, 4 of clubs.

    A. Hold 2-2-2-2.

    B. Hold 2-2-2-2-4.

LOOSE DEUCES STRATEGY

A 2,500-coin jackpot on four 2s with five coins bet is the eye-catcher on this game, and there are some very attractive pay tables. The full-pay version, which pays 17-for-1 on five of a kind and 10-for-1 on straight flushes, returns 101.6 percent with expert play. It is rare. A little more often, you'll find a 15-10 version that returns 101 percent. Some Las Vegas locals casinos and the Las Vegas Hilton sports book area have had this version in recent years. Even a 15-8 version is a better-than-100-percent game, at 100.1 percent. More often, you'll see 12-8, at 99.2 percent, or 10-8, which checks in at 98.6 percent.

The full-pay table is as follows: Natural royal flush 250-for-1 (jumps to 4,000 with five coins wagered); four 2s 500-for-1; royal flush with wild cards 25-for-1; five of a kind 17-for-1; straight flush 10-for-1; four of a kind 4-for-1; full house 3-for-1; flush 2-for-1; straight 2-for-1; three of a kind 1-for-1.

Strategy is very similar to Deuces Wild versions that pay the usual 200-for-1 on four 2s. We can do very little to expand the frequency of four 2s that we aren't already doing in regular Deuces strategy. Our strategy differences are to account for the other pay table variations, mostly on the straight flush payoff.

Let's try some sample hands, concentrating on both the 15-10 version—the best version you'll probably really be able to play—and the more common 12-8 version. Strategy is the same on two-deuce and three-deuce hands: In Loose Deuces, starting with two 2s, we keep pat royal flushes, five of a kind and straight flushes, draw one card to four of a kind or a four-card wild royal, and otherwise just keep the 2s. Starting with three 2s, we just keep the deuces, breaking up even a wild royal.

No-Deuce Hands

36. King of spades, Queen of spades, Jack of spades, 9 of spades, 6 of hearts.

    A. Hold King-Queen-Jack.

    B. Hold King-Queen-Jack-9.

37. 3 of hearts, 7 of hearts, 8 of hearts, 9 of hearts, Ace of spades.

    A. Hold 3-7-8-9.

    B. Hold 7-8-9.

38. 6 of clubs, 7 of hearts, 8 of hearts, 9 of hearts, Jack of spades.

    A. Hold 6-7-8-9.

    B. Hold 7-8-9.

39. Jack of clubs, 10 of clubs, 7 of clubs, King of hearts, 5 of spades.

    A. Hold Jack-10.

    B. Hold Jack-10-7.

    C. Discard all five.

One-Deuce Hands

40. 2 of hearts, 5 of spades, 7 of spades, 8 of spades, King of spades.

    A. Hold the 2.

    B. Hold 2-5-7-8.

    C. Hold all five.

41. 2 of clubs, 5 of diamonds, 6 of diamonds, 7 of diamonds, 10 of diamonds.

    A. Hold the 2.

    B. Hold 2-5-6-7.

    C. Hold all five.

42. 2 of clubs, 5 of diamonds, 6 of diamonds, 9 of diamonds, Jack of diamonds.

    A. Hold the 2.

    B. Hold 2-5-6-9.

    C. Hold all five.

43. 2 of clubs, 7 of hearts, 8 of hearts, 4 of clubs, King of spades.

    A. Hold the 2.

    B. Hold 2-7-8.

44. 2 of hearts, King of hearts, 10 of hearts, 7 of hearts, 5 of hearts.

    A. Hold 2-King-10.

    B. Hold all five hearts.

45. Ace of diamonds, King of diamonds, Queen of diamonds, Jack of diamonds, 2 of hearts.

    A. Hold the wild royal.

    B. Hold the four parts of a natural royal and discard the 2.

Shuffle No. 13: Deuces Wild Answers

DEUCES WILD BASICS

FULL-PAY DEUCES

1. A. Winning hands make up about 45 percent of the total.

This is a very different game from Jacks or Better, with four wild cards and a pay table that starts at three of a kind. But the hit frequency is about the same. With expert play, we'll get some return on 45.32 percent of our hands.

2. B. Royal flushes occur less frequently than in Jacks or Better.

We don't keep single high cards in Deuces Wild, and even with multiple high cards of the same suit, we'll keep 2s that we'd discard in Jacks or Better. The result is a royal flush once every 45,282 hands, instead of the one every 40,400 in Jacks or Better.

3. E. The most frequently occurring winning hands are threes of a kind. We'll hit three of a kind on 28.5 percent of our hands. The next most frequently occurring winning hand is four of a kind, which makes up 6.5 percent of our hands.

4. A. Straights occur more than three times as often as flushes. Wild deuces turn a lot of junk hands into straights. The result is that we hit straights about once per 17.7 hands, and flushes once per 60.3.

Full houses, which occur with about equal frequency as straights and flushes in Jacks or Better, hit only once per 47.1 hands in full-pay Deuces.

5. A. The biggest share of our payoff in full-pay Deuces Wild comes from fours of a kind.

A whopping 32.5 percent of our returns come from fours of a kind, followed by 28.4 percent for threes of a kind, 11.3 percent for straights, 6.4 percent for full houses, 4.8 percent for five of a kind, 4.5 percent for wild royals, 4.1 percent for four 2s, 3.3 percent for flushes, 3.7 percent for straight flushes and 1.8 percent for natural royals.

FULL-PAY, ILLINOIS AND COLORADO DEUCES

6. A. The pay table change that affects our return the most is the reduction of fours of a kind in Illinois and Colorado Deuces.

When casinos and manufacturers realized how narrow their margin was on full-pay Deuces—the edge actually goes to the players with expert play—the first thing they changed was the payoff on fours of a kind. Nearly every version of Deuces Wild you'll come across pays only 4-for-1 on four of a kind, instead of the 5-for-1 in the full-pay version.

We hit four of a kind *a lot* in this game. Those 2s do the trick. Hit three of a kind plus a 2, and you have quads. Hit two pair, with one pair consisting of deuces, and you have four of a kind. Three 2s in the hand, and you have at least four of a kind.

Four of a kind shows up once every 15.4 hands in full-pay Deuces. With that frequency and a 5-for-1 payoff, it's the hand that keeps us going between big wins.

Taking the payback down to 4-for-1 is a huge change. Enormous. Raising both full house and flush paybacks can't overcome that. Neither can raising five of a kind and straight flushes, as we'll see in the next answer.

7. B. From highest payback percentage to lowest, the ranking of these three games is Full-pay, Illinois, Colorado.

Full-pay Deuces Wild returns 100.8 percent in the long run with expert play.

At first glance, many players think Illinois Deuces looks better. We think of full houses and flushes as more frequently occurring hands than fours of a kind, and figure that gaining a unit payback on each of those hands will more than balance out losing a unit on the quads. But Deuces Wild is different. The quads occur more often than the full houses and flushes put together. Illinois Deuces may look better at a glance, but its payback of 98.9 percent can't match up to full-pay Deuces.

Still, that's better than Colorado Deuces. This version reduces payback on the fours of a kind, and increases it on two much less frequent hands, fives of a kind and straight flushes. That leaves a 96.8 percent game with expert play.

I'd like to tell players to stick to the full-pay game and leave the others alone, but I've been in many casinos in which Illinois Deuces was the best game on the floor. And I've been in others in which Colorado Deuces didn't look so bad in comparison to the games around it.

Let's check out the sample hands:

DEUCES WILD STRATEGY

No-Deuce Hands

8. Dealt 8 of hearts, 8 of spades, 5 of hearts, Jack of hearts, Ace of hearts:

FULL-PAY and COLORADO: A. Hold the 8s.
ILLINOIS: C. Hold all four hearts.

Low pairs are a pretty fair building block in Deuces Wild. With a pair of 8s to start, either of the remaining 8s or any of the 2s will give us three of a kind, which is not a far stretch to four of a kind. Occasionally lightning will strike and we'll even wind up with five of a kind. In full-pay and Colorado Deuces, all that outweighs a one-card draw to a flush, which pays only 2-for-1 in those games.

In Illinois Deuces, where we get 3-for-1 on flushes, we have to reverse our strategy. That higher payoff gives the four-card flush an EV of 3.83 in Illinois Deuces, much better than the 2.55 on the other two games. EVs on holding the 8s are 2.80 in full-pay, 2.73 in Illinois and 2.62 in Colorado Deuces.

9. Dealt 9 of clubs, 10 of clubs, Jack of clubs, Queen of clubs, King of clubs:

FULL-PAY, ILLINOIS and COLORADO: B. Hold 10-Jack-Queen-King.

In Jacks or Better, we break up high pairs, flushes or straights for a one-card shot at a royal. The one hand we don't break up is a pat straight flush.

Deuces Wild is different. For a five-coin bet, we're not getting 250 coins on a straight flush, as in Jacks or Better. We're getting only 45 coins in full-pay or Illinois Deuces, or 65 coins in Colorado Deuces. Not only that, the value of the four-card royal is heightened by the presence of the wild 2s. We could draw the Ace of clubs for the natural royal and a 4,000-coin bonanza, but we also could draw any of the four deuces and wind up with a wild royal worth 125 coins for a five-coin bet.

The bottom line is, expected values are in excess of 98 on all three Deuces versions, far better than the certain payoff on a straight flush.

10. Dealt King of diamonds, Jack of diamonds, 10 of diamonds, 9 of diamonds, 5 of diamonds:

FULL-PAY, ILLINOIS and COLORADO: A. Hold the flush.

Since we're only holding three cards to a royal, we're better off taking the sure payoff. We're best off in Illinois Deuces, of course, where our five-coin bet brings back 15 on the flush, but even the 10-coin payoffs on full-pay and Colorado Deuces beat the alternatives. The second-best play is the four-card inside straight flush, which climbs the ladder from an EV of 6.70 in full-pay to 7.34 in Illinois (because of the 3-for-1 flush payback) to 8.83 in Colorado (because of the 13-for-1 straight flush return).

11. Dealt 9 of clubs, 9 of spades, Jack of hearts, Jack of diamonds, Queen of clubs:

FULL-PAY and COLORADO: A or B. Hold either pair.
ILLINOIS: C. Hold the Jacks and 9s.

When full houses pay only 3-for-1, they're almost an after-thought. We don't draw for them; they happen by accident. We're better off holding one pair, giving us a good shot at three of a kind and some chance at four of a kind. In full-pay Deuces, where four of a kind pays 5-for-1, the EVs are 2.81 on holding one pair and 2.55 on holding both. In Colorado Deuces, with a 4-for-1 payback on four of a kind, the margin is narrower, but we get back 2.62 for every five coins bet on one pair, and that same 2.55 if we hold both.

In Illinois Deuces, the value of two-pair hands is heightened because full houses pay 4-for-1 just like fours of a kind. That's a pretty radical change. We have eight ways to complete a full house—any of the four 2s, either of the two remaining Jacks or either of the two remaining 9s. We'll wind up with a losing hand 39 of every 47 times we make this play, but the eight winners will pay 4-for-1. Our EV climbs to 3.40 when we hold two pair, and 2.74 if we hold just one pair.

12. Dealt 5 of spades, 6 of spades, 7 of spades, 8 of spades, 10 of spades:

FULL PAY AND ILLINOIS: A. Hold the flush.

COLORADO: B. Hold 5-6-7-8.

Just as No. 11 plays to the strength of Illinois Deuces, this hand plays to the strength of the Colorado game. Straight flushes pay 13-for-1 instead of the 9-for-1 of the other two games, so we draw for more straight flushes.

Betting five coins, we'll collect 10 on the pat flush in full-pay or Colorado, or 15 in Illinois. But if we hold four to the straight flush, the EV on the Colorado game rises to 10.64 from the 8.09 on full-pay or the 8.62 on Illinois Deuces.

13. Dealt 5 of spades, 6 of spades, 7 of spades, 8 of spades, 9 of clubs:

FULL-PAY and ILLINOIS: A. Hold the straight.

COLORADO: B. Hold 5-6-7-8.

This is a similar problem to No. 12, except that here we're dealing with a pat straight instead of a pat flush. Either way, the pay raise on straight flushes makes the difference in Colorado

Deuces. There, the EV of 10.64 again beats the 10-coin payoff for five wagered on a straight. In the other games, we settle for 10-coin payoffs instead of EVs of 8.72 in Illinois and 8.09 on full pay.

14. Dealt 9 of clubs, Jack of clubs, Queen of clubs, King of clubs, 6 of spades:

FULL-PAY, ILLINOIS and COLORADO: A. Hold 9-Jack-Queen-King.

Here, the three games converge. In all three, it's a lot easier to win with a one-card draw than a two-card draw. It's a fairly close call in full-pay Deuces, with an EV of 6.91 on the four-card inside straight flush compared to 6.58 on the three-card royal. The distance is wider in Illinois (7.56 to 6.82) because of the increased flush payoff, and wider still in Colorado (9.04 to 6.58) because of the 13-for-1 straight flush payback.

15. Dealt 7 of diamonds, 8 of clubs, 9 of diamonds, 10 of diamonds, King of diamonds:

FULL-PAY OR COLORADO: A or B. Hold either 7-8-9-10 or 7-9-10-King.

ILLINOIS: B. Hold 7-9-10-King.

In full-pay and Colorado Deuces, we don't discriminate between four-card flushes and straights. Completing either pays 2-for-1, and we have just as many ways to finish either one off. We complete a straight with any of the four 6s, four Jacks or four 2s—12 cards. We complete the flush with any of the 9 remaining diamonds, including the deuce, or any of the three other deuces—12 cards. In both full-pay and Colorado Deuces, our EVs are 2.55 on the four-card flush, 2.55 on the four-card straight.

Illinois Deuces also has a 2.55 EV on the four-card straight, but the EV on the four-card flush jumps to 3.83. Why? Because flushes pay 3-for-1, a unit more per coin bet than in the other two versions.

16. Dealt Ace of hearts, 3 of hearts, 4 of hearts, 7 of clubs, 9 of spades:

FULL-PAY and COLORADO: B. Discard all five.
ILLINOIS: A. Hold Ace-3-4.

As straight flush possibilities go, this one's pretty limited. We need to draw either two deuces, or a deuce and a 5. That's such a narrow chance that we don't even bother with it in Colorado Deuces, with its heightened straight flush payback. In Colorado, EVs are 1.58 on a full discard and 1.55 on Ace-3-4, while in full-pay, EVs are 1.63 on the discard and 1.44 on Ace-3-4.

However, with a three-card start, we hit a lot more flushes than we do straight flushes, so in Illinois Deuces with its 3-for-1 flush return, we look at Ace-3-4 as better than nothing. EVs are 1.73 on Ace-3-4, 1.62 on a full discard.

17. Dealt King of spades, 10 of spades, 9 of diamonds, 5 of hearts, 3 of spades:

FULL-PAY and COLORADO: B. Discard all five
ILLINOIS: A. Hold King-10.

We don't have high-pair payoffs as in Jacks or Better–based games, so that limits the value of two-card royals. That value is further limited here by the presence of a couple of penalty cards. Discarding the 9 limits our possible straights, and discarding the 3 limits our possible flushes. In both full-pay and Colorado, the EVs of King-10 are 1.56, marginally weaker than the 1.62 in full-pay and 1.57 in Colorado on a complete redraw.

In Illinois Deuces, the higher flush payback makes a difference. King-10 is still a weak start, but at an EV of 1.63 it beats the 1.60 of a redraw.

If there were no penalty cards in this hand—say, if we had an 8 of diamonds instead of a 9 and our 3 was in clubs instead of spades—we would hold King-10 in all three games.

18. Dealt 8 of hearts, 9 of hearts, 10 of hearts, Jack of clubs, 5 of spades:

FULL-PAY: B. Hold 8-9-10-Jack.
ILLINOIS and COLORADO: A. Hold 8-9-10.

The higher flush payback in Illinois Deuces and higher straight flush payback in Colorado Deuces change the way we play this hand. The EVs on the four-card straight are 2.55 in all three games, but the EV on the three-card straight flush rises from 2.49 in full-pay to 2.73 in Illinois and 2.95 in Colorado.

19. Dealt Jack of diamonds, 10 of diamonds, 7 of diamonds, 4 of clubs, 3 of spades:

FULL-PAY: A. Hold Jack-10.

ILLINOIS and COLORADO: B. Hold Jack-10-7.

Even with two gaps on the inside, we want a shot at the straight flush in Colorado Deuces. And in Illinois Deuces, that small straight flush possibility works together with the fact that we'll get that game's higher flush payback more often starting with three cards than with two. Without either of those pay table enhancements, we'll settle for the two-card royal in full-pay Deuces.

EVs on the two-card royal are 1.84 in full-pay, 1.90 in Illinois and 1.86 in Colorado. On Jack-10-7, it's 1.78 on full-pay, 2.07 in Illinois and 2.05 in Colorado.

20. Dealt 5 of hearts, 6 of clubs, 7 of clubs, 8 of clubs, Queen of clubs:

FULL-PAY: A or C. Hold either 5-6-7-8 or 6-7-8-Queen.

ILLINOIS: C. Hold 6-7-8-Queen.

COLORADO: B. Hold 6-7-8.

Isn't diversity interesting? You could walk into a casino and see three video poker machines, all labeled Deuces Wild. They could have three different pay tables, and you could play the same hand three different ways and be right each time.

Just as in No. 15, in full-pay Deuces, it makes no difference whether we go for the four-card straight or four-card flush. Either way, our EV is 2.55.

And just as in No. 15, we prefer the four-card flush in Illinois Deuces, with a higher flush payback that yields a 3.83 EV.

The difference between this one and No. 15 comes in the three-card straight flush, which here is an open-ended draw to 6-7-8 instead of an inside draw. That plays to the strength of the Colorado Deuces pay table, giving us an EV of 2.84 on the three-card straight flush compared to 2.55 on either the four-card flush or straight.

ONE-DEUCE HANDS

21. Dealt 2 of hearts, Queen of spades, Jack of spades, 8 of spades, 6 of diamonds:

FULL-PAY, ILLINOIS and COLORADO: C. Hold 2-Queen-Jack-8

On any pay table, we need to be on the lookout for four-card inside straight flushes. The margin by which it's better than a three-card wild royal increases as we raise the payoffs on flushes and straight flushes. In full-pay Deuces, the four-card straight flush wins by an EV margin of 8.51 to 5.88; in Illinois Deuces it's 9.26 to 6.02; and in Colorado Deuces it's 10.64 to 5.86.

22. Dealt 2 of hearts, King of hearts, 9 of hearts, 8 of hearts, 3 of diamonds:

FULL-PAY, ILLINOIS and COLORADO: C. Hold 2-8-9.

This is a basic play we'll encounter a lot. We're better off with three-card open-ended straight flushes that include a deuce, and we're better off with a deuce alone than with four-card flushes. We don't hold four-card flushes if there's a deuce in hand.

Straight flushes must be open-ended—we don't hold 3-4 or Ace-3 of the same suit along with a 2. To complete those straight flushes, we can build in only one direction—up. The 2 has to be used as a 2.

Here, we're fully open-ended, with EVs on 2-8-9 of 5.47 (full-pay), 5.56 (Illinois) and 5.91 (Colorado), compared with EVs on just the 2 of 5.20 (full-pay), 5.02 (Illinois) and 4.99 (Colorado).

23. Dealt 4 of hearts, 7 of hearts, 8 of hearts, 9 of hearts, 2 of clubs:

FULL-PAY and COLORADO: B. Hold 2-7-8-9.

ILLINOIS: A. Hold 2-4-7-8-9.

On the full-pay and Colorado versions, we'll get only 10 coins for holding the flush, so we're more than willing to go prospecting for a straight flush, with EVs of 11.06 in full-pay and 14.04 in Colorado. But in Illinois, we're already collecting 15 coins on the flush, so we skip the four-card straight flush with its EV of 11.49.

24. Dealt 2 of spades, 5 of clubs, 6 of clubs, 9 of hearts, Jack of spades:

FULL-PAY: A. Hold the 2.

ILLINOIS and COLORADO: B. Hold 2-5-6.

In No. 22, we saw that a three-card fully open-ended straight flush including one deuce is one of the basics of Deuces Wild. But here, the straight flush is not fully open-ended. The cards are low enough to butt up against the wild deuces.

The example in No. 22 used a deuce, plus 7 and 8 of the same suit. Look at all the cards that can be used to complete a straight flush there. Along with deuces, 4s, 5s, 6s, 9s, 10s and Jacks can be used as part of a straight flush. We could have a straight flush with 4, 5, deuce, 7, 8, and we could have one with 7, 8, deuce, 10, Jack. That's a huge range, giving us seven denominations of cards that could be used in addition to the 7 and 8.

With 5 and 6, we can go down only to 4 and 3 before we get to the deuces. We can go up to 7, 8 and 9. That's 2, 3, 4, 7, 8 and 9—six card denominations that can be used to complete the straight flush instead of the seven when the hand is fully open-ended.

In full-pay Deuces, that's enough to make the difference, with an EV of 5.15 on holding the lone 2 beating the 5.00 on 2-5-6. On Illinois Deuces, with the enhanced flush payback, we don't worry as much about the fewer straight flush possibilities. EVs are 5.17 on 2-5-6, and 4.97 on the 2. And in Colorado Deuces, with a pay table that puts an exclamation point on straight flush opportunities, the EVs are 5.35 on 2-5-6 and 4.94 on the 2.

25. Dealt 2 of diamonds, King of clubs, 10 of clubs, 6 of diamonds, 7 of diamonds:

FULL-PAY and ILLINOIS: B. Hold 2-King-10

COLORADO: C. Hold 2-6-7.

For those who have gotten used to lumping Illinois and Colorado Deuces together whenever there's a straight flush possibility, here's a hand with a difference. Remember, in Illinois Deuces it's the flush payback, not the straight flush payback, that is enhanced, and either 2-King-10 or 2-6-7 give us equal flush opportunities. We wouldn't hold an ordinary three-card flush anyway, but this one's a three-card wild royal, with EVs of 5.71 on full-pay and 5.91 on Illinois Deuces that beat the 5.48 in full-pay and 5.63 in Illinois on the straight flush.

In Colorado Deuces, we hold 2-6-7, with an EV of 6.01 that beats the 5.69 on 2-King-10. The edge goes to 2-6-7 even though it doesn't have wild royal possibilities because it is fully open-ended, as opposed to the double-inside draw to 2-King-10.

TWO-DEUCE HANDS

26. Dealt 2 of hearts, 2 of spades, Queen of hearts, 9 of clubs, 4 of spades.

FULL-PAY, ILLINOIS and COLORADO: A. Hold 2-2.

In any Deuces Wild game, we'll hold two deuces alone more often than not. We see big possibilities here—four of a kind, straight flushes, five of a kind, wild royals, even the four-deuce jackpot. With this start we'll wind up with four of a kind once in every 3.9 hands, and four of a kind or better once every 3.35 hands. Our EVs on the 2s are 16.28 (full-pay), 15.16 (Illinois) and 15.49 (Colorado). On 2-2-Queen, EVs are 14.11 (full-pay) 13.16 (Illinois) and 13.19 (Colorado).

No matter what we do, we'll wind up with no worse than three of a kind. I had fun explaining that to my wife Marcy once upon a time at the Rio. We'd had dinner with video poker guru Lenny Frome and his wife Rhoda at the All-American Grill. Afterward, Lenny wanted to take me on a tour of the casino floor. That was his modus operandi every time we got together. He'd take me around the floor to see what video poker games were available and to check out new table games he'd either helped devise or for which he'd done the math for presentation to the Gaming Control Board. While we looked, Marcy and Rhoda chatted and played video poker.

After the Fromes had gone, Marcy had extra rolls of coins in her purse, and we decided to play some Deuces Wild. She hadn't played Deuces much, so when I was dealt a hand with two 2s and nothing else worthwhile, I explained that the 2s by themselves were the play, that no matter what I drew they'd match up with something for three of a kind.

I pushed the draw button, and bam! Up popped the other two 2s, and 1,000 coins started clanging into my tray.

Timing is everything.

27. Dealt 2 of hearts, 2 of spades, Jack of hearts, 10 of hearts, 5 of hearts:

FULL-PAY, ILLINOIS and COLORADO: B. Hold 2-2-Jack-10.

We like the pair of 2s, but four cards to a wild royal is just too powerful to pass up. Either of the remaining 2s, or the Ace, King, Queen of hearts will give us a wild royal worth 125 coins for a five-coin bet. The EVs are 25.1 on full pay, 24.8 on Illinois and 25.7 on Colorado Deuces, which far outdistances the 2s alone, with 16.2 on full-pay, 15.1 on Illinois and 15.4 on Colorado Deuces.

28. Dealt 2 of hearts, 2 of spades, 8 of clubs, 7 of clubs, 4 of hearts:

FULL-PAY, ILLINOIS and COLORADO: B. Hold 2-2-7-8.

Four-card open-ended straight flushes are one of the few non-winning hands we'll keep instead of just holding the 2s. The margin is narrowest on full-pay Deuces, with EVs of 16.60 on 2-2-7-8 and 16.32 on the 2s. The difference is wider on the other games, at 16.38 to 15.21 on Illinois Deuces and 19.36 to 15.52 on Colorado Deuces.

29. Dealt 2 of hearts, 2 of clubs, 4 of spades, 5 of spades, 9 of clubs:

FULL-PAY: A. Hold the 2s.

ILLINOIS and COLORADO: B. Hold 2-2-4-5.

The difference between this hand and No. 28 is that the four-card straight flush is not fully open-ended. We have not much room to go below the 4, limiting the number of cards that will complete a straight flush. (For a more complete explanation, see the similar problem in No. 24.)

In full-pay Deuces, we don't hold four-card straight flushes unless they're fully open-ended, and here we have an EV of 16.35 on the 2s that beats the 15.64 on the flush. In Illinois

Deuces, with its enhanced flush payback, and Colorado Deuces, with its big straight flush return, we're less picky. The four-card straight flush has an EV of 15.53 on the Illinois game and 17.98 on the Colorado version. For the 2s alone, EVs are 15.23 in Illinois and 15.55 in Colorado.

30. Dealt 2 of spades, 2 of diamonds, 6 of clubs, 8 of clubs, Jack of diamonds:

FULL-PAY: A. Hold the 2s.

ILLINOIS and COLORADO: C. Hold 2-2-6-8.

This is a similar problem to No. 29, except with the straight flush draw on the inside instead of too close to the end of the deck. Strategies are the same. We don't draw to four-card inside straight flushes including two 2s in full-pay Deuces. We hold the 2s instead. We do draw to those hands in Illinois and Colorado Deuces, because of the pay table changes.

In full-pay, EVs are 16.24 on the 2s and 15.64 on the straight flush draw; in Illinois they're 15.53 on the straight flush draw and 15.13 on the 2s; and in Colorado we have 17.98 on the straight flush draw and 15.45 on the 2s.

31. Dealt 2 of clubs, 2 of diamonds, 3 of hearts, 4 of hearts, 8 of spades:

FULL-PAY and ILLINOIS: A. Hold the 2s.

COLORADO: B. Hold 2-2-3-4.

Here, we have nowhere to go but up. Only 2s, 5s, 6s or 7s will complete the straight flush, and two of the 2s are already being used. Even the higher flush payback in Illinois Deuces isn't enough to make us hold more than the 2s in that situation. In Colorado Deuces, the possible straight flush is still the better opportunity.

EVs on the 2s alone are 16.39 (full-pay); 15.28 (Illinois); and 15.60 (Colorado). On the straight flush, they're 14.57 (full-pay and Illinois) and 16.49 (Colorado).

32. Dealt 2 of hearts, 2 of spades, 7 of diamonds, 10 of diamonds, Queen of clubs:

FULL-PAY and ILLINOIS: A. Hold the 2s.

COLORADO: B. Hold 2-2-7-10

This is as limited as our straight-flush draws get. We need a 2, 8 or 9 to make the hand. That's enough of a chance for Colorado Deuces (EVs of 16.49 on the straight flush draw, 15.40 on the 2s), but not for the other games, where EVs on the 2s of 16.17 in full-pay and 15.06 in Illinois beat the 14.57 on the straight flush draw in both games.

THREE-DEUCE HANDS

33. Dealt 2 of hearts, 2 of spades, 2 of diamonds, 5 of spades, 4 of spades:

FULL-PAY, ILLINOIS and COLORADO: A. Hold 2-2-2.

Regardless of pay tables on flushes or straight flushes, a pat straight flush is no match for three deuces. In a hand like this, we can smell that fourth deuce, and failing that, we have wild royal and five of a kind possibilities. The least we can wind up with is four of a kind.

Hold the straight flush, and you'll get 45 coins for five wagered in full-pay or Illinois Deuces, or 65 on the Colorado version. Hold just the 2s instead, and you'll get at least 25 coins in full-pay Deuces or 20 in the other games, and have average returns of 74.69 coins in full-pay, 70.97 in Illinois and 73.38 in Colorado.

I make this play whenever I get the opportunity, and I have hit the fourth deuce. On a full-pay machine at the Fiesta in northwest Las Vegas, my 1,000 quarters were pouring out one day when a man stopped to look at my screen.

"Congratulations. You hit the deuces!" he said.

"Thanks. I broke up a straight flush to get it," I replied.

His brow furrowed, and he looked over the pay table. Then he smiled, nodded, and said, "Sure. Of course."

Ah, those Las Vegas locals. Right at home in a video poker environment.

34. Dealt 2 of hearts, 2 of spades, 2 of diamonds, Queen of diamonds, 10 of clubs:

FULL-PAY, ILLINOIS and COLORADO: A. Hold 2-2-2.

Even a four-card wild royal isn't enough to justify holding more than the 2s. EVs on the 2s are 74.67 (full-pay), 70.97 (Illinois) and 73.38 (Colorado). EVs on the wild royal draws are in the 50s.

Which wild royal draw do you think is better, 2-2-2-10 or 2-2-2-Queen? The hand with the 10 is slightly stronger, because it leaves more cards that would complete straights or straight flushes.

FOUR-DEUCE HANDS

35. Dealt 2 of hearts, 2 of spades, 2 of diamonds, 2 of clubs, 4 of clubs:

FULL-PAY, ILLINOIS and COLORADO: B. Hold 2-2-2-2-4.

OK, this really doesn't make much difference. Either way you're going to collect your big jackpot on the four 2s. Unless, of course, the Y2K bug has zapped your machine, and when you draw a fifth 2 shows up. That would be a malfunction, and in case of malfunction the casino can deny your jackpot.

Are we really likely to see this happen? No. Don't worry too much about holding the fifth card.

LOOSE DEUCES STRATEGY

NO-DEUCE HANDS

36. Dealt King of spades, Queen of spades, Jack of spades, 9 of spades, 6 of hearts:

15-10: B. Hold King-Queen-Jack-9.

12-8: A. Hold King-Queen-Jack.

Strategies in various versions of Loose Deuces aren't all that different, but pay table variations do change the odd play. Here's one. With a higher payback on straight flushes, the 15-10 game yields a 7.45 EV on the four-card inside straight flush that beats the 6.58 on the three-card royal. On the 12-8 game, we still have a 6.58 EV on the three-card royal, but the inside straight flush drops to 6.38.

37. Dealt 3 of hearts, 7 of hearts, 8 of hearts, 9 of hearts, Ace of spades:

15-10: B. Hold 7-8-9.

12-8: A. Hold 3-7-8-9.

Even with a three-card open-ended straight flush, we have to make accommodations on the 15-10 paytable. Our EV is 2.60, compared with 2.55 on the four-card flush. On the 12-8 pay table, the EV of the straight flush draw drops to 2.36, while the four-card flush remains at 2.55.

38. Dealt 6 of clubs, 7 of hearts, 8 of hearts, 9 of hearts, Jack of spades:

15-10 or 12-8: A. Hold 6-7-8-9.

In any version of Deuces Wild in which flushes pay the same as straights, percentages are just the same on four-card straight draws as on four-card flushes. This is essentially the same situation as No. 37. We have a four-card straight and and three-card open-ended straight flush. The reason the play is different, and we hold the four-card straight on both pay tables, is the presence of the Jack of spades. It is a penalty card, limiting our opportunities for straights. If it were an Ace, we'd hold 7-8-9 in the 15-10 version, and 6-7-8-9 in 12-8.

The EVs on this hand are 2.55 on the four-card straight on either pay table, 2.53 on 7-8-9 on the 15-10 game and 2.30 on 7-8-9 on the 12-8 game.

39. Dealt Jack of clubs, 10 of clubs, 7 of clubs, King of hearts, 5 of spades:

15-10: B. Hold Jack-10-7.

12-8: A. Hold Jack-10.

Either play is stronger than starting from scratch, but as you probably suspected by now, the three-card double-inside straight flush is a stronger play on the 15-10 pay table. There, we have an EV of 1.85 on Jack-10-7, beating the 1.78 on Jack-10. At 12-8, EVs are 1.76 on Jack-10 and 1.71 on Jack-10-7.

ONE-DEUCE HANDS

40. Dealt 2 of hearts, 5 of spades, 7 of spades, 8 of spades, King of spades:

   15-10: B. Hold 2-5-7-8.

   12-8: C. Hold all five.

There aren't many differences in one-deuce strategies between the 15-10 and 12-8 pay tables. Here's one. With a four-card inside straight flush on the 15-10 game, the EV of 10.32 beats the flat 10-coin payoff for a flush. On the 12-8 game, better to stick with the certain 10 on the flush than try for the average 9.04 on the straight flush draw.

41. Dealt 2 of clubs, 5 of diamonds, 6 of diamonds, 7 of diamonds, 10 of diamonds:

   15-10 or 12-8: B. Hold 2-5-6-7.

Instead of an inside draw as in No. 40, we have a straight flush draw that's open on both ends. That makes the difference so that the straight flush draw is better than settling for 10 coins on the flush on either pay table. EVs on the straight flush draw are 11.81 on the 15-10 game, 10.32 on 12-8.

42. Dealt 2 of clubs, 5 of diamonds, 6 of diamonds, 9 of diamonds, Jack of diamonds:

   15-10 and 12-8: C. Hold all five.

In 15-10 Loose Deuces, we'll make draws to four-card inside straights instead of holding flushes in hands that include a deuce, but we draw the line at double-inside draws. The 10-coin pay for five wagered on the flush is better than four-card straight flush EVs of 8.83 on the 15-10 game or 7.77 on the 12-8 game.

43. Dealt 2 of clubs, 7 of hearts, 8 of hearts, 4 of clubs, King of spades:

   15-10 and 12-8: B. Hold 2-7-8.

Whether in the 15-10 version or the 12-8, three-card open-ended straight flushes, including a deuce, are stronger starts than a lone deuce. The 2,500-coin jackpot on four deuces makes it fairly close. In 15-10 Loose Deuces, the EV on 2-7-8 of 5.50 beats the 5.26 on the lone 2. In the 12-8 version, the 5.23 on 2-7-8 barely beats out the 5.20 on the lone deuce.

44. Dealt 2 of hearts, King of hearts, 10 of hearts, 7 of hearts, 5 of hearts:

15-10 and 12-8: B. Hold all five hearts.

Three-card royals are tempting, especially in Deuces Wild where the wild cards give us so many possibilities. Just be sure you're not throwing out something that gives you more than that three-card royal is worth. The pat flush pays 10 for five-coins wagered in either game. EVs on the three-card wild royals are 5.44 on the 15-10 game, 5.34 at 12-8.

45. Dealt Ace of diamonds, King of diamonds, Queen of diamonds, Jack of diamonds, 2 of hearts:

15-10 and 12-8: A. Hold the wild royal.

Let's leave Deuces Wild on a bit of a cautionary note. I once got a letter from a reader who was having an argument with her husband. He insisted that the 4,000-coin jackpot on a natural royal made it worth breaking up the wild royal. She wanted the sure 125-coin payoff.

She was right. We want deuces in this game. We win when we get lots of deuces. Deuces are good. Period. There are no situations in Deuces Wild in which you want to throw away a wild card.

Toss a deuce away from this wild royal, and you'll get your natural royal once per 47 draws. On average, 47 draws also will include three straights, seven flushes and the other three deuces to take you back to a wild royal. That sounds pretty good, and your average return is 95.21 coins in either 15-10 or 12-8 Loose Deuces. (With King-Queen-Jack-10-2, you'd also have a chance to draw a 9 for a straight flush, and the EV would rise to 96.7 on the 15-10 game, and 96.49 on the 12-8 version.)

But that doesn't match the certain 125 coins for five wagered on a wild royal. Take the sure thing. And don't toss away any deuces.

Shuffle No. 14: Joker's Wild

Joker's Wild is one of the oldest video poker games around. In its full-pay, Kings or Better version, it stood right alongside 9-6 Jacks or Better in spurring the popularity of video poker. With a 200-for-1 payoff on five of a kind—a 1,000-coin jackpot for five coins bet—it gives players a nice potential payday even if they don't hit a royal flush. Even a royal flush with a Joker pays 100-for-1, by far the leading third-best payoff in the days before Double Double Bonus Poker.

Full-pay Joker's Wild, Kings or Better, is a high paying game, returning 100.6 percent with expert play. That payoff was a little too strong for most casinos. The game never spread out of Nevada, and even in Las Vegas all but faded from sight. It did make a little resurgence in the late 1990s.

Most Joker's Wild machines offer reduced pay tables. Maybe you'll find a game that reduces four-of-a-kind paybacks from the 20-for-1 on the full-pay game to 17-for-1, but leaves the rest of the pay table intact. With that change, the payback percentage drops to 98.5 percent, but strategy is not drastically changed. In many jurisdictions, I've encountered a far more radical change, with 5-for-1 paybacks on full houses and 4-for-1 on flushes instead of the 7-5 pay table on a full-pay machine. The drop in the full house payoff is the kind of change that forces some alteration in strategy, so the 20-5-4 game is the one we'll use as a counterpoint to full-pay Joker's Wild in our sample hands.

Even more than in Nevada, Joker's Wild enjoys a hallowed spot in the history of video poker's rise in Atlantic City. There, a version of the game that starts its pay table at two pair or better quickly became a customer favorite. At video poker's dawn, Atlantic City didn't have the 9-6 Jacks or Better that led the charge in Las Vegas. It had much lower pay tables on Jacks or Better, but had a pretty good version of Joker's Wild. Even though the frequency of winning hands was lower than in most games because there were no payoffs on high pairs, the top jackpot hit much more frequently than in other games. That's because the top jackpot wasn't paid on a natural royal flush; it was paid on five of a kind.

Joker's Wild, Two Pair or Better, with the top jackpot on five of a kind, survives in Atlantic City. Much of the rest of the country also has Joker's Wild, Two Pair or Better, but with the top jackpot on a natural royal.

In sample hands below, we'll be looking at four versions of Joker's Wild—two Kings or Better games and two Two Pair or Better games.

JOKER'S WILD, KINGS OR BETTER

Sample hands are based on the following pay tables:

FULL-PAY 20-7-5 KINGS OR BETTER: Natural royal flush 250-for-1 (jumps to 4,000 with five coins wagered); five of a kind 200-for-1; royal flush with Joker 100-for-1; straight flush 50-for-1; four of a kind 20-for-1; full house 7-for-1; flush 5-for-1; straight 3-for-1; three of a kind 2-for-1, two pair 1-for-1; pair of Kings or better 1-for-1.

SHORT-PAY 20-5-4 KINGS OR BETTER: Natural royal flush 250-for-1 (jumps to 4,000 with five coins wagered); five of a kind 200-for-1; royal flush with Joker 100-for-1; straight flush 50-for-1; four of a kind 20-for-1; full house 5-for-1; flush 4-for-1; straight 3-for-1; three of a kind 2-for-1; two pair 1-for-1; pair of Kings or better 1-for-1.

Expert play will bring 100.6 percent on the full-pay version, but only 96.0 on the 20-5-4 version.

KINGS OR BETTER BASICS

1. Winning hands make up about:

- A. 45 percent of the total.
- B. 40 percent of the total.
- C. 35 percent of the total.
- D. 30 percent of the total.

2. Straights occur:

- A. More than twice as often as flushes.
- B. About as often as flushes.
- C. Less than half as often as flushes.

3. The biggest share of our payoff in full-pay Kings or better Joker's Wild comes from:

- A. Fives of a kind.
- B. Fours of a kind.
- C. Threes of a kind.
- D. Two pairs.
- E. Pairs of Kings or better.

KINGS OR BETTER STRATEGY

No-Joker Hands

4. 7 of hearts, 8 of hearts, 9 of spades, 10 of hearts, Jack of hearts.

- A. Hold the straight.
- B. Hold 7-8-10-Jack.

5. Ace of clubs, Ace of diamonds, King of diamonds, Queen of diamonds, 7 of spades.

- A. Hold the Aces.
- B. Hold Ace-King-Queen of diamonds.

6. Ace of clubs, Ace of diamonds, Queen of diamonds, 10 of diamonds, 7 of spades.

    A. Hold the Aces.

    B. Hold Ace-Queen-10 of diamonds.

7. **2 of hearts, 5 of hearts, Queen of hearts, Queen of spades, 10 of hearts.**

    A. Hold the Queens.

    B. Hold the four hearts.

    C. Hold Queen-10 of hearts.

8. **Ace of diamonds, King of diamonds, 9 of clubs, 8 of clubs, 7 of clubs.**

    A. Hold Ace-King.

    B. Hold 9-8-7.

9. **King of spades, 10 of spades, 9 of spades, 8 of hearts, 7 of clubs.**

    A. Hold the King.

    B. Hold King-10-9.

    C. Hold King-10.

    D. Hold 10-9-8-7.

10. **Ace of hearts, King of diamonds, 10 of diamonds, 7 of clubs, 5 of hearts.**

    A. Hold Ace-King.

    B. Hold King-10.

    C. Hold the King.

    D. Hold the Ace.

11. **Ace of hearts, King of diamonds, 10 of hearts, 7 of clubs, 5 of spades.**

    A. Hold Ace-King.

    B. Hold Ace-10.

    C. Hold the King.

    D. Hold the Ace.

12. **Ace of clubs, Queen of spades, 10 of spades, 8 of diamonds, 4 of diamonds.**

A. Hold the Ace.

B. Hold Queen-10.

13. **Queen of diamonds, 7 of hearts, 6 of hearts, 5 of hearts, 6 of clubs.**

   A. Hold the Queen.

   B. Hold 7-6-5 of hearts.

   C. Hold the pair of 6s.

14. **Queen of spades, 10 of hearts, 8 of hearts, 6 of diamonds, 5 of clubs.**

   A. Hold the Queen.

   B. Hold 8-10.

   C. Hold 5-6-8.

   D. Discard all five.

HANDS WITH JOKER

15. **Joker, 6 of spades, 8 of spades, 9 of spades, Queen of diamonds.**

   A. Hold Joker-6-8-9.

   B. Hold Joker-Queen.

16. **Joker, 6 of spades, 9 of spades, 10 of spades, 10 of diamonds.**

   A. Hold Joker-6-9-10 of spades.

   B. Hold Joker-9-10 of spades.

   C. Hold Joker-10-10.

17. **Joker, 3 of hearts, 4 of diamonds, 5 of hearts, 6 of hearts.**

   A. Hold Joker-3-4-5-6.

   B. Hold Joker-3-5-6.

   C. Hold Joker-5-6.

18. **Joker, Ace of spades, Jack of spades, 8 of clubs, 5 of spades.**

   A. Hold Joker-Ace.

   B. Hold Joker-Ace-Jack.
   C. Hold Joker-Ace-Jack-5.

19. Joker, King of diamonds, 10 of hearts, Jack of clubs, 8 of clubs.

   A. Hold Joker-King.
   B. Hold Joker-King-Jack-10.
   C. Hold Joker-Jack-8.

20. Joker, Ace of clubs, 10 of hearts, 8 of hearts, 5 of hearts.

   A. Hold Joker-Ace.
   B. Hold Joker-10-8.
   C. Hold Joker-10-8-5.

21. Joker, 4 of spades, 7 of spades, 5 of clubs, 10 of hearts.

   A. Hold Joker.
   B. Hold Joker-4-7.
   C. Hold Joker-4-5-7.

22. Joker, 6 of hearts, 9 of diamonds, 2 of clubs, 10 of spades.

   A. Hold Joker.
   B. Hold Joker-9-10.
   C. Hold Joker-2-6.
   D. Hold Joker-6.
   E. Hold Joker-10.

JOKER'S WILD, TWO PAIR OR BETTER

Sample hands are based on the following pay tables:

JOKER'S WILD, TWO PAIR OR BETTER, LAS VEGAS: Natural royal flush 250-for-1 (jumps to 4,000 with five coins wagered); five of a kind 100-for-1; royal flush with Joker 50-for-1; straight flush 50-for-1; four of a kind 20-for-1; full house 8-for-1; flush 7-for-1; straight 5-for-1; three of a kind 2-for-1; two pair 1-for-1.

JOKER'S WILD, TWO PAIR OR BETTER, ATLANTIC CITY: Five of a kind 1,000-for-1; natural royal flush 100-for-1; royal flush with Joker 100-for-1; straight flush 100-for-1; four of a kind 16-for-1; full house 8-for-1; flush 5-for-1; straight 4-for-1; three of a kind 2-for-1; two pair 1-for-1.

With expert play, the Las Vegas game returns 98.7 percent, while the Atlantic City version returns 99.0 percent. Similar outcomes, but they get there in very different ways. Note some quirks in the pay tables. The big jackpot on the Atlantic City version is on five of a kind; in the Las Vegas version, it's a natural royal flush. In the Atlantic City game, natural royals, Joker royals and other straight flushes pay the same 100-for-1—a royal is just another straight flush. The Las Vegas version gives back more on flushes and straights.

Keep that in mind for the sample hands below.

TWO PAIR OR BETTER BASICS

23. Winning hands make up about:

    A. 45 percent of the total.
    B. 40 percent of the total.
    C. 35 percent of the total.
    D. 30 percent of the total.

24. The most frequently occurring type of winning hand is:

    A. Two pair.
    B. Three of a kind.
    C. Straight.

25. The biggest share of our payoff in Two Pair or Better Joker's Wild comes from:

    A. Fives of a kind.
    B. Fours of a kind.
    C. Threes of a kind.
    D. Two pairs.
    E. Pairs of Kings or better.

TWO PAIR OR BETTER STRATEGY

No-Joker Hands

26. King of diamonds, Queen of diamonds, Jack of diamonds, 8 of clubs, 5 of diamonds.

    A. Hold King-Queen-Jack.

    B. Hold King-Queen-Jack-5.

27. 8 of hearts, 8 of diamonds, 9 of clubs, 10 of spades, Jack of hearts.

    A. Hold the 8s.

    B. Hold 8-9-10-Jack.

28. 5 of clubs, 6 of clubs, 7 of clubs, 8 of hearts, King of spades.

    A. Hold 5-6-7-8.

    B. Hold 5-6-7.

    C. Hold the King.

29. 9 of spades, 5 of spades, 2 of spades, Ace of diamonds, 10 of clubs.

    A. Hold 2-5-9.

    B. Hold the Ace.

    C. Discard all five.

30. 7 of diamonds, 8 of diamonds, Queen of clubs, 5 of hearts, 2 of spades.

    A. Hold 7-8.

    B. Hold 5-7-8.

    C. Hold the 5.

    D. Discard all five.

31. 8 of spades, 10 of spades, Jack of spades, Queen of spades, Ace of spades.

    A. Hold the flush.

    B. Hold Ace-Queen-Jack-10.

    C. Hold Queen-Jack-10-8.

32. 6 of clubs, 7 of clubs, 8 of clubs, 9 of clubs, Ace of clubs.

    A. Hold the flush.

    B. Hold 6-7-8-9.

33. Ace of hearts, Jack of hearts, 10 of hearts, 9 of clubs, 8 of spades.

    A. Hold Ace-Jack-10.

    B. Hold Jack-10-9-8.

34. Jack of diamonds, 10 of diamonds, 7 of clubs, 5 of diamonds, 2 of hearts.

    A. Hold Jack-10.

    B. Hold Jack-10-5.

35. Ace of spades, King of spades, Queen of spades, Ace of hearts, 9 of diamonds.

    A. Hold the pair of Aces.

    B. Hold Ace-King-Queen of spades.

HANDS WITH JOKER

36. Joker, 8 of hearts, 9 of hearts, 10 of hearts, 2 of hearts.

    A. Hold the flush.

    B. Hold Joker-8-9-10.

37. Joker, 6 of diamonds, 9 of diamonds, 10 of diamonds, 3 of diamonds.

    A. Hold the flush.

    B. Hold Joker 6-9-10.

38. Joker, Ace of spades, Queen of diamonds, 2 of hearts, 3 of clubs.

    A. Hold the Joker.

    B. Hold Joker-Ace.

    C. Hold Joker-Queen.

    D. Hold Joker-Ace-2-3.

39. Joker, King of clubs, 3 of hearts, 4 of diamonds, 5 of spades.

    A. Hold Joker-3-4-5.

    B. Hold Joker-King.

    C. Hold Joker-5.

40. Joker, 6 of diamonds, 10 of diamonds, 7 of spades, 3 of hearts.

    A. Hold Joker.

    B. Hold Joker-6-10.

    C. Hold Joker-6-7.

Shuffle No. 14:
Joker's Wild
Answers

KINGS OR BETTER BASICS

1. A. Winning hands make up about 45 percent of the total.

When we last looked at a Kings or better game in Triple Bonus Poker, we saw that the percentage of hands that bring some money back to us fell to 35 percent. The difference here, of course, is the wild card—there's no Joker in Triple Bonus Poker. In the full-pay Kings or Better version of Joker's Wild, we're right back near the norm on other video poker games with winners on 44.4 percent of our hands.

2. B. Straights occur about as often as flushes.

Unlike Deuces Wild, the other major wild-card game, Kings or Better Joker's Wild takes us right back to the norm for the most basic Jacks or Better games, with full houses, flushes and straights all occurring with about equal frequency. In Deuces Wild, we get straights about three times as often as flushes. But in that game, we have four wild cards, and here we only have one. Joker's Wild is a different game from Jacks or Better, but the difference isn't as extreme as the change to Deuces Wild.

In full-pay Kings or better Joker's Wild, we get straights about once per 60 hands, while flushes and full houses both occur once per 64 hands.

3. C. The biggest share of our payoff in full-pay Kings or better Joker's Wild comes from threes of a kind.

We get 26.8 percent of our total return from threes of a kind. The Joker turns enough threes of a kind into fours of a kind that the second biggest share of our payback, 17.1 percent, comes from quads. We hit four of a kind once per 117 hands in this game, nearly four times as often as we get quads in Jacks or Better–based games.

Next on the list comes pairs of Kings or better, 14.2 percent of our return, followed by two pairs at 11.1 percent, full houses at 11.0 percent, flushes at 7.8 percent, straights at 5.0 percent, straight flushes at 2.9 percent, natural royals at 1.94 percent, five of a kind at 1.88 percent and Joker royals at 1.04 percent.

KINGS OR BETTER STRATEGY

NO-JOKER HANDS

4. Dealt 7 of hearts, 8 of hearts, 9 of spades, 10 of hearts, Jack of hearts:
FULL-PAY: B. Hold 7-8-10-Jack.
SHORT-PAY: A. Hold the straight.

The addition of the wild card means we get straights far more often in Joker's Wild than in Jacks or Better. The tradeoff is that we're paid only 3-for-1. Is that enough for us to settle for the straight rather than draw for an inside straight flush? It is when flushes pay only 4-for-1, as in the short-pay game we're using here. On the short-pay table, if we go for the straight flush we expect a return of 14.38 coins per five coins wagered. That doesn't match the 15-coin payoff for just holding the straight.

On the full-pay version, our EV on the inside straight flush rises to 15.21, pushing it past the pat straight.

5. Dealt Ace of clubs, Ace of diamonds, King of diamonds, Queen of diamonds, 7 of spades:
FULL-PAY: B. Hold Ace-King-Queen of diamonds.
SHORT-PAY: A. Hold the Aces.

The lower flush payback devalues the three-card royal in the short-pay game. We prefer the certain five-coin return and expected value of 6.87 coins per five wagered to the EV of 6.33 on

Ace-King-Queen. However, on the full-pay game where flushes pay 5-for-1, we'll take the EV of 7.06 on Ace-King-Queen over the 7.00 on the high pair.

6. Dealt Ace of clubs, Ace of diamonds, Queen of diamonds, 10 of diamonds, 7 of spades:

FULL-PAY and SHORT-PAY: A. Hold the Aces.

As in No. 5, we have a choice between a three-card royal and a pair of Aces. But this time we keep the Aces in either version of the game. Why the difference? It's because this time we have no King in the hand to give us a second high card along with the Ace that could be paired for a 1-for-1 return. Queen pairs bring no return, so this three-card royal is less valuable than the one in No. 5. In the full-pay game the EV on the pair of Aces remains 7.00, but the suited Ace-Queen-10 is worth only 6.55 coins per five played. On the short-pay game, EVs are 6.87 on the Aces, 6.33 on Ace-Queen-10.

7. Dealt 2 of hearts, 5 of hearts, Queen of hearts, Queen of spades, 10 of hearts:

FULL-PAY and SHORT-PAY: B. Hold the four hearts.

Remember that Queens are basically just low cards in this game, and a pair of Queens is just another low pair. They bring no return by themselves. With nothing better in the hand, we'd hold the Queens and hope for two pairs, threes of a kind, full houses or even more. But in this hand we have something better—the four-card flush. Full-pay EVs are 5.21 on the four-card flush and 3.66 on the Queens. In the short-pay game, it's 4.17 on the four-card flush and 3.53 on the Queens.

8. Dealt Ace of diamonds, King of diamonds, 9 of clubs, 8 of clubs, 7 of clubs:

FULL-PAY and SHORT-PAY: B. Hold 9-8-7.

Straight flushes pay as much in this game as in Jacks or Better, but we hit them much more frequently because of the wild Joker. Actually, we'd play this hand the same way in Jacks or Better, but in Kings or Better Joker's Wild, it's not even a close call. In the full-pay version, EVs are 3.69 on 7-8-9 and 2.88 on Ace-King. On the short-pay game, they're 3.48 and 2.80, respectively.

9. Dealt King of spades, 10 of spades, 9 of spades, 8 of hearts, 7 of clubs:

FULL-PAY: B. Hold King-10-9.

SHORT-PAY: D. Hold 10-9-8-7.

With the higher flush pay in the full-pay game, we'll take our chances with the three-card double-inside straight flush with one high card. It has an expected value of 3.01, compared with 2.81 on the four-card open-ended straight. In the short-pay game, the value of the four-card straight remains the same, but with flushes paying only 4-for-1, the EV on King-10-9 plummets to 2.77.

10. Dealt Ace of hearts, King of diamonds, 10 of diamonds, 7 of clubs, 5 of hearts:

FULL-PAY and SHORT-PAY: B. Hold King-10.

Which would you rather have, two high cards with the potential to pair up for Kings or better pays, or a suited King-10, leaving open royal flush, straight flush and flush possibilities? We're slightly better off with King-10 on both pay tables we're exploring here. On the full-pay version, we'll get an average of 2.35 coins back per five wagered on King-10, and 2.25 on Ace-King. On the short-pay game, it's 2.27 for King-10 and 2.23 for Ace-King.

11. Dealt Ace of hearts, King of diamonds, 10 of hearts, 7 of clubs, 5 of spades:

FULL-PAY and SHORT-PAY: A. Hold Ace-King.

This hand is just the other side of the border from No. 10. Again, we have the option of holding Ace-King of different suits, or two cards to a royal, including one high card. The difference is that the high card here is an Ace, and that limits our number of possible straights. So while we hold the suited King-10 instead of Ace-King of mixed suits, we hold Ace-King of mixed suits instead of a suited Ace-10.

EVs in the full-pay game are 2.25 on Ace-King and 2.16 on Ace-10; on the short-pay game they're 2.24 and 2.16.

As it happens, Ace-10 isn't even the second best play in this hand. The lone King would be a stronger play than Ace-10. But the best play is holding both the Ace and King.

12. Dealt Ace of clubs, Queen of spades, 10 of spades, 8 of diamonds, 4 of diamonds:

FULL-PAY and SHORT-PAY: A. Hold the Ace.

Queen-10 is of limited value because the pay table starts at the pair of Kings. We get no payoff for pairing the Queen. EVs on the lone Ace are 2.29 in the full-pay game and 2.25 in the short-pay version; on Queen-10 it's 1.71 in full-pay and 1.64 in short-pay.

Players may be tempted by the Queen and 10, but the second-best play on this hand is Ace-4. We see just how weak that two-card royal with no high cards is when it's bested by a two-card triple inside straight with one high card but no flush possibilities.

13. Dealt Queen of diamonds, 7 of hearts, 6 of hearts, 5 of hearts, 6 of clubs:

FULL-PAY: B. Hold 7-6-5 of hearts.

SHORT-PAY: C. Hold the pair of 6s.

The return on flushes determines our play here. With the 5-for-1 flush payback in the full-pay game, we hold the three-card straight flush. It has an EV of 3.68 that barely beats out the 3.66 on the low pair. On the short-pay game with the 4-for-1 flush payback, the narrow victory goes the other way. The pair of 6s has an EV of 3.53 that just betters the 3.47 on 7-8-9.

14. Dealt Queen of spades, 10 of hearts, 8 of hearts, 6 of diamonds, 5 of clubs:

FULL-PAY and SHORT-PAY: D. Discard all five.

Even the possibility of a Joker can't induce us to hold a three-card inside straight like 5-6-8, or a two-card inside straight flush like 8-10, and certainly not a lone Queen.

EVs on chucking it all are 1.64 on the full-pay game, 1.61 on the short-pay version. The second best plays are 8-10 with an EV of 1.51 in the full-pay version, and the lone 5 with an EV of 1.46 in the short-pay game. Why the difference? The 8 and 10 give us a better start to a flush, which matters more in the full-pay game. In the short-pay game, the lone 5 at least gives us a clear shot at a straight. But that's all just a mental exercise—neither is good enough to keep.

HANDS WITH JOKER

15. Dealt Joker, 6 of spades, 8 of spades, 9 of spades, Queen of diamonds:

FULL-PAY and SHORT-PAY: A. Hold Joker-6-8-9.

If you've been through the non-Joker hands, this one's just a warmup. Joker-Queen is not a winner by itself, though you'll draw enough winners with that start that its EVs of 6.97 on the full-pay game and 6.80 on the short-pay mean it's a profitable hand. But it's nowhere near as profitable as the four-card straight flush, with an EV of 24.60 on the full-pay game and 23.86 on short-pay.

16. Dealt Joker, 6 of spades, 9 of spades, 10 of spades, 10 of diamonds:

FULL-PAY and SHORT-PAY: C. Hold Joker-10-10.

With that Joker, you're starting with three of a kind, and that's a powerful start. In the remaining 48 cards, there are two more 10s, either of which would give you four of a kind. (That's a big boost from non–wild card games, in which there's only one card in 47 available to you that would give you quads if you started with three of a kind.) Hit both of those 10s and you have the big payday on five of a kind.

All that adds up to a 19.68 EV for Joker-10-10 on the full-pay game, 19.10 on the short-pay. For the inside straight flush with two gaps, EVs are 18.75 full-pay, 17.92 short-pay.

However, things turn around if the gap is narrowed on the inside straight flush. Make it Joker-7-9-10 and we'd be drawing for the straight flush instead of holding the three of a kind.

17. Dealt Joker, 3 of hearts, 4 of diamonds, 5 of hearts, 6 of hearts:

FULL-PAY and SHORT-PAY: B. Hold Joker-3-5-6.

In the last couple of hands, we've seen how powerful those four-card straight flushes are, even with inside draws. Here we have just one gap, as in No. 15, with EVs of 24.27 on the full-pay game and 23.58 on short-pay. Either is far better than the flat 15-coin payoff for sticking with the straight.

18. Dealt Joker, Ace of spades, Jack of spades, 8 of clubs, 5 of spades:

FULL-PAY: C. Hold Joker-Ace-Jack-5.

SHORT-PAY: B. Hold Joker-Ace-Jack.

In Joker as well as non-Joker hands, a change in the payoff on flushes makes a big difference in strategy. The 5-for-1 payoff on flushes in the full-pay game dictates that we hold all three spades along with the Joker. That one-card draw for a flush has an EV of 10.10, compared with 9.59 on the three-card royal. In the short-pay game the lower flush payback drops the EV on Joker-Ace-Jack-5 to 9.06, below the 9.32 on the three-card royal. In that case, we'll take our chances with Joker-Ace-Jack, giving ourselves a two-card draw to hit a third—or even fourth—Ace, or pair up the Jack for two pairs, or pull a full house, or even the miracle wild royal.

Either way, we come out of this hand with no worse than a pair of Aces.

19. Dealt Joker, King of diamonds, 10 of hearts, Jack of clubs, 8 of clubs:

FULL-PAY: A. Hold Joker-King.

SHORT-PAY: B. Hold Joker-King-Jack-10.

We have a winning hand no matter what, with the Joker and King giving us a high pair. The question is, do we settle for a one-card draw for a straight, or go for something bigger? Hold Joker-King-Jack-10, and we can complete a straight by drawing an Ace, Queen or 9—there are 12 cards to complete the straight. If we draw another King, Jack or 10 to go with the Joker, we'll have three of a kind. With all that going for us, the EV on holding the four-card straight is 8.44 on either game.

In the short-pay game, that beats the 8.30 EV on Joker-King, but in the full-pay version, the higher flush pay nudges Joker-King into the lead at 8.47.

20. Dealt Joker, Ace of clubs, 10 of hearts, 8 of hearts, 5 of hearts:

FULL-PAY and SHORT-PAY: A. Hold Joker-Ace.

Neither a four-card flush (Joker-10-8-5) nor a three-card straight flush (Joker-10-8) can beat Joker-Ace. It's a pair of Aces to start, and it's also two cards to a wild royal. The EV for Joker-Ace is 8.55 on the full-pay game and 8.38 on short-pay, a bit better than the 8.43 on full pay and 8.18 on short-pay for the four-card flush.

21. Dealt Joker, 4 of spades, 7 of spades, 5 of clubs, 10 of hearts:

FULL-PAY and SHORT-PAY: B. Hold Joker-4-7.

The three-card inside straight flush, Joker-4-7, is the best play, even with a couple of gaps. The EVs are 7.82 on the full-pay version and 7.52 on short-pay. What do you think is the second-best play? It's neither of the others listed in the question.

The second best play on this hand, with EVs of 7.39 on full-pay and 7.23 on short play, is Joker-10. The 10 has the advantage of being a royal flush card that also allows for a full range of straight draws. The only card we'd be tossing out of this hand that would affect a straight draw to Joker-10 would be the 7.

22. Dealt Joker, 6 of hearts, 9 of diamonds, 2 of clubs, 10 of spades:

FULL-PAY and SHORT-PAY: D. Hold Joker-6.

We've hinted at this a couple of times, but now let's come right at it. Draws in which we hold a lone Joker and dump everything else are rare. Holding a second card starts us with at least a low pair, and who knows where we might go from there?

We'd rather start with four cards to a flush or straight, or three cards to a straight flush, but in a pinch we'll settle for something like Joker-6. Choose a card with a full range of straight possibilities, with the fewest discards penalizing our potential flush or straight draws.

Here, our EVs on Joker-6 are 7.37 in the full-pay game and 7.20 in short-pay. Our second best draw is Joker-10, with EVs of 7.32 and 7.15. Joker-10 is slightly weaker than Joker-6 because we'd be discarding the card just beneath it in rank, the 9, limiting our straight possibilities. If the 9 in this hand were a 3 of diamonds instead, we'd hold Joker-10.

When would we discard everything but the Joker? It would have to be a hand with no middle-type cards, just highs and lows, but none high enough to give us a paying high pair when combined with the Joker. An example of such a hand would be Joker, 2 of spades, 3 of hearts, Jack of hearts, Queen of diamonds. All the cards are either high enough or low enough to limit our straight possibilities, there are no high pair chances, no four-card flushes or straights and not even any three-card straight flushes.

In a word, yuck.

But you know what? Even with that start, just holding the Joker, we'll get back an average of 7.22 coins for every five we bet on the full-pay game. The wild card is that powerful.

TWO PAIR OR BETTER BASICS

23. D. Winning hands make up about 30 percent of the total.

With the elimination of any payoffs on high pairs, our percentage of winning hands plummets. Forget the 45 percent or so on most Jacks or Better based-games or the 44.4 percent on Kings or Better Joker's Wild. Forget even the 35 percent on the Kings or better game Triple Bonus Poker. Even with a Joker, we win on only 30 percent of our hands in Two Pair or Better Joker's Wild, in either the Las Vegas or Atlantic City version. That makes for an extremely streaky game.

24. B. The most frequently occurring type of winning hand is three of a kind.

Here's a rarity: the winner we hit most often isn't the hand at the bottom of the pay table. In the Las Vegas version, we hit three of a kind about once per 8.1 hands, compared to once per 9.6 for two pairs. In the Atlantic City version, it's once per 8.0 hands for three of a kind and once per 9.5 for two pair.

Other winners in the Atlantic City game: straights once per 38.5 hands; flushes once per 49.4; full houses once per 66.1; fours of a kind once per 121.7; straight flushes once per 1,313;

royal flushes with Joker once per 13,088; fives of a kind once per 10,972; and natural royals once per 63,301.

In the Las Vegas version, we get straights once per 35.4 hands; flushes once per 44.3; full houses once per 67.1; fours of a kind once per 123.8; straight flushes once per 1,683; royal flushes with Joker once per 13,900; fives of a kind once per 11,053; and natural royals once per 52,183.

Note that natural royals occur less frequently in either version than in most video poker games, but that in the Atlantic City version, where we'd rather have five of a kind, our strategies make natural royals truly scarce.

25. C. The biggest share of our payoff in Two Pair or Better Joker's Wild comes from threes of a kind.

In this game, the most frequent winning hand also contributes the most to our bottom line. In the Las Vegas version, we get 24.5 percent of our return from three of a kind, while in the Atlantic City game the figure is 25.1 percent.

The Las Vegas game gives us 16.1 percent of our return on fours of a kind, 15.8 on flushes, 14.1 on straights, 11.9 on full houses, 10.4 on two pairs, 3.0 on straight flushes, 1.5 on natural royals, 0.9 on five of a kind and only 0.4 on Joker royals.

In the Atlantic City game, fours of a kind make the second biggest contribution to our payback at 13.1 percent of the total, followed by full houses at 12.1 percent, two pairs at 10.5, straights at 10.4, flushes at 10.1, fives of a kind at 9.1, straight flushes at 7.6, Joker royals at 0.8 and natural royals at just 0.2.

Note the big difference in the percentage of our payback we derive from five of a kind. The 9.1 percent of our payback from the top hand on the pay table makes the Atlantic City version of Joker's Wild, Two Pair or Better, the most top-heavy game in video poker. With a low overall frequency of winning hands, but a top jackpot that occurs about four times as often as the top jackpot in most other games, quarter players will walk away with more small losses but also more $1,000-plus wins than on any other game.

TWO PAIR OR BETTER STRATEGY

No-Joker Hands

26. Dealt King of diamonds, Queen of diamonds, Jack of diamonds, 8 of clubs, 5 of diamonds:

LAS VEGAS and ATLANTIC CITY: B. Hold King-Queen-Jack-5.

Time and again, we've come back to how flush payoffs affect the way we play video poker hands. Some of you probably looked at the 7-for-1 return on flushes in the Las Vegas game, and said, "Aha! Here we want to keep the four-card flush." And you're right. The EV of 7.29 on King-Queen-Jack-5 beats the 6.82 on the three-card royal.

If you then went on to say, "In the Atlantic City game, the flush pays only 5-for-1, so we keep the three-card royal instead," you'd be mistaken. With five coins played, we're not getting any big 4,000-coin jackpot on a natural royal as in the Las Vegas game. We get a mere 500 coins. That drops the EV on the three-card royal all the way to 4.08, below the 5.21 on the four-card flush.

27. Dealt 8 of hearts, 8 of diamonds, 9 of clubs, 10 of spades, Jack of hearts:

LAS VEGAS: B. Hold 8-9-10-Jack.

ATLANTIC CITY: A. Hold the 8s.

There are a couple of factors at work here. The Las Vegas game has a higher straight return, 5-for-1 instead of the A.C. 4-for-1. With that at work, this hand is not a close call, with an EV of 4.69 on the four-card straight easily beating the 3.69 on the pair of 8s.

The smaller straight payback in the A.C. game depresses the expected value of the four-card straight to 3.75. Not only that, we have to remember that the big payoff is on five of a kind in this game. Just as we have to keep one eye on royal flush opportunities in other games, here we have to have five of a kind in the backs of our minds. The EV on the pair rises slightly to 3.80, just enough to make it the better play.

28. Dealt 5 of clubs, 6 of clubs, 7 of clubs, 8 of hearts, King of spades:

LAS VEGAS: A. Hold 5-6-7-8.

ATLANTIC CITY: B. Hold 5-6-7.

Here's a switch for you: the game that offers the lower flush payback is the game in which we go for the three-card straight flush instead of the four-card straight. In the Atlantic City game, straight flushes pay twice as much as in the Las Vegas game, and with the Joker they happen often enough to make a difference. EVs in the Atlantic City game are 5.30 on 5-6-7, 3.75 on the four-card straight.

In the Las Vegas game, which doesn't have the bigger straight flush payoff but does pay more on garden variety straights, 5-6-7-8 is a better play, with an EV of 4.69 that beats the 4.38 on the three-card straight flush.

29. Dealt 9 of spades, 5 of spades, 2 of spades, Ace of diamonds, 10 of clubs:

LAS VEGAS and ATLANTIC CITY: A. Hold 2-5-9.

In both games, we hold the three-card flush not so much because it's a good play, but because it's the best among bad ones. Expected values are only 1.98 on the Las Vegas game and 1.50 in Atlantic City. For those tempted by the Ace, remember that a pair of Aces wins nothing in this game. You need at least two pair.

30. Dealt 7 of diamonds, 8 of diamonds, Queen of clubs, 5 of hearts, 2 of spades:

LAS VEGAS and ATLANTIC CITY: A. Hold 7-8.

With nothing better, we hold two-card straight flushes in Joker's Wild, Two Pair or Better. That's largely because we get no payoffs on high pairs, and that limits the value of a complete five-card redraw. EVs on 7-8 are 1.75 in the Las Vegas version and 1.71 in Atlantic City. Redraws are 1.22 in Las Vegas and 1.16 in A.C. Even holding a lone Queen or lone 5 would be better than a redraw, although not by much.

31. Dealt 8 of spades, 10 of spades, Jack of spades, Queen of spades, Ace of spades:

LAS VEGAS: B. Hold Ace-Queen-Jack-10

ATLANTIC CITY: B or C. Hold either Ace-Queen-Jack-10 or hold Queen-Jack-10-8.

In the Las Vegas version here, holding a four-card royal is an obvious call, just as it would be on almost any other video poker game. The EV of 95.2 dwarfs the 35-coin payback for holding the flush.

But on the Atlantic City game, a royal is just another straight flush. You'd get the same 100-for-1 return whether you drew the King to Ace-Queen-Jack-10 or the 9 to Queen-10-Jack-8. It makes no difference which you hold; either way you have an EV of 25.73 that nips the sure 25-coin payoff on the flush.

32. Dealt 6 of clubs, 7 of clubs, 8 of clubs, 9 of clubs, Ace of clubs:

LAS VEGAS: A. Hold the flush.

ATLANTIC CITY: B. Hold 6-7-8-9.

In the Las Vegas game, the flush is a certain 35-coin payback, and the EV of going for a straight flush is only 23.12. But in the Atlantic City game, flushes pay only 25 coins for a five-coin bet. The enhanced 100-for-1 payoff on straight flushes more than makes up the rest of the difference, giving the four-card straight flush an expected value of 36.88 coins per five wagered.

33. Dealt Ace of hearts, Jack of hearts, 10 of hearts, 9 of clubs, 8 of spades:

LAS VEGAS: A. Hold Ace-Jack-10.

ATLANTIC CITY: B. Hold Jack-10-9-8.

The big royal flush jackpot, combined with the 7-for-1 return on flushes, makes the three big hearts the best play in the Las Vegas game. EVs are 6.25 on the three-card royal, 4.69 on the four-card flush. In the Atlantic City game, with smaller payoffs on both royals and flushes, the one-card draw to a straight is stronger, with an expected value of 3.75 that beats the 3.13 on Ace-Jack-10.

34. Dealt Jack of diamonds, 10 of diamonds, 7 of clubs, 5 of diamonds, 2 of hearts:

LAS VEGAS: B. Hold Jack-10-5.

ATLANTIC CITY: A. Hold Jack-10.

With no high-pair payoffs in this game, we're looking at expected values below 2, so this hand isn't exactly a bankroll-padder no matter what you do. But in Las Vegas, we'll take the three-card flush and hope for the best (EVs: 1.99 on Jack-10-5, 1.89 on Jack-10). In Atlantic City, we'll leave open the possibility of a miracle draw to a straight flush instead (EVs: 1.66 on Jack-10, 1.49 on Jack-10-5).

35. Dealt Ace of spades, King of spades, Queen of spades, Ace of hearts, 9 of diamonds:

> **LAS VEGAS: B.** Hold Ace-King-Queen of spades.
>
> **ATLANTIC CITY: A.** Hold the pair of Aces.

On either version of Two Pair or Better, we'll take a start as close to the big one as we can get. Its just that we're talking about a different big one in each game. In Las Vegas, we have one eye on the royal as we hold Ace-King-Queen. That hand has an EV of 6.29, which is much stronger than the 3.69 on the pair of Aces. In Atlantic City, we'll settle for a third Ace while we dream of the fourth and fifth. The five of a kind jackpot nudges the EV on the pair up a trifle to 3.80, while the smaller payoff on royals sends the EV of Ace-King-Queen tumbling to 3.08.

HANDS WITH JOKER

36. Dealt Joker, 8 of hearts, 9 of hearts, 10 of hearts, 2 of hearts:

> **LAS VEGAS: A.** Hold the flush.
>
> **ATLANTIC CITY: B.** Hold Joker-8-9-10.

Easy does it: in Las Vegas, we stand pat for the 35-coin flush payoff for five wagered instead of settling for a 32.6 EV on the four-card straight flush; in Atlantic City, with the bigger jackpot on straight flushes, we hold Joker-8-9-10 for an EV of 51.14 instead of settling for 25 coins on the pat flush.

37. Dealt Joker, 6 of diamonds, 9 of diamonds, 10 of diamonds, 3 of diamonds:

> **LAS VEGAS: A.** Hold the flush.
>
> **ATLANTIC CITY: B.** Hold Joker 6-9-10.

In Atlantic City, even with two gaps on the inside, we like the four-card straight flush (EV 28.85) enough to pass up the 25-coin flush payoff. In Las Vegas this is an easy decision—the inside gaps make the straight flush draw (EV 20.52) no stronger an option than the open-ended draw we passed up in No. 36.

38. Dealt Joker, Ace of spades, Queen of diamonds, 2 of hearts, 3 of clubs:

LAS VEGAS: D. Hold Joker-Ace-2-3.

ATLANTIC CITY: C. Hold Joker-Queen.

The higher straight payback in Las Vegas means we'll take the four-card straight draw, which we can complete with a 4 or 5. (EV 6.04 on Joker-Ace-2-3, 5.99 on Joker-Queen.) In Atlantic City, with only a 4-for-1 payoff on straights, we'll pass on that. Instead, we'll keep the Joker and one card, choosing the one with the fewest impediments to straight or flush draws. That's the Queen. (EV 5.85 on Joker-Queen, 5.78 on the next best option, the Joker alone). We'll settle for a third Queen or a second pair, and hope for better.

39. Dealt Joker, King of clubs, 3 of hearts, 4 of diamonds, 5 of spades:

LAS VEGAS and ATLANTIC CITY: A. Hold Joker-3-4-5.

This is a four-card open-ended straight, better in either game than keeping the Joker alone, or a Joker and another card. In the Las Vegas game, the EV is 10.20, and the next best is actually on a three-card straight, Joker-4-5. In Atlantic City, the four-card straight is easily the best with an EV of 8.54, but second-best is Joker-5 at 6.28.

40. Dealt Joker, 6 of diamonds, 10 of diamonds, 7 of spades, 3 of hearts:

LAS VEGAS and ATLANTIC CITY: B. Hold Joker-6-10.

Better three-card flushes than three-card straights, especially if there's a straight flush opportunity, however slim. In Las Vegas, the expected value per five coins wagered is 6.72 on Joker-6-10, and 6.45 on the three-card straight, Joker-6-7. In the Atlantic City game, we don't worry about the three-card straight. Joker-6-10 remains the best play with an EV of 6.65, but next on the list is

Shuffle No. 15: A Sampler

If variety is the spice of life, then video poker is spicy indeed. Covering every video poker game on the market just isn't possible. Not only would it take several volumes the size of this one, but by the time the job was finished, there'd be another raft of new games out there! So up till now we've focused on the major types of games and their pay table variations.

For a taste of what else is available, let's sample a few of the more unusual video poker games. Mostly these are niche games, not offered by every casino and usually available in limited quantities even where they have a foothold.

Sometimes these niche games become popular local favorites. That's what happened with Pick 'Em Poker in Atlantic City. Pick 'Em Poker machines are sparse in other jurisdictions, and in Nevada you'll mainly find the game on a limited number of Bally's Game Maker multiple-game units.

And since gaming has become a nationwide enterprise, Nevada isn't always the first place to look for a game. For example, you're more likely to encounter Multi-Pay Poker on a riverboat or a Native American casino than on the Strip.

Some of these unusual games are:

PICK 'EM POKER

All the video poker games we've discussed so far are based on five-card draw poker. Pick 'Em Poker is different. It's based on five-card stud.

Upon making a bet, the player sees four cards. The two on the left will remain part of the hand no matter what decision is made. The two on the right are the tops of two three-card stacks. The player decides which of those two stacks go best with the initial two cards. Select a stack, and its cards are all turned face up to complete the five-card hand.

Since this is stud poker, that's where it ends. There is no further draw. That makes winning combinations more difficult to come by than in most video poker games. We won't get a royal flush once per 40,400 hands as in 9-6 Jacks or Better, or even once per 63,300 hands as in the Atlantic City version of Joker's Wild, Two Pair or Better. We'll hit a royal flush only once per 351,818 hands.

That makes some adjustments necessary. The pay table starts at a pair of 9s or better to increase the frequency of winning hands. Even so, we hit winners only 33.2 percent of the time. So the game is further refined so that the lowest payoff on the game, the pair of 9s or better, returns 2-for-1.

Here's the full pay table: Royal flush 1000-for-1 (jumps to 6,000 coins on a five-coin bet); straight flush 200-for-1 (jumps to 1,199 coins on a five-coin bet); four of a kind 100-for-1 (jumps to 600 coins on a five-coin bet); full house 18-for-1; flush 15-for-1; straight 11-for-1; three of a kind 5-for-1; two pair 3-for-1; pair of 9s or better 2-for-1.

That leaves a 99.95 percent payback game with expert play—accounting for its popularity in Atlantic City.

Let's try a few strategy problems:

1. **Initial cards: 10 of spades, Jack of spades. First stack: Queen of spades. Second stack: Jack of hearts.**

    A. Hold the Queen of spades.
    B. Hold the Jack of hearts.

2. **Initial cards: 9 of diamonds, 10 of diamonds. First stack: Jack of hearts. Second stack: 6 of diamonds.**

   A. Hold the Jack.
   B. Hold the 6.

3. **Initial cards: 8 of clubs, 3 of spades. First stack: 9 of hearts. Second stack: 3 of diamonds.**

   A. Hold the 9.
   B. Hold the 3.

4. **Initial cards: 2 of diamonds, 6 of diamonds. First stack: Jack of hearts. Second stack: 8 of diamonds.**

   A. Hold the Jack.
   B. Hold the 8.

5. **Initial cards: 4 of hearts, 6 of diamonds. First stack: 7 of clubs. Second stack: Queen of spades.**

   A. Hold the 7.
   B. Hold the Queen.

MULTI-PAY POKER

Usually found on Williams Multi-Pay Plus multiple-game machines, Multi-Pay Poker seems to have carved out a small following in Las Vegas, but has more floor space on riverboats and in tribal casinos.

At first glance the pay table looks awful: Royal flush 250-for-1 (jumps to 4,000 coins for a five-coin wager); straight flush 100-for-1; four of a kind 20-for-1; full house 7-for-1; flush 5-for-1; straight 4-for-1; three of a kind 3-for-1; two pair 2-for-1; pair of Kings or better 1-for-1.

The player who just glances at the pay table and doesn't read what the game is about will walk swiftly in the other direction. Kings or better? That will chop the proportion of winning hands down to about 35 percent. Full houses only 7-for-1 and flushes only 5-for-1? The other major Kings or better game with no wild cards, Triple Bonus Poker, has an 11-7 pay table on full houses and flushes. And what's with only 20-for-1 on four of a kind? What is this, about an 80-percent game?

Investigate further, and it all becomes clear. This is no 80-percent game. It's a 99-percenter with some well-hidden bonuses. The key is the name of the game. What "Multi-Pay" means is that you're paid on every type of winner in a given hand. If you have three 6s and two Kings, you're not just paid 7-for-1 on a full house. You also get 3-for-1 on three of a kind, 2-for-1 on two pair and 1-for-1 on the pair of Kings. The bottom line is that a full house is really worth 13-for-1 if it includes a high pair, and 12-for-1 if it doesn't.

That works all the way up the pay table. Once upon a time, my father, brother and I were on a rare getaway together in Las Vegas. We found a bank of Multi-Pay Plus games on the mezzanine level at the Tropicana. The machines also had a good blackjack game that since has been removed at the Trop and in many other casinos. That's the game my dad wanted to see, while my brother wanted to see Multi-Pay Poker. I was switching back and forth between the games, explaining some features on the blackjack game to my dad on my right, then explaining the multi-pays to my brother on my left.

Then it happened. A royal flush. The speaker started blaring "The Stars and Stripes Forever." And the jackpot amount displayed on the screen wasn't a mere $1,000 on this quarter machine. It was $1,136.25—4,000 coins for the royal, 500 for the straight flush, 25 for the flush and 20 for the straight.

That apparently was all new to the folks at the Trop. An attendant paid me off, but after a shift change, another attendant came over to double-check, wondering why I had been paid such an odd amount on a non-progressive machine. She sat down and played a while until she was satisfied that the game really did pay back on more than one combination per hand.

(Incidentally, in the timing is everything department, that turned into quite a day. Later on, I reinvested some of my winnings in a $2 game, and hit another royal for $8,000. A woman and her daughter who saw it happen went to the gift shop while I was waiting to be paid and bought me a pin displaying a royal flush in spades. I still wear it when I give seminars.)

Try a few sample hands for Multi-Pay Poker:

6. **Queen of hearts, Queen of spades, 8 of spades, 7 of spades, 2 of spades.**

    A. Hold the pair of Queens.
    B. Hold the four spades.

7. **4 of hearts, 6 of diamonds, 7 of spades, 8 of hearts, Jack of clubs.**

    A. Hold the Jack.
    B. Hold 4-6-7-8.
    C. Discard all five.

8. **4 of hearts, 6 of diamonds, 7 of diamonds, 10 of hearts, Queen of clubs.**

    A. Hold the Queen.
    B. Hold 4-6-7.
    C. Hold 6-7.
    D. Discard all five.

9. **King of diamonds, King of clubs, Queen of diamonds, Queen of spades, Jack of diamonds.**

    A. Hold the two pair.
    B. Hold King-Queen-Jack of diamonds.

10. **Ace of spades, King of clubs, 9 of diamonds, 8 of diamonds, 7 of diamonds.**

    A. Hold Ace-King.
    B. Hold 9-8-7.

BONUS DEUCES WILD

Can't decide between a wild card game and a big bonus game? You might like Bonus Deuces Wild, combining elements of Deuces Wild and the Bonus Poker variations. When the fifth card is an Ace, the payoff on four 2s kicks up a notch to 400-for-1—a 2,000-coin jackpot for five played. There also are bonuses on fives of a kind. With a five-coin wager, you'll get 100 coins back on five 6s through Kings, 200 on five 3s, 4s or 5s, or 400 on five Aces.

Bonus Deuces is not a common offering. I've never seen it outside Nevada—if you have, I'd like to know about it. It seems to show up mainly in Boyd Gaming casinos, including the Stardust and Sam's Town in Las Vegas.

With the following pay table, it's a 99.4-percent game: Natural royal flush 250-for-1 (jumps to 4,000 coins for five wagered); four deuces with Ace as fifth card 400-for-1; four deuces 200-for-1; royal flush with wild cards 25-for-1; five Aces 8-for-1; five 3s, 4s or 5s 40-for-1; five 6s through Kings 20-for-1; straight flush 9-for-1; four of a kind 4-for-1; full house 4-for-1; flush 3-for-1; straight 1-for-1; three of a kind 1-for-1.

Let's try a few sample hands:

11. 5 of hearts, 6 of hearts, 7 of clubs, 9 of spades, Jack of clubs.

    A. Hold 5-6-7-9.
    B. Discard all five.

12. 2 of hearts, 2 of spades, Ace of clubs, King of hearts, 9 of diamonds.

    A. Hold 2-2.
    B. Hold 2-2-Ace.
    C. Hold 2-2-Ace-King.

13. 2 of hearts, 7 of clubs, Ace of clubs, King of hearts, 9 of diamonds.

    A. Hold 2.
    B. Hold 2-Ace.

14. 2 of diamonds, 2 of spades, 3 of hearts, 9 of clubs, Jack of spades.

    A. Hold 2-2.
    B. Hold 2-2-3.

C. Hold 2-2-9.

15. 2 of clubs, Ace of spades, Ace of clubs, Jack of spades, 8 of spades.

A. Hold 2-Ace-Ace.
B. Hold 2-Ace of spades-Jack.
C. Hold 2 and the three spades.

DOUBLE DOWN STUD

This five-card stud poker game has a small but loyal following. Rarely does a month go by that I don't receive a letter requesting information on where the game can be found. Most recently, I've seen it at the Stardust and some locals casinos in Las Vegas, but it does not appear to be widespread.

It's an easy game, and four cards are dealt. Before receiving the fifth card, the player has the option of doubling his bet.

The following pay table yields a 97.8 percent return with expert plays. Royal flush 1,000-for-1 (jumps to 20,000 on a 10-coin bet); straight flush 200-for-1; four of a kind 50-for-1; full house 12-for-1; flush 9-for-1; straight 6-for-1; three of a kind 4-for-1; two pair 3-for-1; pair of Jacks through Aces 2-for-1; pair of 6s through 10s 1-for-1.

If you know the best play on the sample hands below, you know all you need about Double Down Stud:

16. 5 of hearts, 5 of spades, 2 of clubs, Jack of diamonds:

A. Double.
B. Don't double.

17. 3 of clubs, 4 of diamonds, 5 of clubs, 6 of diamonds:

A. Double.
B. Don't double.

18. 3 of clubs, 4 of spades, 6 of spades, 7 of clubs.

A. Double.
B. Don't double.

19. 3 of hearts, 5 of hearts, 7 of hearts, Ace of hearts.

    A. Double.

    B. Don't double.

20. 4 of spades, 5 of diamonds, 8 of clubs, 10 of hearts.

    A. Double.

    B. Don't double

Shuffle No. 15: A Sampler Answers

PICK 'EM POKER

1. A. Dealt initial cards of 10 of spades, Jack of spades, with first stack showing Queen of spades and second stack showing Jack of hearts, hold the Queen of spades.

No matter what stack you choose in Pick 'Em Poker, there are 1,128 possible outcomes. Starting with a pair of Jacks, every outcome will be a winner, while if you start with Queen, Jack and 10 of the same suit, 672 of the 1,128 will be losing hands. That makes it awfully tempting to hold the Jack. But if you hold the Jack, there will be no straights, no flushes and no royal flush. Our average return for five coins wagered will be 15.86 coins if we hold the Queen, but only 13.16 if we hold the Jack.

However, if the three-card royal includes an Ace, we're better off to stick with the paying pair. That's because the Ace limits the number of possible straight draws.

2. B. Dealt initial cards of 9 of diamonds, 10 of diamonds, with first stack showing Jack of hearts and second stack showing 6 of diamonds, hold the 6.

Either of our initial cards could be paired for a 2-for-1 payoff. Presented with no better choice, we'd be happy to add a third high card to that mix. The Jack would not only give us another card with high pair potential, it would give us a three-card open-ended straight. But the 6 of diamonds gives us a double-inside straight flush, and that's worth pursuing. The expected value on the inside straight flush is 7.54, compared to 6.17 on the 9-10-Jack.

3. B. Dealt initial cards of 8 of clubs, 3 of spades, with first stack showing 9 of hearts and second stack showing 3 of diamonds, hold the 3.

A low pair brings no payback by itself, but is far more valuable than a single high card. Either way, we'll lose more hands than we win, but our wins will be big enough when we start with the pair that in the long run we'll turn a profit with this play.

Of the 1,128 possible draws, 840 will be losers if we hold the 3, and 950 will be losers if we hold the 9. Not only that, but hold the 9, and 150 of the 178 potential winners are high-pair hands at the bottom of the pay table. Hold the 3, and every one of the 288 winners will be at least two pairs.

Bottom line: the EV of 5.71 on the 3 dwarfs the 1.76 on the 9.

4. B. Dealt initial cards of 2 of diamonds, 6 of diamonds, with first stack showing Jack of hearts and second stack showing 8 of diamonds, hold the 8.

Even with no straight flush possibilities, a three-card flush has greater potential than a single high card. EVs are 3.84 on the three-card flush, and 1.86 on the high card.

5. A. Dealt initial cards of 4 of hearts, 6 of diamonds, with first stack showing 7 of clubs and second stack showing Queen of spades, hold the 7.

This play will take some getting used to for most players. In draw poker games, we don't look for three-card inside straights. We do in Pick 'Em. The 4-6-7 is worth an average return of 2.41 coins for every five we wager, while the single high card is worth only 1.86.

MULTI-PAY POKER

6. B. Dealt Queen of hearts, Queen of spades, 8 of spades, 7 of spades, 2 of spades, hold the four spades.

A pair of Queens is not a winning hand in this game, so we go with the four-card flush. The Queens have some value because they give us a head start toward some multi-pays. If we draw a pair of Aces or Kings, for example, we'd be paid 3-for-1 on our two pair instead of the usual 2-for-1. (That breaks down into 2-for-1 on two-pair plus 1-for-1 on a high pair.) And if the alternative was a four-card open-ended straight, we'd hold the Queens. But here, we hold the four-card flush.

7. B. Dealt 4 of hearts, 6 of diamonds, 7 of spades, 8 of hearts, Jack of clubs, hold 4-6-7-8.

In Jacks or Better, we'd hold the Jack, and if we substituted the 10 of clubs for the Jack in the sample hand, we'd discard all five. Not in Multi-Pay. The Jack is of limited value since we get no payoff on a pair of Jacks. Not only that, but making this a Kings or better game depresses the value of a complete redraw. So given no better options, we hold four-card inside straights, even with no high cards.

8. C. Dealt 4 of hearts, 6 of diamonds, 7 of diamonds, 10 of hearts, Queen of clubs, hold 6-7.

We not only have no high pair possibilities, but also have no four-card inside straight, and we won't stoop quite so low as a three-card inside straight. However, we will hold two cards to a straight flush with zero or one gap. That gives us both straight and flush possibilities and we'll hit the odd high pair, two pair or even more.

9. A. Dealt King of diamonds, King of clubs, Queen of diamonds, Queen of spades, Jack of diamonds, hold the two pair.

Tempted by my tale of the multi-pays on my royal flush? Don't be, not with only three parts of the royal and two pair in hand. In good old Jacks or Better, the two pair would be a much better play than King-Queen-Jack. Here, the two pair are even better, since they include the Kings that will give us a multi-pay. But even if we had Queens and Jacks instead, the pairs would be much the better play.

10. B. Dealt Ace of spades, King of clubs, 9 of diamonds, 8 of diamonds, 7 of diamonds, hold 9-8-7.

It's tempting to hold Ace-King, and most of the time we will. But here, the three-card open-ended straight flush is the stronger play. We'd make that same play in Jacks or Better. Here, the play is strenghtened by the 100-for-1 return on straight flushes, double the payoff offered by Jacks or Better.

BONUS DEUCES WILD

11. B. Dealt 5 of hearts, 6 of hearts, 7 of clubs, 9 of spades, Jack of clubs, discard all five.

This is the most frequently occurring strategy difference between Bonus Deuces and other Deuces Wild games. We have more ways to make inside straights in Deuces Wild than in games with no wild cards. To finish off this straight, we can use any of the four eights or any of the four wild 2s. That gives us enough of a fighting chance that in most Deuces Wild games, we draw to inside straights.

Not in Bonus Deuces. Why? Because here straights pay only 1-for-1, instead of the 2-for-1 in other deuces games. Our potential earnings are cut in half, and slip below the point at which we discard all five cards.

The expected value is a return of less than one coin—0.85 to be precise—for every five coins we wager when we hold the inside straight. Tossing away the entire hand gives us an EV of 1.49.

12. B. Dealt 2 of hearts, 2 of spades, Ace of clubs, King of hearts, 9 of diamonds, hold 2-2-Ace.

With two deuces and an Ace, we give ourselves a chance at some pretty good stuff. We could hit the 1-in-1,081 shot and hit the 2,000-coin jackpot on four 2s and an Ace. We could draw two Aces or an Ace and a deuce and get 400 coins for five Aces. We could draw two more high clubs or one high club and a deuce and get 125 coins for a wild royal.

We also could draw nothing else of use and wind up with five coins for three of a kind, the bottom end when we start with two 2s.

In the long run, we'll get 16.00 coins back per five wagered when we hold 2-2-Ace, and only 15.13 when we hold just the 2s.

The bonuses make the difference. Without the enhanced pays on four 2s plus and Ace or five Aces, we'd hold just the deuces.

13. A. Dealt 2 of hearts, 7 of clubs, Ace of clubs, King of hearts, 9 of diamonds, hold 2.

There's a limit to how far the potential bonuses can push our strategy. With only one 2 in the hand, the bonus possibilities are too remote to worry about. We hold just the deuce, with an EV of 4.74, instead of 2-Ace, at 4.42.

We'll hold the Ace kicker with two, three and, of course, four deuces. With one, we have to worry about drawing any kind of winner and can't get too starry-eyed over bonuses.

14. A. Dealt 2 of diamonds, 2 of spades, 3 of hearts, 9 of clubs, Jack of spades, hold 2-2.

We play this one the same way we would in other Deuces Wild games. Neither the 3 nor the Jack give us what we'd get from an Ace. With a 3, we have an outside shot at a 200-coin payoff for five wagered if we fill in five of a kind. But that's only half the jackpot we'd get on five Aces; the 3 does not help us as a kicker if we pull the other two 2s, and it doesn't even give us a shot at a wild royal. The Jack would give us a shot at a wild royal, but it's still no use as a kicker to four 2s. Plus, the jackpot on five Jacks, 100 coins for five played, is only half that on the 3s.

The EV on the 2s is 15.36, a good-sized step up from the 12.74 on 2-2-Jack and 12.25 on 2-2-3.

15. A. Dealt 2 of clubs, Ace of spades, Ace of clubs, Jack of spades, 8 of spades, hold 2-Ace-Ace.

By a wide margin, we hold the deuce and two Aces, with an expected value of 12.40 coins per five wagered. In fact, the next best play would be to hold 2-Ace-Ace with either the Jack or the 8, giving us a shot at four of a kind if we pull a 2 or Ace, or a full house by pairing the Jack or 8. EVs on those plays are 7.55.

Even in regular Deuces Wild, holding the deuce and two Aces would be the best play. Here, it's a no-brainer.

DOUBLE DOWN STUD

16-20: Let's answer all of these together, since Double Down Stud has the easiest strategy in video poker.

In our sample hands, we double on No. 17 (3 of clubs, 4 of diamonds, 5 of clubs, 6 of diamonds) and No. 19 (3 of hearts, 5 of hearts, 7 of hearts, Ace of hearts). One is a four-card open-ended straight, the other a four-card flush. We also double if our first four cards include a winning hand—if you already have a pair of 6s or better, make the most of it.

That's it. We don't double on pairs lower than 6 (No. 16: 5 of hearts, 5 of spades, 2 of clubs, Jack of diamonds); four card inside straights (No. 18: 3 of clubs, 4 of spades, 6 of spades, 7 of clubs) or the chance to pair up high cards (No. 20: 4 of spades, 5 of diamonds, 8 of clubs, 10 of hearts).

The entire strategy for this game is to double with a winning hand, a four-card flush or a four-card open-ended straight, and not to double with anything else.

Easy enough. If only the game paid a little better...

Shuffle No. 16:
The Readers Write

I frequently receive mail from readers with questions about casino games. See if you can figure out the answers before you check out my responses:

1. I have a friend who, when she gambles, plays only video poker. In the last 10 months—and she gambles maybe every four to six weeks—she has hit a royal flush *six times*! She's done this at different locales: Indiana, Las Vegas and Iowa. Sometimes she's playing dollars, sometimes quarters, sometimes one coin, sometimes five, but altogether she's won at least $4,500. Is she just very, very lucky or would you consider her to be an expert player?

2. I hit a royal flush on a video poker machine. I was thrilled, but now I get lectures from everyone when I tell them I was playing only one quarter at a time. Everyone tells me I should have been playing five coins at a time so I'd have won $1,000. I thought my 250 quarters for only one bet was pretty good, but everyone wants to rain on my parade. Did I make a mistake?

3. Why is that a royal flush comes up an average of once every 48,000 hands in Double Bonus Poker but only once every 40,000 hands in 9-6 Jacks or Better? Is it because of the different strategies used?

4. I've read in your column that blackjack and video poker give skilled players a chance to get an edge on the casino, while other casino games have a fixed percentage in favor of the house.

I understand that. What I want to know is which game, blackjack or video poker, gives the player a better chance to win? If I'm going to study and practice on the computer, does it make a difference which game I play? Should I just go with the game that's more fun?

5. In video poker, are the new cards drawn affected by the amount of time it takes for the player to press the draw button?

In other words, does the random number generator continue to rearrange the other 47 cards in the deck between the time the player gets his original five-card hand and the time the player presses the button to receive the new cards?

6. Having read your book *The Casino Answer Book*, I understand that all video poker machines are controlled by a random number generator that determines which cards are dealt. I assume then that all 9-5 machines pay out the same percentage, based on expert play, regardless if they are nickel machines or $100 machines. In my experiences, it seems that the higher the denomination of the machine, the more payouts. Wrong, huh?

7. On a recent trip to Green Bay, I was playing 25-cent video poker and I won with a royal flush. Could you please give the guidelines for tipping, either at the bar or on the floor?

I waited about 30 minutes for my money, which seems to be the policy. Is that about right?

8. On a three-month trip to Las Vegas, I played video poker, mostly 25-cent Double Double Bonus with a progressive jackpot. Sometimes I played $1 machines but never slots or tables.

I played so much video poker and watched my discards and those that fell in their place and began noticing a pattern.

When being dealt three of a kind, which I would save, approximately 90 percent of the time a 4 of any suit would fall in instead of the fourth card. Even if I saved a pair, a 4 would fall in as one of the three cards on the draw.

This was starting to drive me crazy. Why a 4? One day at the Fiesta, the woman sitting next to me said, "Oh, yes, that is true. My friend works for a company that makes slots, and a 4 of any suit is called a 'blocker card.'"

Is this true?

It happens to me playing video poker on riverboats and on my hand-held machine, but not nearly the percentage of time it happens in Las Vegas. You may ask if I ever got four 4s. Yes. Once in 90 days.

9. On a recent trip to Las Vegas, I was playing progressive 25-cent poker and I was the only one at that bank. I always play the limit, and after playing two rolls of quarters and any credits I had won, I noticed the progressive dollar amount had not changed since I sat down to play. This was a big-name casino and everyone I talked to had no answer. They just closed the machine and said it was out of order.

What percent of a player's limit wager goes into the progressive pot? Can the casinos set the percentage or are they regulated? Have you ever noticed any rules posted by these progressive banks?

10. I was recently playing a 25-cent Bonus Poker machine. I bet the maximum number of coins and up came the 7, 10, Jack, Queen and King of clubs. Without thinking, I held all five clubs for a flush and a payout of 25 coins. As soon as I did this, I was kicking myself for not going for the straight flush or royal flush for a payout of 250 coins or 4,000 coins. I also had six other cards to make my flush and six to make a straight.

I believe I should have thrown the 7 of clubs away and drawn one card. What is the correct play and what are the percentages?

11. It is my impression (I have not kept any records) that in video poker, four-card non-winning combinations, such as four cards to a flush, straight, straight flush, royal flush or wild royal flush, seem to come up a lot. Do you have any explanation, other than pure chance?

A related question: Is this where the phrase "four-flusher" comes from?

12. On the Bonus Poker Deluxe video poker machines, whenever two pairs show up I discard one pair. I go for three of a kind, or better yet, four of a kind.

Am I doing the right thing? Four of a kind pays 80-for-1. (I always play the maximum coins.)

I am the kind of player who is satisfied with small winnings, but will go for the big one on occasion. So in your estimation, what machines should I look for?

Also, in layman's terms, can you explain payback percentages, such as 99 percent or 94 percent on a machine?

13. Lately I've been seeing more multigame video poker machines in the local casinos. It would seem to me that the better video poker machines to play would be the ones that have the highest payback percentages and also receive a lot of activity. My question is, do the multigame machines record activity for each individual game separately or for the machine as one unit?

14. I play Double Bonus Poker. It seems I rarely hit the flush when I start with four cards of the same suit. Logic tells me I should make it one out of four hands, since there are four suits and one wins. I don't make it nearly that often. Should I break up a four-card flush if I have a pair or a high card?

15. I am strictly a video poker player, and I thank you for helping me improve my game and winnings.

One question I must ask, and I've now seen this twice on progressive video poker at difference casinos in different parts of the country. When I see progressive quarter video poker at close to $2,000, that means that no one in *days* has hit the royal flush. Yet all around you see people winning hundreds every hour on the regular slots.

Why can't the casinos give away at least a lousy thousand dollars per day on what is probably their biggest moneymaker?

16. My favorite game is video poker (Deuces Wild or Jacks or Better). In the thousands of hands that I've played, I have hit everything but the royal flush. I've never even seen anybody else hit it.

What are the odds of hitting a royal flush? Many times I have sat for hours playing the optimum without even coming close. I'll be going to Las Vegas in the next few weeks. Is there something besides the odds to look for?

17. I have always considered a 1-for-1 payoff to be no payoff at all. If I, as the bettor, wager three coins on a Jacks or Better machine and get back three coins for my pair of Jacks, I am merely getting the return of the money that I have put up to bet. In effect, the house has put up nothing on the wager.

I feel that there should be nothing less than a 2-for-1 payoff. If the bettor puts up one, two or three coins, then the house should have to put up one, two or three coins, and any minimum winning payout would have to include the return of the original bet plus the equal amount in payout.

How does one get this changed—if that's at all possible?

18. Video poker machines can be programmed to pay off for any hand. So why can't an inside straight, which has only four chances to win, pay more than an open-ended straight that has eight chances to win? Also, why does a flush pay more than a straight? When you have a four-card flush, you have nine cards remaining with which to make a flush, while on an open-end straight, you have only eight cards remaining to make a straight?

19. I recently came across some video poker machines that took eight quarters at a time. They were 7-5 Bonus Poker machines, and were in the same bank as machines that take only five quarters at a time. I know I'm risking more money faster if I play the eight-quarter machines, but given a sufficient bankroll, does it make any difference which machine I play?

20. I play video poker at an Indian casino in California. They have machines that allow you to double up after a win. A card spins and you have to pick high (9 through Ace) or low (2 through 7). An 8 is a push. This seems to me like a true even-money bet and therefore the best bet in the casino aside from the craps table.

Is this correct, and is there any strategy as to when to do it or not? Also, if you win the first, do you double again? You can double up to four times.

Shuffle No. 16:
The Readers Write
Answers

1. Even expert players are lucky when they hit a royal flush, and royal flushes alone are not enough to tell whether a player is an expert. In fact, some non-expert plays will yield more royals in the long run than expert strategy.

Let's say you start with 6 of clubs, 6 of hearts, 8 of diamonds, 9 of spades and Queen of clubs. If you're trying to force as many royals as possible, you hold just the Queen and discard the rest. But the expert play here is to hold the pair of 6s. The frequency of hitting two pair, three of a kind, full houses or four of a kind when you hold the low pair more than makes up for giving up the long-shot chance at a royal.

The amateur's play will bring more royals, but the expert play will bring more money. The idea for experts is to find an optimal balance between going for the big one and making plays that will bring enough return to keep them going between royals.

Is your friend an expert or just very lucky? I don't have enough information to tell whether she's an expert, but there's no doubt she's been lucky.

2. If your bankroll and comfort level with wagering tell you that you should play one coin at a time, then that's what you should bet. You get a better payback percentage if you bet five coins at a time—that royal would have paid 800-for-1 instead of 250-for-1. I play five coins at a time, and if I can't afford to do it, I don't play. But if you're enjoying your day's entertainment while settling for the lower percentage, it's your quarter.

That being said, there is a price for playing fewer coins than the maximum. When we say that 9-6 Jacks or Better is a 99.5 percent game with expert play, well, part of expert play is betting maximum coins. If you bet fewer coins, it's only a 98.4 percent game.

I would warn you against betting four coins at a time. Then, you're paying most of the price of video poker without getting the best benefit. Look at it this way. If we break 9-6 Jacks or Better down to five one-coin bets, on the first coin we're getting a 250-for-1 payoff on a royal flush, and our return is 98.4 percent. Same on the second coin, the third and the fourth. But on the fifth coin, our royal pays 3,000-for-1, right? If we bet four coins, we get only 1,000 back on a royal, but if we bet five, we get 4,000. With that bonus payback in mind, our return on the fifth coin is 106.2 percent.

That's true on nearly every video poker game. The return on the fifth coin brings back in excess of 100 percent of what we put in. When we stop at four coins, we give away so much return in exchange for so little savings.

Betting one coin at a time may be budget-conscious; betting four is penny-wise and pound-foolish.

3. If we used the same hold/draw strategy, the frequency of royal flushes would be the same in every video poker game. But we don't. We adust our strategies to take advantage of what the game offers throughout the pay table.

In full-pay 10-7 Double Bonus Poker, flushes pay 7-for-1, a step up from the 6-for-1 on 9-6 Jacks or Better or the 5-for-1 on lesser Jacks or Better games. That leads us to hold more partial flushes in Double Bonus than in Jacks or Better.

Dealt Queen, Jack and 8 of hearts, 6 of clubs and 3 of spades, in 10-7 Double Bonus we hold all three hearts, giving up the possibility of a royal flush for the stronger chance at a flush. In 9-6 Jacks or Better, we hold just the Queen and Jack of hearts, leaving our chance at a royal intact.

Plays like that lead to the higher frequency of royals in Jacks or Better than in 10-7 Double Bonus.

4. First off, let's start with a warning that it's not easy to gain an edge in either blackjack or video poker. It takes knowledge, discipline and practice. Most players don't play at anywhere close to expert level.

Now then, a blackjack player with sufficient skills, discipline and bankroll can get a little bigger edge than a skilled video poker player. Depending on house rules and playing conditions, a blackjack card counter might be able to squeeze out an edge of 1 percent to 1.5 percent.

Potential player edges in video poker are smaller. In 10-7 Double Bonus Poker, in which full houses pay 10-for-1 and flushes 7-for-1, the expert player has an edge of 0.17 percent— the long-term payback percentage is 100.17 percent, which we've rounded to 100.2 in most of this book. Full-pay Deuces Wild, with four of a kind paying 5-for-1, is better, with a payback percentage to experts of 100.78 percent. That player edge of 0.78 percent is still less than the 1 percent or more a blackjack card counter can gain.

Player edges in video poker can be augmented by slot club cash back, a bonus few player tracking systems offer to table players. In most casinos in the United States, video poker players who use a slot club card can expect a cash rebate. At Empress Joliet, which offers 10-7 Double Bonus, the basic cash back rate is 0.25 percent of all coins played. Play on double points day, and experts have a total edge of 0.67 percent—0.17 percent on the basic game plus the cash back.

But comparing potential player edges is the tip of the iceberg. Learning video poker strategy is roughly akin to learning basic strategy in blackjack. It's not easy to play video poker at expert level—if it were, games with potential player edges would disappear. Still, gaining an edge is less complex than it is at blackjack, where after learning basic strategy the player still must learn to count cards and vary bets and strategy with the count.

On the other hand, video poker players face the problem of finding machines that give them profit potential. Unless you're playing in Nevada, 100 percent–plus machines are few and far between.

Also, blackjack is a less volatile game than video poker. A player who has mastered all the skills that go with counting cards and has sufficient bankrolls will win more sessions than he loses—even though there will still be losing sessions, sometimes with large deficits. Video poker experts lose more sessions than they win, then make it up when they hit the rare royal flushes.

Which should you play? That depends largely on your temperament.

Do you have the necessary discipline and concentration to master all facets of expert blackjack play? Then, if you have the bankroll to sustain short-term losses, blackjack is a better percentage play than video poker.

Do you have the patience to deal with a high frequency of losing sessions while you wait for a big hit? Video poker, a little easier than blackjack to play at expert level, might be your game.

5. In video poker, the entire outcome of a hand is set at once. When you drop a coin in the slot, hit the bet-one-coin button or hit the maximum-bet button to signal the machine that you are going to play, the random number generator stops shuffling for that hand. Not only are the first five cards you'll see on the screen set, so are the next five that are possible draws. If you decide to draw one card, you get the next card off the top of the deck; draw two cards, and you get the next two, and so on.

Waiting a little longer to draw after receiving your initial hand does not change the outcome of the draw. If you draw a royal flush, you wouldn't have ruined it by hitting the button a little earlier or a little later. And if you miss a one-card draw to a royal, you'd still have missed it if your timing were different on the draw.

I mentioned in Shuffle No. 4 that in the early days of video poker, 10 electronic cards were dealt out at once, with your five potential draws as a shadow hand beneath the five cards you saw on the screen. Then, as now, the entire hand was set at once; the random-number generator did not shuffle potential draw cards after dealing the initial hand. The only difference now is that cards are now dealt serially, off the top of the electronic deck, instead of with a shadow hand.

6. If the rest of the pay tables are equal, all 9-5 machines pay the same percentage, regardless of denomination. Programs to make them do otherwise are illegal in many jurisdictions. That includes Nevada, where most games are manufactured. That's one of the big advantages video poker players have over slot players—video poker players can tell a good machine from a bad one at a glance while identical-looking slot machines can have wildly different payback percentages.

If you've noticed a difference between denominations, it's strictly chance. In five-card poker, there are about 2.6 million pre-draw hands. It takes a very long time for percentages to even out. In the casino statistics, a 9-5 quarter machine and a 9-5 dollar machine will show the same rate of return. But the player is just there for a small slice of time. It's easy for a few hot or cold streaks to give the player a misleading impression.

7. Players who have hit royal flush jackpots may have noticed that usually most of their winnings are paid out in $100 bills, but the last $100 is paid in $20 bills. Attendants are hoping you'll take the clue and pass on a $20 tip.

If you want to pass on $20, that's fine—you're being generous. A $5 or $10 tip would be appropriate. Just as at the tables, you want to reward someone who makes the overall casino experience more enjoyable, but you don't want to tip so much you dramatically change the odds of the game.

The majority of players don't tip change persons or the slot floorpersons who accompany them to make the payoff. Tipping levels were never high, and have declined now that most players make change by sliding currency into the machine instead of seeking out a change person.

I do tip on hand-paid jackpots. Change persons' wages are not high, but these people help the whole operation run more smoothly, not only by pushing those carts around but also by keeping their eyes open for players having problems with mal-functioning machines or coins stuck in the slots, hoppers that need filling and jackpots that need to be paid.

Thirty minutes seems like a long wait for a jackpot that does not require IRS paperwork. (Jackpots of $1,200 or more require the player to sign an IRS form W-2G; the typical quarter royal flush jackpot with five coins played is $1,000.) A 15-minute wait for jackpot verification, and to bring a change person and super-visor to make the payoff, seems more normal. In busy periods at the casino, waits are sometime longer.

8. Blocker cards are illegal. A casino using machines with blocker cards, or a manufacturer producing such things, would risk losing its license to operate in Nevada.

Under Nevada law, video poker games must deal from a ran-domly shuffled 52-card electronic deck in which any card has an equal probability of turning up as any other. Operators who have used non-random programs have been prosecuted on felony charges.

My first thought when somebody tells me a particular draw has been coming up 90 percent of the time is that there's some selective memory at work. A player sees something happen a few times, thinks there's a pattern, and then every time it occurs thereafter it's regarded as further evidence. Sometimes the player just doesn't notice hands that don't fit the pattern. Try keeping track with pencil and paper sometime. Each time you start with three of a kind, mark down the two cards you draw. I think you'll find that the pattern disappears.

9. The operator sets the percentage of wagers that goes into the progressive pot. That percentage must be reported and cleared with the state gaming board, but the casinos are allowed a lot of leeway. The casino does not have to post rules for build-ing the progressive jackpot, nor have I ever seen anyone do so.

There is no one set, regulated amount per bet added to pro-gressive jackpots. I've seen video poker progressives that add as much as 1 percent per wager to the royal flush jackpot, and others that add as little as one-tenth of 1 percent per bet.

Expected return on the basic game may affect the jackpot percentage. Several locals casinos in Las Vegas have progressive jackpots on 9-6 Jacks or Better—a 99.5 percent game with expert play even without a progressive meter. Naturally, most progressive jackpots on the 9-6 game build more slowly than most on 8-5 Jacks or Better, a 97.3 percent game. The casino has more room to invest in the jackpot when it makes 2.7 percent on the basic game than when it makes 0.5 percent.

Progressive jackpots are there to attract players' attention, to lure customers to play. If the casino thinks it can accomplish that goal by investing relatively little of its profit per pull, it will build the jackpot at a lower rate than if it thinks it needs eye-popping amounts on the meter to attract players.

10. The correct play in that situation is to discard the 7 of clubs and give yourself a chance at a royal.

Once you have seen your initial five cards, there are 47 possible one-card draws. One, the Ace of clubs, gives you a royal flush worth 4,000 coins, and another, the 9 of clubs, gives you a straight flush for 250 coins. Any of six cards—the 2, 3, 4, 5, 6 or 8 of clubs—gives you a flush worth 25 coins. Any of six others—the 9s and Aces of hearts, spades and diamonds—gives you a straight worth 20 coins. In addition, any of nine cards—the Jacks, Queens and Kings of hearts, spades or diamonds—gives you a high pair worth a five-coin return.

That's 23 cards that complete a winning hand; any of the other 24 would leave you with a loser. Per 47 times you make this play, your expected return is one royal flush for 4,000 coins, one straight flush for 250, six flushes for 150, six straights for 120 and nine high pairs for 45. That's a total of 4,565 coins per 47 plays, an average of 97 per hand.

If you stand pat on the flush, per 47 plays your return is 1,175 coins, or 25 per play. You're nearly four times better off taking the chance with a one-card draw.

The only time to stand pat on a hand that includes four cards to a royal flush is when it includes a pat straight flush.

11. You don't need any better explanation than random chance. That's because there are many more four-card near misses than five-card winners.

Take royal flushes. There is only one combination that constitutes a royal flush in hearts—Ace, King, Queen, Jack and 10 of hearts. But there are 235 four-card near-miss heart royals—the other four, minus the Ace, plus each of the other 47 cards in the deck gives you 47 possible near-misses. There are another 47 near-misses for each combination missing the King, as well as 47 each when missing the King, Queen, Jack or 10.

Multiply all that by the four suits, and you have four possible royal flushes, and 940 possible four-card near misses. Naturally, you'll see near misses much more frequently than you see winners.

You're hot on the trail of the derivation of "four-flusher." A four-flusher was a cheater in poker games in the old West who tried to pass off four cards to the flush as the real thing. When caught, four-flushers had very short life expectancies.

12. You need to adjust your strategy on Bonus Poker Deluxe. By breaking up two pair, especially if neither pair is a paying hand by itself, you're costing yourself quite a bit of play in the long run.

Let's say you have two 6s and two 9s, along with one other card that will be discarded. Neither pair pays anything by itself, but together they return your bet on a 1-for-1 payoff. If you break up the two pair and draw three cards while holding a single card, you actually wind up worse off than if you'd held all five cards. If you hold all five cards, you at least have a five-coin payoff for your five-coin maximum bet. On an 8-5 machine, with full houses paying 8-for-1, holding only one pair lowers your expected payback to 4.05 coins per five played.

On the other hand, if you hold both pairs, your expectation rises to 7.98 coins per five played. That's because you're guaranteed at least the two-pair payoff, and you have four chances in the 47 cards remaining to draw a full house.

That 1-in-11.75 shot at a full house vastly outweighs the chance at four of a kind you're giving up by holding both pairs. If you discard one pair, you'll hit four of a kind only 45 times in 16,215 possible draws, or once per 360 hands. In fact, 11,520 of those 16,215 draws—or 71 percent—are losing hands on which you'll get no return.

It is a closer call if one of your pairs consists of Jacks or better and is a paying hand by itself. Then, by holding the high pair, you still get at least the 1-for-1 payoff. But the full house possibilities are still stronger than breaking up the pairs. If full houses pay 8-for-1, you can expect to get back 7.98 coins per five played by holding both pairs, or 7.60 coins per five played by holding only the high pair.

On 7-5 machines, paying 7-for-1 on full houses, it's largely a matter of player preference as to whether you hold just the high pair or two pair. The expected values still favor holding both pairs, but by an extremely low margin—7.553 for holding both pairs, 7.551 for holding just the high pair.

But even on 7-5 Bonus Poker Deluxe machines, it's nowhere near a close call if both pairs are lower than Jacks. Get in the habit of always holding two pair.

As for which games to play, you've chosen one that I rarely choose for myself. The higher-paying 8-5 version of Bonus Poker Deluxe returns only 97.4 percent of all coins played in the long run, while the 7-5 version pays 96.3 percent with optimal play.

I choose machines with higher long-term payback percentages. If you want the shot at big bonuses on four of a kind, I'd recommend a switch to Double Bonus Poker. Four-of-a-kind payoffs are lower at 50-for-1 on 5s through Kings, but you'll get the 80-for-1 you're used to on 2s, 3s and 4s and a big 160-for-1 on Aces.

Not only that, you'll get increased payoffs on full houses, flushes and straights. Most Double Bonus Poker pays 5-for-1 on straights. If you see a machine that pays only 4-for-1, don't play it. The best version pays 10-for-1 on full houses and 7-for-1 on flushes. There also are 9-7 and 9-6 versions. Again, if you see a version that pays less than 9-for-1 on a full house or less than 6-for-1 on a flush, don't play it.

The long-term payback percentage on 10-7 Double Bonus Poker approaches 100 percent with expert play, while the 9-7 version pays 99.1 percent and the 9-6 version pays 97.8 percent.

What those percentages mean is that in the long run, a player using expert strategy will have returned in payoffs that percentage of all coins played. If I play 20,000 hands of 9-6 Jacks or Better, meaning I wager 100,000 coins, my expected return is 99,500 coins and my expected losses are 500 coins.

The average player will not get that kind of return. Mistakes will cost them a couple of percentage points. But if you can answer the questions in this book, you'll be very close to getting optimal return.

13. The multiple-game machines do track which games get played, but that data is not released to the public. Even if I had that information, it wouldn't affect which games I played.

If the same machine has 9-7 Double Bonus Poker, returning 99.1 percent in the long run with expert play, 25-15-9-4-4 Deuces Wild, returning 98.9 percent to experts, and 8-5 Jacks or Better, returning 97.3 percent with optimal play, I'm going to play either Double Bonus or Deuces, and skip the Jacks or Better. It doesn't matter to me if others make a different choice.

14. You don't really have a 1 in 4 chance of completing a flush because four cards of your suit have already been dealt out. A 52-card deck starts with 13 cards in each suit.

But let's say your hand consists of four hearts and one spade. Of the 47 cards remaining, only nine are hearts. So when you discard the one spade, your chances of drawing a heart to complete the flush are 1 in 5.2.

That remains your chance each time you draw one card to a four-flush. Even though on the average you should hit 10 flushes for each 52 times you make this play, if you've gone 51 tries with only, say, five flushes, the chance of hitting on your next try is still 1 in 5.2.

Even so, keeping four to a flush remains a better play than holding a low pair or a single high card.

15. Video poker is unlike reel slots in that the casino is not permitted to have the manufacturer program the machine to pay out a big jackpot more or less frequently. Reel slots can be programmed so that a top jackpot appears once per 5,000 pulls, once per 10,000 pulls, once per 50,000 pulls or more. The size and frequency of smaller payouts are adjusted to stay in balance with the size and frequency of the top award.

In video poker, frequency of winning hands is governed by the same odds that govern a game played with a physical deck of cards. Video poker is dealt from a randomly shuffled 52-card electronic deck. Given expert strategy, royal flushes in Jacks or Better video poker will occur about once per 40,400 hands. It doesn't matter whether there's a progressive jackpot on the royal, or even whether the cards are dealt electronically or whether you practice at home with a regular deck.

Royal flushes aren't on a schedule. If 40,399 hands have passed since the last one, that doesn't mean a royal is bound to turn up on the next hand. It could take 80,000 hands, 120,000 hands or more. Over billions of trials, on the average there will be one royal flush per 40,000 hands played. But we don't know when they'll show up—there could be two in 15 minutes, or none for two weeks.

In Las Vegas, where there are people who make a living playing video poker, pros look for progressive machines that haven't hit in a while. Given equal payouts on other hands, the bigger the royal flush jackpot, the better the overall payout percentage.

16. Royal flushes do hit, but there can be dry spells. I once went two years without one, but then hit six in the next four months. I've seen other players hit royals; a family member even hit two in the same day on one of the Illinois riverboats.

With expert play, royal flushes turn up about once per 40,000 to 50,000 hands in most games, with variations depending on pay table and strategy. A fast player can get in about 800 hands per hour; for an average player, 500 hands per hour seems like a comfortable pace. So an average-speed player should hit a royal an average of once per 80 to 100 hours of play on Jacks or Better.

There is no guarantee that a player will hit an average number of royals. It's well within the range of chance that a player could play 160 hours, 320 hours or more without a royal turning up.

The chances of hitting a royal are the same on each hand. If you are playing your first hand of Jacks or Better, your chances of hitting a royal are 1 in approximately 40,000. If you have played 40,000 hands, your chances of hitting on the next hand are still 1 in 40,000. At any time, the best estimate of when you can expect a royal is sometime within the next 40,000 hands.

All you can do is make the right strategy decisions and hope that soon you'll be in the right place at the right time.

17. Video poker machines that merely return your bet for a pair of Jacks, Queens, Kings or Aces are so well entrenched that I don't think you could change it. I also don't think a change would be desirable.

A 1-for-1 payoff on the minimum winning hands are video poker's equivalent of a push in blackjack—and many's the time I've sat with a 17 against a dealer's Ace and been grateful to get a push when the dealer turned up a 6. From ties in baccarat to split hands in pai-gow poker, pushes are enough a part of the fabric of gaming that I don't see 1-for-1 payoffs as a problem.

That aside, I think video poker games that had no payoffs of less than 2-for-1 would be unplayable. The pay table would have to be kept in balance—a casino that offers 7-5 Jacks or Better, paying 96.2 percent to experts, isn't suddenly going to start paying 120 percent or so by raising payoffs on high pairs to 2-for-1 without making some adjustments. Pairs of Jacks and Queens would have to become zero-pay hands. That would drastically reduce the number of paying hands and make results more volatile—most of the time, you'd be heading for the exit quickly.

In most games, the 1-for-1 payoffs are the most common paying hands on the machine, and they keep you going until something better comes along. They are important to the player—too important to give up for a belief that a bet ought to be met with more than a push.

18. For those who are wondering, questions No. 17 and 18 came from different readers. The short answer to the question—why not pay more on tougher draws such as inside straights?—is that the video poker plays better as it is than it would with a more complicated pay table.

If you're playing five-card draw around the kitchen table and you win with a straight, you don't get extra credit for drawing to the inside, do you? The video poker pay table is not meant to be a precise mathematical model of the relative frequency of paying hands. It's meant to draw players in by giving them a familiar-type game, one in which full houses outrank flushes and flushes outrank straights even though those three hands occur with about the same frequency in video poker.

To give a bonus for hitting a straight on an inside draw would mean that the pay table would have to adjusted down elsewhere to keep the payback percentage the same. By splitting hairs like that, we'd create the need for a more complex strategy.

You can find situations like that all the way up and down the pay table. Instead of 800-for-1, shouldn't royal flushes pay closer to the 40,000-1 odds of hitting one? The answer is no, because other paybacks would have to be adjusted down so far that the game would be unplayable.

19. I've seen the type of machine you describe, and yes, it makes a difference. The 7-5 Bonus Poker machines that take eight quarters at a time offer a slightly lower payback percentage than those that take only five quarters.

The reason is that while almost all payoffs rise in proportion to the number of coins played, the top jackpot for a royal flush with full coins played is 4,000 coins on both machines. A full house that pays 35 coins for five played pays 56 for 8, but the royal payout remains at 4,000 coins for five played on the five-coin machine, and 4,000 for eight played on the eight-coin version. In order for the payback percentages on the two machines to be the same, the eight-coin royal would have to pay 6,400 coins.

How much difference does that make? The overall return, assuming expert strategy and maximum coins bet, is 98.0 percent on five-coin 7-5 Bonus Poker. If it takes an eight-coin wager to get the 4,000-coin return on a royal flush, the payback percentage drops to 97.3 percent.

20. The Double-Up bet you describe is, indeed, an even wager with no house edge, provided the machine draws the cards randomly. There are six denominations from 2 through 7, and six more from 9 through Ace. And since the remaining cards, the 8s, are a push, there's no edge on this bet either way, just as there's no edge on the free odds wager in craps. It's the electronic equivalent of a coin flip.

Remember, though, that although the house has no edge here, neither do you. If you enjoy the doubling option, play it; if not, don't. In the long run, you'll wind up the same either way.

Let your own tastes and bankroll guide you in deciding when and how many times times to double up. On an even bet, the odds against winning two consecutive trials are 3-1; the odds are 7-1 against winning three in a row and 15-1 against winning four in a row. However, the odds on winning your next bet are always even. If you've already won three in a row, the odds of winning the fourth are not 15-1; they're even.

Appendix: Strategy Charts

The charts that follow will give you basic strategies for attacking the basic games mentioned in this book—Jacks or Better, Double Bonus Poker, Deuces Wild, Kings or Better Joker's Wild and Two Pair or Better Joker's Wild.

Hands are listed in order of value. If your initial deal includes more than one type of the hands listed, the proper play is to keep the combination highest on the list and break up the others. For example, if you're playing 9-6 Jacks or Better and dealt 7, 8, 9 and Jack of spades and a Jack of clubs, you have both a four-card inside straight and a high pair. Look down the strategy chart and you'll see the four-card inside straight flush listed before the high pair, so you keep the four spades and discard the Jack of clubs.

9-6 JACKS OR BETTER

1. Royal flush.
2. Straight flush.
3. Four of a kind.
4. 4-card royal.
5. Full house.
6. Flush.
7. Three of a kind.

8. Straight.

9. Open-ended four-card straight flush.

10. Two pair.

11. Four-card inside straight flush.

12. High pair.

13. Three-card royal flush.

14. Four cards to a flush.

15. 10-Jack-Queen-King of mixed suits.

16. Low pair, 2-2 through 10-10.

17. 9-10-Queen-Jack or 8-9-10-Jack of mixed suits.

18. Queen-Jack-9 or Jack-10-9 of the same suit.

19. Four-card open-ended straight.

20. Three-card open-ended straight flush.

21. Three-card inside straight flush with two high cards.

22. Three-card inside straight flush with one high card.

23. Queen-Jack of the same suit.

24. Ace-King-Queen-Jack of mixed suits.

25. Two-card royal, no 10.

26. Four-card inside straight with three high cards.

27. Three-card inside straight flush with two gaps and one high card.

28. Three-card inside straight flush with one gap, lowest card 3 or higher.

29. King-Queen-Jack of mixed suits.

30. Queen-Jack.

31. Jack-10.

32. King-Queen or King-Jack.

33. Ace-King, Ace-Queen or Ace-Jack.

34. King-10 of the same suit.

35. Jack.

36. Queen.

37. King.

38. Ace.

39. Three-card inside straight flush, two gaps, no high cards.

40. Redraw.

10-7 DOUBLE BONUS POKER

1. Royal flush.

2. Four of a kind.

3. Straight flush.

4. Four-card royal.

5. Three Aces.

6. Full house.

7. Flush.

8. Three of a kind.

9. Straight.

10. Four-card straight flush.

11. Two pair.

12. Pair of Aces.

13. Queen-Jack-10 of the same suit.

14. High pair.

15. Four cards to a flush.

16. Three-card royal.

17. Open-ended four-card straight.

18. Pair of 2s, 3s or 4s.

19. Jack-10-9 or Queen-Jack-9 of the same suit.

20. Pair of 5s through 10s.

21. Three-card open-ended straight flush.

22. Ace-King-Queen-Jack of mixed suits.

23. Three-card inside straight flush, at least one high card.

24. Four-card inside straight with three high cards.

25. Queen-Jack of the same suit.

26. Three-card inside straight flush, one gap, no high cards.

27. Three-card inside straight flush, two gaps, one high card.

28. Three-card flush, two high cards.

29. King-Queen or King-Jack of the same suit.

30. Ace-King, Ace-Queen or Ace-Jack of the same suit.

31. Four-card inside straight, two high cards.

32. King-Queen-Jack or Queen-Jack-10 of mixed suits.

33. Four-card inside straight, one high card.

34. Jack-10 of the same suit.

35. Queen-Jack of mixed suits.

36. Three-card straight flush, two gaps, no high cards.

37. Three-card flush, one high card.

38. Queen-10 of the same suit.

39. King-Queen or King-Jack of mixed suits.

40. Ace.

41. Jack.

42. King-10 of the same suit.

43. Queen.

44. King.

45. Four-card inside straight, no high cards.

46. Three-card flush, no high cards.

47. Redraw.

FULL-PAY DEUCES WILD

No-Deuce Hands

1. Royal flush.

2. Four-card royal.

3. Straight flush.

4. Four of a kind.

5. Full house.

6. Three of a kind.

7. Flush.

8. Straight.

9. Four-card straight flush.

10. Three-card royal.

11. One pair.

12. Four-card flush.

13. Four-card open-ended straight, low card 4 or higher.

14. Three-card open-ended straight flush, low card 5 or higher.

15. Three-card inside straight flush, one gap, high card 7 or higher.

16. 4-5-6 or 3-4-5 of the same suit.

17. Jack-10 of the same suit.

18. Three-card inside straight flush, two gaps, high card 7 or higher.

19. Queen-Jack or Queen-10 of the same suit.

20. 3-4-6 or 3-5-6 of the same suit.

21. Four-card inside straight, not Ace low.

22. Redraw.

ONE-DEUCE HANDS

1. Wild royal.

2. Five of a kind.

3. Straight flush.

4. Four of a kind.

5. Four-card wild royal.

6. Full house.

7. Four-card open-ended straight flush, low non-deuce 5 or higher.

8. Three of a kind.

9. Flush.

10. Straight.

11. 2-3-4-5 or 2-4-5-6 of the same suit.

12. Four-card inside straight flush with one gap, high card at least a 6.

13. Four-card inside straight flush with two gaps, high card at least a 7.

14. 2 with Ace-3-4, Ace-3-5 or Ace-4-5 of the same suit.

15. Three-card wild royal, no Ace.

16. Three-card open-ended straight flush, low non-deuce at least a 6.

17. Three-card wild royal, including Ace.

18. Deuce only.

TWO-DEUCE HANDS

1. Wild royal.

2. Five of a kind.

3. Straight flush.

4. Four of a kind.

5. Four-card wild royal.

6. Four-card open-ended straight flush, low non-deuce at least a 6.

7. Two deuces only.

THREE-DEUCE HANDS

1. Wild royal.

2. Five of a kind.

3. Three deuces only.

FOUR-DEUCE HANDS

1. Hold all five.

7-5 JOKER'S WILD, KINGS OR BETTER

NO-JOKER HANDS

1. Royal flush.

2. Straight flush.

3. Four of a kind.

4. Four-card royal.

5. Full house.

6. Flush.

7. Open-ended four-card straight flush.

8. Three of a kind.

9. Four-card inside straight flush.

10. Straight.

11. Two pair.

12. Three-card royal, no Ace.

13. Three-card royal, with both Ace and King.

14. Pair of Aces or Kings.

15. Three-card royal, with Ace but no King.

16. Four-card flush.

17. Low pair.

18. Three-card open-ended straight flush.

19. King-Queen-Jack-10.

20. Three-card inside straight flush, one gap, low card at least a 3.

21. Three-card inside straight flush, two gaps, one high card.

22. Ace-King of the same suit.

23. Four-card open-ended straight.

24. Three-card straight flush, two gaps, no high cards.

25. King-Queen, King-Jack or King-10 of the same suit.

26. Ace-King of different suits.

27. Ace or King.

28. Two-card royal, no Ace or King.

29. Redraw.

HANDS WITH JOKER

1. Five of a kind.

2. Joker royal.

3. Straight flush.

4. Four of a kind.

5. Full house.

6. Four-card Joker royal.

7. Four-card open-ended straight flush, low non-Joker 3 or higher.

8. Flush.

9. Four-card straight flush, one gap.

10. Four-card straight flush, two gaps, one high card.

11. Three of a kind.

12. Four-card straight flush, two gaps no high cards.

13. Straight.

14. Three-card wild royal, with King but no Ace.

15. Four-card flush, one or two high cards.

16. Joker with Jack-10 of the same suit.

17. Three-card wild royal, with Ace.

18. Three-card open-ended straight flush, low card at least a 4.

19. Joker with King-9, Ace-2, Ace-3, Ace-4s or Ace-5 of the same suit.

20. Joker with Queen-Jack of the same suit.

21. Three-card inside straight flush with one gap, low card at least a 3.

22. Joker-Ace.

23. Joker-King.

24. Three-card straight flush, two gaps, low card at least a 3.

25. Four-card flush, no high cards.

26. Joker with 2-3, 2-4, 2-5 or Queen-9 of the same suit.

27. Four-card open-ended straight, low-card at least a 4.

28. Joker plus a 6, 7 or 8.

29. Joker plus a 10, no Jack or 9 among discards.

30. Joker plus a 5.

31. Joker plus 9-10-Jack.

32. Joker plus a 9.

33. Joker only.

ATLANTIC CITY JOKER'S WILD, TWO PAIR OR BETTER

No-Joker Hands

1. Royal flush.
2. Straight flush.
3. Four of a kind.
4. Full house.
5. Four-card straight flush (includes four-card royals).
6. Flush.
7. Three of a kind.
8. Straight.
9. Two pair.
10. Three-card open-ended straight flush, low card at least a 3, high card no greater than a Queen.
11. Four-card flush.
12. Three-card royal, King high, or three-card inside straight flush, one gap (includes 2-3-4).
13. One pair.
14. Four-card open-ended straight.
15. Three-card royal, Ace high.
16. Three-card straight flush, two gaps.
17. Four-card inside straight.
18. Two-card open-ended straight flush, no more than Jack high.
19. Two-card inside straight flush, one gap, low card at least a 3.
20. Queen-Jack or Queen-10 of the same suit.
21. Three-card flush.

22. Three-card open-ended straight, low card at least a 3, high card no greater than a Queen.

23. King-Queen, King-Jack or King-10 of the same suit.

24. Two-card inside straight flush with two gaps.

25. Single card, 5 through 10.

26. Jack only.

27. 4 only.

28. Redraw.

HANDS WITH JOKER

1. Five of a kind.

2. Joker royal.

3. Straight flush.

4. Four of a kind.

5. Four-card straight flush, zero or one gap (includes four-card royals, except Ace-high).

6. Full house.

7. Four-card Joker royal, Ace high.

8. Four-card straight flush, two gaps.

9. Flush.

10. Three of a kind.

11. Straight.

12. Three-card open-ended straight flush, at least 4 low and no more than Jack high.

13. Three-card straight flush with one gap, low card at least a 3.

14. Joker with Queen-Jack or Queen-10 of the same suit.

15. Four-card open-ended straight, low card at least a 3, high card no greater than a Queen.

16. Three-card inside straight flush, two gaps.

17. Joker with King-Queen, King-Jack or King-10 of the same suit.

18. Four-card flush.

19. Four-card inside straight, one gap.

20. Three-card straight flush, three-gaps.

21. Three-card Joker royal, including Ace.

22. Joker plus a single card 5 to 10.

23. Joker-Jack.

24. Joker-4.

25. Three-card open-ended straight, low card at least a 4, high card no greater than a Jack.

26. Joker-Queen.

27. Joker-3.

28. Joker only.

LAS VEGAS JOKER'S WILD, TWO PAIR OR BETTER

NO-JOKER HANDS

1. Royal flush.

2. Straight flush.

3. Four of a kind.

4. Four-card royal.

5. Full house.

6. Flush.

7. Straight.

8. Four-card straight flush.

9. Three of a kind.

10. Two pair.

11. Three-card royal, Queen-Jack-10.

12. Four-card flush.

13. Three-card royal, Ace or King high.

14. Four-card open-ended straight.

15. Three-card open-ended straight flush, low card at least a 3, high card no greater than a Jack.

16. Three-card inside straight flush, one gap, low card at least a 3.

17. One pair.

18. Three-card straight flush, two gaps.

19. Four-card inside straight.

20. Three-card flush.

21. Two-card royal, Queen or Jack high.

22. Two-card open-ended straight flush, low card at least a 4.

23. Three-card open-ended straight, low card at least a 3.

24. Two-card royal, King high.

25. Two-card straight flush, one gap, low card at least a 3.

26. Two-card royal, Ace high.

27. Two-card straight flush, two gaps.

28. Single card, 5 to 10.

29. Two-card straight flush, three gaps.

30. Jack.

31. 2-3-4 or Jack-Queen-King.

32. 4.

33. Redraw.

HANDS WITH JOKER

1. Five of a kind.

2. Joker royal.

3. Straight flush.

4. Four of a kind.

5. Full house.

6. Flush.

7. Four-card open-ended straight flush, includes inside draws with one gap and Joker royals with no Ace.

8. Straight.

9. Four-card inside straight flush, two gaps, includes Ace-high Joker royals.

10. Three of a kind.

11. Four-card open-ended straight.

12. Three-card open-ended straight flushes, low card at least a 4 and high card no greater than a Jack.

13. Four-card flush.

14. Three-card Joker royals, Queen high.

15. Three-card inside straight flush, one gap, includes Joker-3-4.

16. Four-card straight, one gap.

17. Three-card straight flush, two gaps.

18. Three-card Joker royal, King high.

19. Three-card straight flush, three gaps.

20. Three-card Joker royals, Ace high.

21. Three-card open-ended straight, low card at least a 4.

22. Joker plus single card 5 to 10.

23. Joker plus Jack.

24. Joker plus 4.

25. Joker only.

Video Poker Resources

As a game in which player strategy actually makes a difference in outcome, video poker has become a favorite topic of gambling writers and analysts. The resources listed below are among those I use myself, and I have no doubt you'll benefit from them, too.

BOOKS

America's National Game of Chance: Video Poker and *Winning Strategies for Video Poker* by Lenny Frome, Compu-Flyers, 5025 S. Eastern Avenue, Las Vegas, NV 89119.

Victory at Video Poker by Frank Scoblete, Bonus Books, 160 East Illinois Street, Chicago, IL 60611.

Video Poker Precision Play and *The Best of Video Poker Times* by Dan Paymar, published by Dan Paymar, 2540 S. Maryland Parkway, Suite 141, Las Vegas, NV 89109.

SOFTWARE

I used four pieces of software in selecting and analyzing sample hands for this book. WinPoker, Video Poker Tutor and Strategy Pro all can be used as games as well as teaching tools, with warnings when you misplay a hand. Strategy Master generates strategies, pure and simple. It cannot be played as a game, but if you plug in the pay table, it will generate playing strategies.

Bob Dancer Presents WinPoker by Zamzone, published by Zamzow Software Solutions, 15628 Mustang Drive, Fountain Hills, AZ 85268. Phone (480) 816-8995. Available for download online. Go to http://www.zamzone.com

Video Poker Strategy Master by TomSki, distributed through Zamzow software solutions, at the same address and Web site as WinPoker.

Masque Video Poker Strategy Pro by Masque Publishing, P.O. Box 5223, Englewood, CO 80155. Phone (303) 290-9853.

Panamint's Video Poker Tutor by Panamint Software, 316 California Ave. #863, Reno, NV, 89509.

NEWSLETTERS

Frank Scoblete's *Chance and Circumstance*, published quarterly by Paone Press, P.O. Box 610, Lynbrook, NY 11563. $40 for one year, single issue $11.95. Includes articles by Scoblete, Alene Paone, John Robison, Henry Tamburin, Walter Thomason and John Grochowski.

Anthony Curtis' *Las Vegas Advisor*, published monthly by Huntington Press, 3687 South Procyon Avenue, Las Vegas, NV 89103. $50 for one year; single issue $5. If you want to get the most out of Las Vegas, from gambling to dining to entertainment, this is your guide.

Other Books by John Grochowski

The Slot Machine Answer Book, Bonus Books, 160 East Illinois Street, Chicago, IL 60611. $12.95. John Grochowski answers nearly 200 questions on slot machines, from their colorful history with tidbits such as how the bars and fruit symbols wound up on slot reels, to how to best take advantage of modern bonus slots, slot clubs and tournaments.

The Casino Answer Book, Bonus Books, 160 East Illinois Street, Chicago, IL 60611. $12.95. In the first of the series of Answer Books, John Grochowski focuses on blackjack, video poker and roulette, with everything from how an English game called roly-poly led to the development of modern roulette, to the right times to double down at the blackjack table.

Gaming: Cruising the Casinos with Syndicated Gambling Columnist John Grochowski, Running Count Press, P.O. Box 1488, Elmhurst IL 60126, or call Huntington Press at (800) 244-2224. $11.95. A compilation of 67 essays on casino gambling, from blackjack to baccarat and slot clubs to progressive betting.

Winning Tips for Casino Games, Publications International, 7373 N. Cicero Avenue, Lincolnwood, IL 60646. $4.99. This 144-page small format paperback is a basic primer on how to play casino games.

The Experts' Guide to Casino Games, edited by Walter Thomason, Carol Publishing, 600 Madison Avenue, New York,

NY 10022. $16.95. John is one of eight co-authors, and provides a brief history of gaming in the United States as well as a chapter on blackjack. Other co-authors are Frank Scoblete, Henry Tamburin, Walter Thomason, Alene Paone, Steve Bourie, Jim Hildebrand and John Rainey.

About the Author

John Grochowski lends his expertise to players and the gaming industry alike through his books, magazine articles and seminars. Readers of *Midwest Gaming and Travel* magazine will know him as the monthly Answer Man, and he's also a regular in *Chance: The Best of Gaming* and in Frank Scoblete's *Chance and Circumstance* magazine. Twice a week, John writes a column on gaming for the *Chicago Sun-Times*.

On the industry side, he's a regular in *Casino Executive*, *Slot Manager* and *International Gaming and Wagering Business* magazines. For *Casino Executive*, a monthly magazine targeted at the movers and shakers in the industry, John is the new games expert, offering reviews and ratings of new slots, video poker machines and table games.

A popular speaker at seminars, John lives in the Chicago area with his wife and son.